Management

Fredmund Malik

Management

The Essence of the Craft

Translated from German by Jutta Scherer, JS textworks
(Munich, Germany)

Campus Verlag
Frankfurt / New York

Bibliographic information published by Deutsche Nationalbibliothek:
The Deutsche Nationalbibliothek lists this publication in the Deutsche
Nationalbibliografie; detailed bibliografic data is available in the internet at
http://dnb.d-nb.de.
ISBN 978-3-593-39129-8

Cover design: Hißmann, Heilmann, Hamburg
Typesetting: Publikations Atelier, Dreieich
Printing: Druckhaus "Thomas Müntzer", Bad Langensalza
Illustrations: Alex van de Hoef, Walldorf
Printed in Germany

www.campus.de

For Peter F. Drucker
in gratitude for everything I have learnt from him.

He was the first to see, capture, and solve the key problems of management – namely the conflicting priorities of continuity and change, conservation and innovation, community and society, great ideas and the work of man. He is the founder of the ecology of society – both in theory and practice.

Contents

Author's Preface to
the English Edition 2010

In this book I am presenting a new kind of management for a new kind of world. It is my concept of right and good management for functioning organizations in functioning societies of exceeding complexity.

The need for such a concept arises because conventional management – by which, basically, I mean the US-type management theory and practice now applied worldwide – has come to its very limits as it is unable to deal with the consequences of its own success. The result of its tremendous achievements is a world of inextricably interrelated dynamic systems which are incomprehensibly complex. This has largely been ignored by the dominating US management approach because it was never designed for such conditions. It now fails exactly for this reason, thereby causing the present crisis. I have actually been predicting this for years in many of my publications, including the German version of this book which was first published in 2005.

The fact that success almost inevitably breeds its own failure is often overlooked, although it is well known in many fields and in particular in those that accept complexity explicitly as their research subject such as biology or ecology. Albert Einstein already remarked that one cannot solve problems with the same methods which produced them.

Failure to manage complexity as the major cause of the world-crisis

What, at present, a majority – at least in the West – considers to be a mere financial crisis can probably be much better understood if it is looked at from an altogether different perspective: the failure to understand and manage complexity.

Business and society seem to be undergoing one of the most fundamental transformations in history. Only on the surface, and only if perceived in conventional categories, do present changes appear to be financial and economic in nature.

What is happening might better be understood as an Old World dying because a New World is being born. There will hardly be any bridges back to the old state of affairs. Perhaps the most practical premise to navigate by is that whatever can change will change.

If so, we are witnessing no less than the almost complete collapse of the formerly so efficient US management approach, which was developed mainly in the context of business administration and taught in business schools as the ultimate wisdom with regard to the running of corporations in a world where its premises applied to an ever lesser degree. Its realities have already been changing for quite some time but this went largely unnoticed because most people tend to see only the old familiar patterns in the new realities.

We are experiencing in particular the failure of the US-type of corporate governance and the kind of top management which is dominated almost exclusively by financial variables only. We see the collapse of the shareholder value approach, which due to its short term profit orientation is largely ignoring the customer and is hostile to future-oriented investing and innovating, thereby systematically misdirecting the allocation of societal resources. The failure of the US-approach is, among other aspects, the consequence of mistaking financial investment for real investment, thereby undermining the former strengths of the US-economy, of confusing mountains of bad debts with sustainable wealth, and of failing to distinguish between healthy and pathological growth.

Ironically, what collapsed first was the financial system which appeared to be the most highly developed and sophisticated system ever designed. It was believed to be free of systemic risk by most experts and run by the world's most excellent executives educated in what were thought to be the best universities and business schools worldwide.

However, complex systems have properties and laws of their own. Their driving forces – if systematically ignored – make them inevitably go out of control. Such systems are incomputable and unpredictable in principle and incomprehensible to the conventionally educated mind. They are non-linear, self-dynamic and continuously self-changing and self-restructuring in unforeseeable ways. They are largely self-organizing and self-regulating.

Nevertheless, they can be – up to a degree – controlled and regulated albeit only by a fundamentally different kind of thinking, a new approach for managing complexity and by applying the right methods and tools which are the subject of this book and its companion volumes.

Reliable Functioning by Wholistic Management Systems

Economic and financial measures on the macro level alone will hardly cure the crisis. What it takes on the level of societal institutions is a new way of functioning which is described in my six volume series *Management: Mastering Complexity* in which I present my Malik Wholistic General Management Systems. This first volume contains an overview of the system as a whole whereas the other five volumes will describe the constitutive parts of the system. The second volume "Corporate Policy and Governance: How Organizations Self-Organize", was published in 2008 in German and will be available in English soon. The third volume on strategy is still due in 2010. The remaining three volumes will be dedicated to the new structure for functioning complex organizations, their appropriate culture and the kind of executives who have to be able to understand and master complexity.

Together these six volumes will contain the essence of the most comprehensive General Management System worldwide. To the best of my knowledge my Wholistic General Management Systems are globally the only ones explicitly designed to ensure reliable functioning under conditions of exceedingly high and dynamic complexity.

For this reason and because my Management Systems are universally applicable conventional business administration plays a limited role in my book. For practical reasons, however, I am going to illustrate the application of my systems mainly in the context of the business enterprise. Familiar concepts and terms are left unchanged wherever possible in order to avoid confusion for the practitioner whereas their meaning and most contents are new and different.

The important new knowledge for mastering complex systems does not come from economics or business administration but from what I call the Complexity Sciences, i.e. Systemics, Bionics and Cybernetics, which can also be called the Sciences of Functioning.

For the term "Functioning" I often use the synonym "Right and Good Management" as opposed to wrong and bad management. By this I want to point to the need to understand management as a true profession with its own standards of craftsmanship as indicated in the subtitle of this book.

If the institutions of today's and more so of tomorrow's societies are supposed to function, management needs to liberate itself from fashions and fads and has to become a profession of the same status as for example the profession of the surgeon, the aircraft pilot or the lawyer all of which have as a matter of course their standards of professionalism. The foundation for a profession of effective management for functioning institutions is to be found in my earlier book *Managing Performing Living.*

My General Management Systems – with the support of the experts of my own organization – have been developed, tested and implemented in numerous cases over more than 30 years in all sorts of institutions in business and non-business areas mostly in Europe and particularly in the German speaking world including their worldwide subsidiaries. What works in the complexities of these areas will almost certainly work worldwide. Having discussed the structure, functioning principles and effects of my systems with tens of thousands of executives of all levels I have strong arguments that there is only one kind of management that works effectively, namely Right and Good Management as I present it in my books, and that it is – contrary to mainstream thinking – universally valid and culturally invariant. Fashionable arbitrariness which so often characterizes management should not be given any place in what is one of the most important social functions.

In most respects my Wholistic Management Systems for Functioning are the opposite of what is taught in most business schools. That they will have to change fundamentally as a consequence of the global crisis is hesitatingly becoming apparent to some – among them also a few leading ivy league schools. But it might be a long and hard way for them to recover from the fallacies of their own teachings and partly from the application of wrong management to themselves. At the same time, however, if they manage to change radically and fast it is one of the greatest opportunities for them to show effective leadership in the service of a functioning society in times of great change.

Fredmund Malik

St. Gallen, January 2010

Preface to the New German Edition 2007

> "Two roads diverged in a wood,
> and I – I took the one less traveled by,
> and that has made all the difference."
> *Robert Frost*

If the genome is the code to human life, good management is the code to man's ability to master life. It determines both the ability of the individual to survive in society, and the ability of society and its institutions to function and perform. Few things could be more important. Few raise so many questions. Few are as complex.

But what is management? Concepts abound. If they all worked reliably there would be no failures. Unfortunately there are many, as the world-wide crisis tragically makes visible – which, in my view, is primarily a crisis of functioning, which in turn is synonymous with a crisis of management. Obviously it does not suffice to ask what management is – the question must be more precise: what is right management? And, proceeding from there: what is good management?

So what is right and good management? This first volume of the six-volume series "Management: Mastering Complexity" provides an overview of my concept of a wholistic, systemic, cybernetics-based general management theory in the sense of right and good management. In the following volumes[1] I will elaborate on and define the different topics pertaining to right and good management.

---

1 The second volume on "Corporate Policy and Governance" was published in 2008 in German. The third on "Strategy" will be published in the fall of 2010. The English translations are expected in 2011.

Critical readers may wonder about the principles and characteristics of the management theory presented here. Management, in my view, is not an empirical science in the usual sense but an application-focused discipline – or, in other words, a practice. It does, however, draw on numerous empirical sciences and their findings. The best evidence of management being practiced rightly is when it works. This book was written for German-speaking countries. Most of its content is contrarian to mainstream thinking in these countries and even more so in the Anglo-Saxon world. The crisis shows that conventional mainstream management is dead wrong and caused the mess we are in. So, my approach may prove to be the best solution for getting out of this mess.

My views on the subject, set forth in this book and in the following volumes of the series, have evolved in over thirty years of research on management, of developing management systems, and of employing them in my own as well as in other businesses, organizations and institutions, both in German-speaking countries and internationally. What has been particularly valuable is the feedback I obtained from my ongoing interaction with thousands of managers in different functions and at different levels, as well as with many of my readers.

In addition, I make a point of drawing on the insights of other management thinkers who, like me, focus on management in its entirety – that is to say, on general management. Among them I consider the works of Peter F. Drucker, Stafford Beer, Hans Ulrich, Aloys Gälweiler, and Frederik Vester to be my most valuable sources, along with the essential publications existing on cybernetics. To answer the question of what right and good management is, proven findings and reliable principles must be amalgamated, as this is the only way to achieve further insights. By contrast, the widespread trend in management literature – starting from scratch every time and reinventing the wheel over and over again – is a roadblock to progress.

My publications on the subject of management are designed for thematic continuity and for consistency of content and language. They are based on my application of cybernetics, as described in my book *Strategie des Managements komplexer Systeme* ["Strategy for the Management of Complex Systems"]. Readers familiar with my previous publications will immediately realize this. Others may find it difficult to view some of my remarks in the context of right and good management. This series of books, therefore, is an attempt to provide an overview of essential issues and interrelations and depict them in a comprehensible way.

My sincere thanks go to my colleagues at Malik Management for many helpful discussions. I also thank Linda Pelzmann, professor of business psychology, for her invaluable feedback, Tamara Bechter for the critical review of my first draft and numerous suggestions for improvement, Maria Pruckner for helping with the new edition of this book, and the staff of the Campus Verlag publishing house. Last but not least, I thank my wife Angelika for her limitless patience.

Fredmund Malik

St. Gallen, August 2008

Concept and Logic of the Series "Management: Mastering Complexity"

This six-book series entitled "Management: Mastering Complexity" has a modular structure. The first volume, *Management. The Essence of the Craft*, lays the foundation, giving an overview of the overall layout of my model for right and good management. The remaining volumes elaborate on the topics of each chapter.

In other words, each of the volumes to follow deals with a subject matter en bloc. They can be read independently of one another and in random sequence. However, readers of succeeding volumes may find it useful to consult this introductory volume *Management. The Essence of the Craft*, as this will enable them to put the individual subject matters in context (as visualized in figure 1).

A key concept for this series of books is my Basic Model of Right and Good Management, frequently referred to as "The Management Wheel" due to its shape. In my book *Managing Performing Living*[2] it is described in detail. The statements I make in this book are an essential prerequisite for correctly understanding the contents of the series "Management: Mastering Complexity".

The basis for all my books and essays is my book *Strategie des Managements komplexer Systeme* ["Strategy for the Management of Complex Systems"][3], a considerably expanded version of my habilitation thesis. It was based on *Systemmethodik* ["System Methodology"], Volumes I and II[4], the joint doctoral thesis by Peter Gomez, Karl-Heinz Oeller, and myself. These books lay out the theoretical principles of cybernetics and system sciences which represent the cornerstones of all my deliberations.

---

2   *Managing Performing Living* was published by Campus Verlag in 2006.
3   Meanwhile the 10th edition has been published in 2008.
4   Both volumes were published in 1975.

Figure 1: Structure of the series "Management: Mastering Complexity"

The dynamics of a cybernetic system are best explored in dialogue-like interaction. To familiarize yourself with the *Malik Management System* and the way it works, please visit www.malik.ch.

Introduction

"The very first step
toward success in any occupation
is to become interested in it."
Sir William Osler (1849–1919), physician

Our increasingly complex world cannot function without management, and it can hardly function without precise management. This is true for all kinds of societal institutions, be it commercial enterprises or other organizations. The purpose of this book is to help their managers and employees fulfill their demanding occupational tasks in a professional manner.

In the midst of a jumble of doctrines, ideologies, and true innovations, this book will provide the overview required to distinguish right from wrong and useful from useless. These distinctions are indispensable for meeting both individual and shared responsibilities at each stage of a professional career. They are also crucial for successful and productive interaction.

This book is a compact compendium for right and good management – for *general management* – in that it provides the necessary overview of what it entails. In the following volumes of this series, each of the elements of right and good management will be described in greater detail, including both theoretical content and recommended implementation approaches. Interested readers will be able to familiarize themselves with the tools and practices of the craft, along with numerous practical examples. As such, the present book is a prelude to a practical, comprehensive guide to what the management craft and managerial professionalism must entail.

Sound general management is not about doing something new, modern, or fashionable. What matters is that it is right, that it works, and that it helps practitioners fulfill their tasks to the best of their abilities. The subject of this book – and of the rest of my publications – is not the "management thinking of today". Rather, all my books are practical guides to effectiveness. They point out my personal opinions on different matters, which are often not in sync with mainstream thinking.

Management. The Essence of the Craft continues, enlarges upon, and complements my book *Managing Performing Living*. While the latter deals with the conduct and actions of the individual manager, the present book goes much further in that it deals with the institution as a whole – with system-oriented *general management*.

The book contains a series of propositions which, compared to mainstream thinking, may be regarded as provocative, unusual, and frequently even wrong – at least initially. In this book, and the books to follow, I am putting my arguments forward for discussion.

Central Propositions

1. Management is society's most important function. The functioning of society depends on management. Only management turns resources into results.
2. Management can largely be acquired by learning. It is a profession and a craft. It follows the same rules of professionalism that are known and have proven useful in other professions. Talents are useful but not essential.
3. The only kind of management a person needs to learn is right and good management. Right and good management is universal, invariant, and independent of culture. It is equally valid for all kinds of organizations and all countries. There is no need for international, multicultural, or global management. All effective institutions function in the same way. They employ the same functional principles.
4. Apparent differences are not related to management but to the nature of the different tasks to be fulfilled in different organizations.
5. Not everyone can manage just any organization. This is not due to management skills but to the difference in operational tasks.
6. All managers in all organizations and across all hierarchy levels need the same kind of management skills. Not all, however, need them in the

same degree of comprehensiveness and detail. Disregarding this principle leads to a lack of orientation and direction, which, in turn, means the end of communication and function.

7. In my view, most of the management ideas prevailing over the past fifteen years or so are false, misleading, and harmful. This is true in particular for anything related to the doctrine of shareholder value and its consequences – such as value-increasing strategies and a way of thinking that focuses predominantly on financial aspects. The stakeholder approach is equally wrong.

8. The economic difficulties of our time, which I believe will inevitably deepen, are largely due to factors other than political errors. They are results of misguided management, of faulty and poor management. As a result, the question as to what right and good management is gains all the more importance.

A Word on the Terms Used

In management – as opposed to other, more advanced and mature disciplines of learning – there is no such thing as uniform or common parlance. Quite to the contrary: most authors attempt to impress readers by inventing their own terms and slogans. This is a roadblock to progress and to acquiring management skills. For this book, I essentially draw on the terms used in the St. Gallen Management Model, the first and so far only wholistic, system-driven management model, as well as on the linguistic usage of Peter F. Drucker, the doyen of management theory. As far as cybernetics and system sciences are concerned, I draw on the terms used by Stafford Beer, the originator of management cybernetics, and my own book *Strategie des Managements komplexer Systeme* ["Strategy for the Management of Complex Systems"].

1. The terms "company", "organization", and "institution" are largely used in the same sense. Certain variances in meaning relate to the degree of generality, or the special limitation to a segment of society. The most general terms are "institution" and "organization". They refer to all organizations existing in a society, no matter what kind or legal form. The term "company", in essence, belongs to the business sector. When-

ever no specific pointers are provided, it will be clear from the context what I mean when using each of these terms.

The term most frequently used in this book is "company" and other terms related to it, such as "corporate policy". The statements made will generally be applicable to all kinds of institutions. Depending on the field of usage, the terms might need to be adapted somewhat, as in "educational policy" or "health policy".

2. The term "management" itself can be understood in several ways:

Firstly, as a function that exists in any kind of organization and is indispensable for its functioning. This is the so-called functional dimension of management. It is neither linked to specific persons nor to organizational elements. This function is not perceptible to our senses. It is incorporated in certain actions taken by individuals and in this way its impact is perceived.

Secondly, the term "management" can be understood to be the sum of the legal and/or organizational authorities in an institution. Examples include the executive board of a private company, the executive committee of a public company, a national government, or a university's board of directors. This is referred to as the institutional dimension, and it also includes expanded boards of managers, group management, management circles, or partners' conferences. As far as mandatory and/or higher-level authorities are concerned, the respective responsibilities, rights, obligations, and accountabilities are governed by laws, articles of incorporation, or statutes. Those of other organizational entities are determined by common sense and habits.

Thirdly, management can be understood to include the persons that belong to the institutional authorities mentioned. This is the personal dimension of management. In particular the terms "top management" and "top manager" frequently carry that meaning.

3. I use the term "management" in the same meaning as its German equivalent "Führung". Both terms mean the same. In all my German-language publications, I use the two terms synonymously. By contrast, the terms "management" and "leadership" do not mean the same.

4. In the chapter on structure, the term "organization" carries two different meanings: the first, as mentioned above, is what we refer to when we speak of an institution *being* an organization; the second is what we

mean when we speak of an institution *having* an organization. Which one of the two meanings applies should be clear from the particular context.

Part I

What Management Is and What It Is Not

Chapter 1

What Management Is Not

"The deeper the problem that is ignored,
the greater the chances for fame and success."
Heinz von Foerster, Cybernetician and philosopher[5]

Many people think management is the art of attaining wealth, fame and power. Those are the categories in which PR people and the media often report on management. They have about as much in common with professional management as does a low-budget thriller with the realities of police work.

There is much confusion about what management is, what it should be, and what it must not be. As management gains importance, countless definitions, concepts and ideas have emerged. Most of them are not only useless, they are also absurd and misleading. Some demonstrate a total lack of expertise in the field.

This confusion is one of the main drivers of deep-rooted misunderstandings, misapprehensions and ambiguous interpretations of management. It is also one of the main reasons why the advancement of this topical area progresses so slowly, if at all, and why there are so many recurrent trends and fashions. Another, highly expensive consequence is the alarming ineffectiveness of much of the existing management training, for it is a prerequisite for any training, no matter what kind, that the subject matter is unmistakably clear.

A good way to get started is by clarifying what management is not, thus helping to clear up some of the many widespread misunderstandings. My

---

5 Foerster, Heinz v., "Responsibilities of Competence, Keynote Address at the Fall Conference of the American Society for Cybernetics", Dec. 9, 1971, published in: Foerster, Heinz v., *Observing Systems*, Seaside, California, 1981, p. 206.

own understanding of what management is not has resulted from three decades of studying management in theory and practice; it has undergone thousands of revisions during that time and proven its worth over and over again. As we are not dealing with laws of nature here but with choices to be made in every organization for the sake of clarity, there is no obligation for readers to adopt my views. Those disagreeing with my suggestions are free to make their own choices, according to whatever seems more useful to them. These choices may be better or they may be worse. At any rate, the riskiest of all conceivable options is to not make exceedingly clear what management is and what it is most definitely not.

Management Is Not Status, Rank, and Privileges

If you understand management to mean rank and status, you will never be a good manager. Status and privileges are possible side effects rather than core elements of management. In most cases they can even interfere with professionalism. They are temptations which can easily result in extravagance, ego trips, and a general lack of contact with reality.

Management must be understood from the point of view of its function. It is about fulfilling tasks, performing, making a contribution. No contribution is made simply by being important. Personality cults have no place in management. Whoever aspires to achieve fame will be better off trying his luck in the world of entertainment.

Management Is Not Business Administration

In German-speaking countries, one of the most popular misconceptions is that *Betriebswirtschaft* – the discipline of business administration – and management (or management theory) are the same. This is wrong. And every new generation of business administration graduates contribute their share to the dissemination and strengthening of this erroneous belief.

Business administration and management are two entirely different things. Knowledge of business economics alone is never sufficient to manage a company. Rather, it requires additional skills which to this date have not been introduced to the academic discipline of business administration.[6]

While a certain degree of knowledge of business economics is without doubt important for managing a commercial enterprise, it is not that relevant for the management of other types of organization. For instance, marketing is important for every commercial enterprise but a minor issue for most hospitals (with the exception of certain fashionable clinics). Cost accounting is important for hospitals but less so for political parties. Production, logistics, purchasing, and research and development are functions not every type of institution requires. Indeed they have little significance for banks and insurance companies, and none at all for a multitude of other organizations.

In short, all organizations need management, but few need business administration. As a matter of fact, those that do are in the minority. For many, a business administration way of thinking would be downright harmful, as, for example, in the case of philharmonic orchestras.

Management Is Not Limited to Commercial Enterprises

The equating of management with business economics is attributable to the basic belief that management is predominantly or exclusively relevant for the world of business – that is to say, that mainly, or solely, commercial enterprises need to be managed – and also to the belief that management evolved in the business sector. At the same time, representatives of other organizations, sometimes condescendingly, tend to consider management something purely business-related and thus profane and materialistic. They do not realize that what they do is essentially also management, even though applied to another field.

Management is a universal societal function. It is needed in all societal institutions. The names used for it in each particular case are meaningless. For instance, the principal of a university is a manager with regard to a major share of his or her tasks – even if he or she may not like to see it that way. The same is true for the director of an opera house or an orchestra,

---

6   A detailed discussion of this subject can be found in my book *Strategie des Managements komplexer Systeme,* Bern/Stuttgart, 1984, 9th edition, 2006.

for top-level government officials, principals of schools, and head physicians in hospitals. What matters is the function, not its name. This is something that top people outside the business world often fail to understand, which is why they frequently fail to get appropriate training.

Management did not evolve in the business world – this is only where its impact is most visible, and where the difference between right and wrong management can best be observed. One reason is that in commercial enterprises there is access to data that does not exist in other organizations. Many things can be measured that cannot be quantified in other sectors. Here, the impact of management errors and mistakes manifest themselves in facts and figures, and become evident much earlier than they would in many other organizations. This does not necessarily mean that in those other organizations management mistakes will always go undetected – rather, a possible dysfunction is revealed in other ways: in a hospital, for instance, it may be a patient operated on the wrong leg; in schools it may be an increase in violence among students.

Management Is Not Management of People

A rather widely held belief is that management is about managing people. It is a misconception, and its root cause lies in the fact that the term "management" is often used in the sense of managing individuals, groups or teams, not in the sense of managing entire organizations. The logical consequence is that management training is often understood to deal solely with management of people, and thus the major emphasis is put on psychological issues. Communication, too, is perceived to refer to the communicative interaction between people – although, in fact, this is where the fewest problems lie. The greatest challenge regarding communication is its organization: when to communicate what to whom; who needs to be told what when and by whom? These questions cannot be answered by psychological means – they require solid, system-driven general management.

Management does include management of people, but it is much more than that. Wherever people fail to understand that management must be applied to the institution as a whole, all their efforts are doomed to fail. For one thing, management of people is not simply about managing people but about managing people in organizations – which is different from people in their private lives. Likewise, organizations are often dealt with unilaterally if it is not understood that management refers to organizations made up of people. In short: what is often overlooked is that organizations and the people that constitute them are mutually dependent.

What we are dealing with is the management of people *in organizations*, and the shaping of organizations *made up of people*. And this is precisely what makes everything so difficult. In and by itself, each of these tasks would be relatively easy to solve; yet both in conjunction with one another are rather difficult to handle. This leads us to yet another problem: if people management is not viewed as having an inextricable connection with the functional requirements of organizations, the risk is that issues relevant to people's private lives will be transferred to the organization – where they will be out of place in many cases. This phenomenon is reflected in large parts of motivation theory, but also in the question of whether a profession should or can be expected to be fun. Conversely, principles that are crucial for people in organizations (as organizations cannot function without them) are inconsiderately transferred to people's private lives, where they do not belong and may even do harm.

In my experience, three quarters of the training programs on people management are useless or even misleading, as they leave such ambiguity, confusion, and existing differences unconsidered.

When management is understood to be people management, the result is a certain prevalence of psychological factors with partially detrimental effects. Management problems are mistaken for psychological problems; solutions are sought in the field of psychology. Efforts focus on so-called "difficult" employees although the "normal" ones – those without problems – are by far in the majority, which causes problems of bias. Those in functions of responsibility forget that their task is not to change, diagnose, and therapeutically treat people, but to accept them as they are and make use of their strengths. The bottom-line result is a massive disorientation, as everything is seen in purely psychological categories and the whole thing moves further and further away from what good management actually is. Management means adapting organizations to human nature, not the other way round. Whoever practices good management will also need psychology – but of a very different kind, as people-oriented organizations do not develop neuroses or provoke avoidable conflicts.

Management Is Not Doing Business

20 years ago, only few people outside English-speaking countries knew and used the term "management". Today it has worldwide currency, and apart from having lost its original meaning it has gained numerous others, including some rather absurd ones.

For instance, the term "management" is often used when referring to business transactions – including everything from the activities of honorable merchants to downright shady deals. As a result, even such crucial differences are veiled in contemporary usage of the term.

Many think that by studying the subject of management they will learn how to get better bargains. That, however, has nothing to do with management. These people would probably be better off attending a sales training. Of course companies need to do business, but that is not what we refer to in business management theory when we use the term management; rather, we refer to managing *the company that does business*. "Doing business" and "managing a company" are two things that need to be clearly distinguished. The latter requires management – the former hardly does.

When it comes to making a deal, management might even be an obstacle. Why? Because management requires thinking in greater dimensions and longer time horizons. From this perspective a short-term business deal may appear counterproductive, for instance, if it is inconsistent with overriding strategic goals. Just think of a business selling a bad product, which will drive customers to the competition and, in the longer term, cause an erosion of trust in the brand or company.

Management Is Not Entrepreneurship

The perception just described, of management being about doing business, is closely related to another one: of management training helping you become a better entrepreneur, or simply become an entrepreneur. This is another thing management cannot accomplish (nor, by the way, can a course of study in business management,).

Being an entrepreneur – initiating a business venture and taking the associated risk – is not the same as being a businessperson, and it is not identical to *managing* a business. That does not mean that both skills cannot coincide in one person – which does happens occasionally though only in rare cases.

This is another differentiation which is often neglected. It is drowned in the maze of arbitrary conceptions, terms, and interpretations – although there are dozens of examples from day-to-day experience that should make the difference clear. It is usually most evident wherever entrepreneurs fail to pass on their business to the next generation: it either goes down with them or it is sold. It takes management to make one's business independent of oneself.

Being successful as an entrepreneur is difficult enough. The real challenges, however, emerge with the next step, the business's next development phase. It may be right and true when it is said that an entrepreneur must have certain personal qualities, but that has nothing to do with what the business needs in order to be independent of him or her.

My suggestion to distinguish between entrepreneurs and managers also refutes the theory so adamantly upheld, according to which profit is seen as being the chief motivation for entrepreneurs: what an entrepreneur wants is usually different from what a business needs. This is where we must clearly differentiate. It is also the reason why management is not the same as entrepreneurship.

Management Is Not Only Top Management

Further misconceptions result from the fact that, when hearing the word "management", many people reflexively think of top management – that is to say, the most senior managers of an organization who, as corporate organs, act on behalf of and commit the organization. Usually that would be the board of directors and/or managers.

Those familiar with the inner workings of a company know that management does not only consist of the organization's top levels. It also includes the second and third levels, often more.

Still, this does not suffice for a truly function-based understanding of management. On principle, *anyone who manages* is part of management. This also includes production supervisors. This very perception provided one of the bases for the development of the St. Gallen Management Model, which was initiated back in the late 1960s, as well as that of the System-Oriented Management Theory. To date, the model differs from virtually all other concepts and theories in this regard. Numerous postulates, methods, and tools of the St. Gallen Model are based on this broader understanding of management, and on the belief that management will only make sense in this wider context.

Put somewhat crudely, anyone who is a boss is part of management. I suggest, however, we go one step further and include not only those in management training who are bosses themselves, but also everyone who has a boss (without necessarily being one). A training program for that second group would not have the same content as for the first. Regardless, for anyone with a boss it is extremely important to know how bosses think, by what criteria they act, why they act that way, and why they have to act that way. This would help prevent significant misunderstandings and a good deal of communication effort, and even render a considerable degree of conflict management superfluous. Yet another reason is that not only must subordinates be managed, but so must superiors – by their subordinates. This is a fact neglected in most training programs outside Malik Management, but it is highly recommended and has proved to be effective. People who know how to manage their superiors will seldom face difficulties at the workplace.

Management Is Not Identical with U.S. Management

For the most part, globalization is nothing other than an Americanization of the world. As a consequence, many people unthinkingly assume that America has the world's best economy, only because it has the largest – and that its management is also the best worldwide. Both assumptions are wrong. It is simply an optical illusion based on statistical deception. Many of my monthly management letters deal with this subject.[7]

America is massively overrated, both economically and in terms of management, as I have shown (and provided evidence of) in many of my

---

7   See, for instance, *m.o.m.*® *Malik on Management Letters* Nos. 12/00, 10/03, 2/04 and 3/04.

essays. Size is not strength. And the endless repetition of erroneous beliefs in the media does not make them any truer.

U.S. management is good for simple situations; in complex ones, it usually fails. U.S. management works under U.S. conditions. Wherever they do not apply, its impact is questionable, if not disastrous.

Along with the world's Americanization, US management has also been exported. In Asia, it is the only kind available. Alternative concepts are unknown – not because they do not exist but because they are not available in English. It is easily possible that this will create an enormous advantage for Europe in the near future.

Management Is Not Identical with MBA programs

Along with the proliferation of MBA programs, the widespread belief has taken hold that these programs are the ultimate in management education. Wrong again. Management is not identical with business administration theory, be it at business schools or universities.

It is not without reason that these study courses are entitled "Master of Business Administration" rather than "Master of Management". What North Americans call Business Administration is one variety of what German-speaking people call *Betriebswirtschaftslehre*.

Although study courses often carry the term "management" in their names, such as Marketing Management, Production Management, or Finance Management, their content usually includes little management – rather, what they teach is simply marketing, production, and finance. Consequently, an MBA degree alone will not make you a capable manager. Yet many MBA graduates and those around them seem to believe just that – which is one of the causes of the sometimes horrendous managerial performance we see.

As a result of the management disasters that occurred over the past ten years, not least owing to the influence of Americanized corporate governance and MBA trainings, a countermovement is now gradually forming. As one example of many, I will only mention the book *Managers not MBAs*[8] by the Canadian management professor Henry Mintzberg.

---

8   Mintzberg, Henry, *Managers not MBAs,* San Francisco, 2004.

The majority of MBA programs do not properly qualify people for managing complex systems. One reason is that MBA trainings place much emphasis on quantification. As a consequence, and influenced by the general discussion on corporate governance, the management of a business is degenerating into the manipulation of financial data.

Management Is Not Identical with Operational Tasks

Plenty of confusion results from the fact that management tasks and operational tasks are not clearly distinguished. The typical functions existing in economic organizations, such as research and development, marketing, production, finance, accounting, human resources, logistics, and so on, are often mistaken for management tasks when they are really functual or subject-specific tasks. Above all, it takes functual and subject-specific skills to fulfill them.

If in the course of one's education someone has studied subjects like marketing, finance, accounting, production, human resources, and such, he will hopefully make a good subject-specific expert. It is not sufficient, however, to make him a manager. Contrary to what most people think, graduates in business economics have received little or only superficial management training. Due to this confusing of business administration tasks with management tasks, people tend to think that business administration graduates will make good managers, or at least well-trained ones.

Management, however, includes tasks of a different kind: providing goals, organizing, making decisions, supervising, developing and supporting people.

Fulfilling operational tasks *well* will always *include* management. Likewise, management cannot be performed without any reference to a operational task. Management is always "the management of something".

The question as to what is more important, management skills or specific expertise, cannot be answered in general and is therefore pointless. In principle, both belong together; in individual cases there may be some emphasis on one or the other.

Subject-related expertise alone will not produce results, let alone optimal ones. Management skills alone will evaporate if there is no field of application for the operational task.

The widely held belief that a manager without any subject-specific expertise can be employed anywhere and will be able to manage anything is wrong in my opinion. There have been precious few cases in which a successful bank manager had previously led an automotive company or vice versa. Personally, I would not even entrust the Chief Financial Officer of an automotive group, who will surely have ample finance-related skills, with the management of a large bank.

Management Is Not Leadership

A new wave of confusion has resulted from the fashionable trend to differentiate sharply between management and leadership.[9] The way this has been going forward is blocking any gain of insight.

The term "management" is used to subsume anything considered bad and perceived as "low-level", such as everyday business and operative issues, but also planning, control, and budgeting.

Conversely, "leadership" stands for anything considered good and important; that is to say, anything far-sighted, future-related, innovative, and visionary – in short, everything perceived to be desirable.

The increasing use of the term "leadership" is the result of a mistranslation – this time from German into English and not, as usual, the other way round. The German word *Führung* is translated into English as "leadership". This is one of the consequences of introducing English as the corporate language of German-speaking organizations – which, incidentally, has benefited neither the quality of management nor the language. Mistakes are bound to happen in a process like this; yet it is amazing how serious and how misleading related errors have been.

But to get back to our subject: management, translated into German, is *Führung*. Likewise, the German *Führung* will almost invariably have to be translated as "management". There is hardly an instance where the German term for "manager", which is *Führungskraft*, will have to be translated back into English as "leader".

---

9   I have repeatedly explained this in my *m.o.m.® Malik on Management Letter*, for instance in Nos. 4/00 and 5/00, and expanded on the subject in my book *Die neue Corporate Governance*, Frankfurt, 1997, 3rd edition, 2002.

In most cases a person referred to as *Führungskraft* in German will correctly be called a "manager" in English. And senior managers will be called "officers" or "directors". People in charge of a department, such as Research, will be called "Head of", not "Leader of" that department. The general term for senior managers would be "executives". A CEO is a Chief Executive Officer, not a "Chief Executive Leader".

Chapter 2

What Management Is

> "A great society is a society in which men of
> business think greatly of their functions."
> *Alfred N. Whitehead, logician and philosopher*

From Resources to Value

What is management? Management is the transformation of resources into value.

In my view, this is the most useful definition of the term. It enables the most productive access to this societal function and opens the broadest perspective possible.

The following rationale should clarify what is to be understood by right and good management. It follows from the fact that both resources and value can only be found outside a business, outside any kind of institution.

In developed economies, the most important resource today – if not the only one – is knowledge. It exists mainly outside the company: it arrives in people's heads in the morning and leaves the company in the evening to go back to people's homes. There is no guarantee it will be back the next morning. The "knowledge" most knowledge-management experts speak of – the kind that can be recorded as computer-processable data – has little relevance by comparison. Put more succinctly, we might say that management is the transformation of *knowledge* into value. This variation of management being the transformation of *knowledge* into value, provides the basis for the 21st-century understanding of society and economy.

Value, too, only arises outside a business organization. It accrues at the place where services are received – at the customer's. It is the value a business must create in order to exist. It is the value through which a business fulfills its purpose. I am speaking of "value", not "utility" as economists do. And there is only one kind of value which everything comes down to: it is customer value – not shareholder value, not stakeholder value, no kind of internal value, as I will explain later. Value accrues where invoices are paid. In a literal sense of the word, the only one doing that is the customer – and conversely, anyone paying an invoice can be considered a customer. This insight alone suffices to eliminate numerous errors prevailing around the issue of corporate governance.

Management at all levels, therefore, is under natural pressure whilst located in the external to have to focus on the internal. The logical consequence from all that is that institutions, companies, and organizations must be managed outside-in. At this point, critical readers will surely recognize the most persistent of all misunderstandings around management: it is very common to manage inside-out.

What Further Sharpens the View on Management

Younger managers in particular often ask for definitions. It is one of the negative consequences of modern university education. They think a definition can tell them something about the matter itself, that is, the nature of the thing or notion defined. I do not share that view but will not expand on it at this point.[10] Definitions say nothing about the matter as such. Under certain circumstances they define what is common parlance. Linguistic terms, however, are not decisive per se. What matters are the statements we make when using the terms, and thus the verbal communication they enable.

In order to facilitate an understanding of management, the following two definitions might be useful.

My first example was written by Hans Ulrich in 1972:[11] "Management is the driving force whenever it comes to jointly accomplishing something

---

10 Anyone interested in these questions might best start by consulting Popper, Karl R., *The Open Society and Its Enemies,* Vol. 2, Chapter 1, on the 'Aristotelian Roots of Hegelianism'.

11 Ulrich, Hans, *Das St. Galler Management-Modell,* 1972; republished in: Hans Ulrich, *Gesammelte Schriften,* Vol. 2, Bern/Stuttgart/Vienna, 2001, p. 13.

by way of collaboration and through division of labor among many people, be it in national defense, the church, the field of education, health care, or the business world." Hans Ulrich, one of the groundbreaking conceptional management thinkers, is a co-founder of the St. Gallen System-oriented Management Theory and, together with Walter Krieg, a co-founder of the St. Gallen Management Model. From the very start, Ulrich has consistently defined management as the *shaping, guiding, and developing of complex, productive, social systems.*

He based his thinking on the work of Stafford Beer, the renowned management cybernetics pioneer. Beer says: "… if cybernetics is the science of control, management is the profession of control – in a certain type of system."[12] This makes cybernetics the *foundation of management*, as it is the science of comprehensive regulation, steering, guidance, and development – in short: "control" – of certain systems, in particular highly complex systems serving a clearly defined purpose. This perspective has proved to be by far more productive than the economic view of business economics or the American discipline of business administration.

My second excample is by Peter F. Drucker, the doyen of management. In his most comprehensive book he writes:[13] "The first thing is that management, that is, the organ of leadership[14], direction, and decision in our social institutions, and especially in business enterprise, is a generic function which faces the same basic tasks in every country and, essentially, in every society. Management has to give direction to the institution it manages. It has to think through the institution's mission, has to set its objectives, and has to organize resources for the results the institution has to contribute. … This means, above all, that managers practice management. They do not practice economics. They do not practice quantification. They do not practice behavioral science. These are tools for the manager. But he no more practices economics than a physician practices blood testing. He no more practices behavioral science than a biologist practices the microscope. He no more practices quantification than a lawyer practices precedents. He practices management."

---

12 Beer, Stafford, *Decision and Control*, London 1966, 2. edition 1994, p. 239.
13 Drucker, Peter F., *Management – Tasks, Responsibilities, Practices*, London 1973, p. 17.
14 The reader should not let himself be confounded by Drucker's using the term "leadership" – Drucker shares my points of view regarding terminology.

Both quotations entail the most essential things for the right understanding of management. As you can see, it has nothing to do with being rich, famous, and powerful. And it has nothing to do with the apparently ineradicable dogma of the economic sciences – profit maximization –, which was resurrected and falsely legitimized in the wake of the shareholder doctrine.

What Does "Craft" Mean?

For many years I have proposed to view management as a *profession*. I speak of the profession of effectiveness or of achieving results. On principle, management is a profession like any other. Consequently, we must have the same aspirations and make the same demands on management as on any other profession.

The most important thing in any profession is an appropriate degree of professionalism, as we would expect, for instance, of dentists, lawyers, or directors of orchestras. Professionalism has always been expected of merchants. The same should be required of, or at least aspired to, by managers in any kind of organization. It should be the goal of their education and training. They should be measured by it. Particular elements required for individual professions will be outlined in the chapter on the Standard Model of Right Management.

I very deliberately chose the word "craft", despite the fact that it is the brainworker, rather than the craftsman, who is at the center of attention nowadays – and rightfully so. I have already mentioned the significance of knowledge as a resource. All societies are undergoing a rapid transformation process to become knowledge societies. Knowledge societies are mainly characterized by the fact that they are dominated and shaped by a group of people working with their knowledge rather than their physical strength and manual skill. As a consequence, the element of *crafting* – of tangible action – is becoming all the more important for management.

Management is acting, doing, accomplishing. Knowledge alone has little importance so long as it is not used to produce results. Management is not knowledge alone, nor the production or sharing of that knowledge – it is the transformation of knowledge into results, as I said before. Educational knowledge alone is not enough. For knowledge to create value, it must be active knowledge. It is surprisingly seldom, however, that people talk about *action* in the management context. The much more common term is *behavior*. Admittedly, acting is one kind of behavior and behavioral sciences may prefer the latter term. In my view, it is too pale – too neutral, too passive – to capture the essence of management. Managers behave one way or another – so much is clear. It is also meaningless. Rather than behavior, what really matters is the kind of action that leads to effectiveness and useful results.

Another significant point is that the term "craft" refers to something that can be *learnt*. I am often asked whether it is possible to learn how to manage. The question cannot be answered like this. It must be rephrased to "*What* about management can be learnt?"

To this date there are people – even in the business world – still clinging to the obsolete notion (and telling it to the world) that management is something you must be born for. People can learn much more than most seem to be aware of. This is not to say, however, that anybody could learn anything. Some people have better abilities than others. Some make more of an effort than others. Some work harder on themselves than others to become better managers. Finally, it is an accepted fact that some people are simply not suited for the management profession. I personally think, however, that their number is limited. Only very few are unable to make certain advances.

Also, I do not contend that the entire high art of management can be learnt. Everybody has their limits somewhere, and there are tasks for which it will not suffice to practice what can be learnt. In such cases, natural talents will probably have the decisive effect. Nevertheless, the fact that studying and learning alone may not suffice to reach the highest levels of management should not keep anyone from learning what can be learnt.

From an Art to a Profession

What we call 'management' today had to be viewed as an art, as long as there was no general understanding of what it was about and what it consisted in. Successes of great entrepreneurs, for instance, were marveled at and considered unique or even ingenious. No-one thought to look closer to find out how these people had managed to be so successful, what they had done and what they had focused on, what approaches they had taken. They were idolized by those in favor of business dealings, and demonized by those against them. No-one went to the trouble of doing a sober analysis.

Peter F. Drucker was the first to *put in words* a clear understanding of management, one that could be learnt and partly taught. Drucker recognized the essential elements, since all his life he never contented himself with survey results and clichés. He worked with managers and entrepreneurs, helped them solve their problems, and watched them in the process.

Drucker's approach was to ask: *This man is successful. What makes him successful? What is the basis for his success? That woman is considered to have charisma. What causes people to think that?* With his research approach, Peter Drucker has immensely contributed to the practice of mangement. And not only that: he has also created a new, largely unsurpassed standard of scientific quality.

Management in itself is a profession, not a science, and it should not attempt to become one. Management is a practice, a "clinical" practice, a discipline. Yet it does require scientific approaches to capture the subject conceptually, to think it through, to formulate, to discuss, and to reason. This is not empirism for empirism's sake; it has nothing to do with succumbing to quotation trends or going with the mainstream. Science is not congruent with what happens at universities. Working scientifically, above all, means speaking and writing intelligibly, clearly and precisely, as well as challenging, arguing, reviewing, and reasoning. It means facing up to the general discussion and continuing the search for better solutions to the problems raised. For management, specifically, these must be problems relevant in practice, not problems conceived in academic ivory towers.

Management Is Dealing with Complexity

"Greater Skill
only arises from greater complexity"
Carsten Bresch, biologist[15]

"… in a certain type of system …" Remember I mentioned Stafford Beer earlier, with his pioneer work on management cybernetics. What type of system is Beer referring to?

---

15 Bresch, Carsten, *Zwischenstufe Leben – Evolution ohne Ziel?* Munich, 1977.

In order to understand management, we need a minimum understanding of complex systems. We cannot sensibly talk about the purpose of societal functions and their functional requirements if we have not understood complexity and the nature of systems.

Many of the elements of my management theory which may appear controversial at first can easily be clarified when considering the actual complexity of management in practice. Otherwise these points will remain unintelligible. For instance, my criticism of the shareholder value concept, which I will elaborate on later in the book, is owed mainly to the issue of complexity. Shareholder value is an illusionary solution: it seems plausible due to its reductionism, but is clearly (and demonstrably) inept and even detrimental. Together with the general focus on profit maximization, the shareholder value concept is one example of outdated 20th century thinking. Business organizations adopting such illusionary solutions cannot function properly.

In order not to complicate things too much for the readers of this book, I will be sparing in the use of cybernetic terminology. Systemics and cybernetics are already contained in my concepts, proposals, and solutions. In other words, they *are* cybernetic and systemic – which means there is no need to elaborate on these theories much further. A few hints here und there will suffice.

Complexity has been one of the terms used most frequently in recent years. There is much talk of complex systems, complex interactions, complex issues, and so on. Hardly a presentation or management-level discussion is held without referring to complexity – of markets, of products, and/or of processes. Where does the term come from? In what context was it created? Why is it important?

Most people have a rather intuitive understanding of complexity. They take it to mean something difficult, inscrutable, and hard to understand. Such an intuitive understanding may suffice for everyday life. In a management context, in particular for senior-level management tasks, we need a more precise knowledge of complexity. This applies for all kinds of organizations.

In a sense, management can be defined as the ability to successfully cope with complex systems, steer them in the desired direction, and influence their behavior in such a way that certain targets can be reached. Another way to put it is, management means *getting and keeping a system under control.*

This latter formulation often meets with harsh criticism, mainly by those who, when hearing the word "control", mainly associate with it the notion of power, force, and dominance. This is only *one* of the meanings of control, and it mainly applies to non-English languages. In the English language, "to control" has another meaning: it means regulate, rule, steer, guide. In this second meaning, the English term "control" is the chief subject of research for the science we call cybernetics – almost as physics is the science of matter and energy. The 1948 book by which the mathematician Norbert Wiener provided the foundation for cybernetics as a modern science, carries a subtitle that is very much to the point here: *Cybernetics, or Control and Communication in the Animal and the Machine.*

What Is Cybernetics?

The word "cybernetics" is derived from the Greek "*kybernetes*" which means helmsman or navigator. It is present in terms like governor (or gouverneur in French) and governance. In the volume on Corporate Governance I will talk about this some more. Cybernetics, then, can be understood to mean the art of navigation – or, in more general terms, the art of control, regulation, and steering. The fact that this art is backed by a whole science can largely be neglected in everyday business. It only becomes interesting and significant when problems arise for which a general, everyday understanding is no longer sufficient.

How Norbert Wiener discovered cybernetics, why he called his book *Cybernetics*, and who else has stood out in this field is another story altogether. Although cybernetics has not caused much of a stir in public attention, it may well be considered the most significant science of the 20th century. Although there was much more public discussion about nuclear physics than about cybernetics, the latter is the science that has driven the transformation of the 20th into the 21st century. Its full impact will be noticeable throughout the 21st century. It will fundamentally change our lives. Without cybernetics, there would be no computers or robots, no electronics, no information sciences. There would be no breakthroughs in biological disciplines, nor in genetic engineering. The progress enabled by cybernetics creates risks but even greater opportunities. Whoever wishes to avoid the first and capture the latter will have to deal with cybernetics.

It was *cybernetics*, along with the related fields of *system sciences* and *information theory*, which has enabled us to understand, explain, and systematically use the third basic element of nature: *information*. Until that point, science had only known two basic elements, *matter* and *energy*. They are the topics that the supreme disciplines of natural sciences – physics and chemistry – dealt with in the era of Enlightenment, in an attempt to *reduce* all manifestations of nature to these two elements. No doubt this research approach has brought us enormous increases in insight and, as a result, in technical possibilities.

Truly excellent scientists, however, were never satisfied with this basic philosophy of natural sciences. Something was missing – and it was something crucial. If you know, for instance, that a given object consists of some 15 kg carbon, 4 kg nitrogen, 1 kg calcium, ½ kg phosphor and sulfur, about 200 g of salt, 150 g potash and chlorine, and around 15 other materials, as well as plenty of water – what do you know? Nothing, really.

Owing to conventional scientific thinking, and educated on the basis of its logic, only few will think of answering: *it all depends on how you organize these materials ...* but that is precisely what matters.

These materials are what we are when we break down the human body into its basic components. If we deprive a living being from the very essence of its being, nothing remarkable remains. The *materials* are not important – what is important is their *organization*, the *pattern*, the *order* in which they are arranged, or the *information* that puts them into an order. Life is not simply matter or energy – it is informed matter and energy. After all, the Gospel of John does not say: *in the beginning there was carbon*. It says, "In the beginning was the Word" – meaning information or order.

That is what makes cybernetics so important. One of its most significant insights is that matter and energy are relatively insignificant for the nature and capabilities of a system. It is not important what a system's constituent parts are.[16] The important thing is the information that *sorts* and *organizes* its basic elements. It enables these basic elements to *become* a system.

The most interesting developments today, by the way, do not occur in technological areas or information sciences, even though these are what

---

16 See also: Beer, Stafford, "The World, the Flesh and the Metal"; 1964 Stephenson Lecture; in: *How Many Grapes Went into the Wine*, Harnden, Roger and Leonard, Allena, Eds., Chichester 1994.

people talk about the most. The strongest impulses go into and emerge from the *life sciences*, most specifically the *neurosciences* – the investigation of the brain and the central nervous system. This is not very surprising; after all, it is the central nervous system which steers, controls, and guides an organism. Modern brain research is no longer imaginable without cybernetic findings and concepts.

Cybernetics derives important impulses from brain research, but it is not identical with it. It is a science of its own. Cybernetics is based upon the insight that there are *natural laws* determining the control and function of *all* systems. It does not matter whether they are natural or man-made, whether they are biological, physical, technical, social, or economic systems. That is what makes cybernetics a cross-boundary – a transdisciplinary – science (which, by the way, is not the same as interdisciplinary). And that is what caused Norbert Wiener to give his book the meaningful subtitle: ... in *the Animal and the Machine* ..., thus postulating that the gap between the natural and the artificial world, which had blocked the understanding of complex systems since antiquity, be closed.

Simple and Complex Systems

After this brief excursion into scientific and historic foundations, let us return to our main subject – complexity. In cybernetics, it is important to differentiate between *simple* and *complex* systems. Simple systems do not pose much of a problem in terms of control, regulation, and steering. Serious problems emerge – all the more adamantly – in complex systems.[17]

What is it that must be brought under control? In truth, it is not "the system", as we say in an abbreviated manner. Strictly speaking, it is the system's complexity. The core questions of cybernetics, then, are these: *how can the complexity of a system be brought under control? How can*

---

17 On this subject, and the entire chapter here, see Maria Pruckner's book *Die Komplexitätsfalle – Wie sich Komplexität auf den Menschen auswirkt: vom Informationsmangel zum Zusammenbruch*, Norderstedt 2005. The author presents different aspects of the issue of complexity in new and very creative ways.

we control and regulate a system that is complex? What must the structure or architecture of a system be like in order to enable its complexity to be controlled?

Yet that is only one part of what makes cybernetics so interesting and complexity so important. The other, much more important part is based on the insight that simple systems cannot have certain, highly desirable capabilities. In his book *Zwischenstufe Leben – Evolution ohne Ziel?* ["Life as an Intermediate Stage – Pointless Evolution?"][18] the biologist and geneticist Carsten Bresch put it very succinctly when he wrote that "greater capabilities only arise from greater complexity"

This fact is often disregarded. Numerous books on the subject contain passages expressing, in so many words, that the complexity of a system must be reduced in order to control that system. That is only half the story. What is often left unmentioned is the risk of destroying the system itself, along with its most important characteristics and capabilities. In order for an organism to be capable of learning in a higher and sophisticated sense, it needs a minimum of complexity. Below a certain level, learning is impossible. The same is true for perception or communication. And it is true, among other things, for the capabilities of thinking and awareness. The same considerations apply to technical fields. Higher performance – for instance, in neurosurgery or avionics – calls for adequately complex systems. Seasoned managers are familiar with this aspect of complexity because they know that, for instance, it takes complex methods and means to be successful in a complex market.

The Dominance of Reductionism

The greatest deficit of management literature, management theory, and management understanding is the reductionism that can be observed almost throughout. One example is the reduction of management to people management, as mentioned before; another is the misconstrued contradiction between management and leadership. Also, management cannot be reduced to the purely economic aspects of an organization, as suggested by the typical business administration theories. Least of all, can management

---

18 Bresch, Carsten, *Zwischenstufe Leben – Evolution ohne Ziel?* Munich, 1977.

be reduced to the maximation of profits – not even in a purely commercial context.

Management is a multidimensional function. It cannot be reduced to one or some of the many facets of the organization to be managed, because that organization would then become unstable and, at a later stage, get out of control. The end result would be total collapse. Management, understood properly, goes beyond the functional areas of an organization; it would therefore be detrimental to an organization were we to treat it as a mere aggregate of finance, marketing, accounting, personnel, and so on. Reductionism in management, as in any other area, causes misconceptions and false doctrines. The recent economic crisis has not only been caused by politics. Its roots also lie in false management doctrines about corporate governance, reducing organizations to vehicles of shareholder interests and profit maximization.

The significance of a non-reductionist understanding of systems becomes evident when looking at the stages of evolution with their different forms of life. Lower organisms are not capable of certain behaviors and achievements. Higher organisms, due to their greater complexity, are capable of them. Remember the example I used above, of the raw materials making up a human body: the same raw materials are contained in many other organisms. The difference is not in the materials; it is in the way these materials are organized, in the degree of their complexity.

The same is true, in a sense, for technical devices and organizations. It is therefore necessary for managers to gain a basic understanding of complexity. The higher they climb (or wish to climb) on the career ladder, the deeper that understanding must be. Competent fulfilment of top management tasks, in particular, requires the ability to expertly deal with complexity. This will be the key skill of the 21st century.

The more complex a system, the greater its *range of behaviors*, or in other words, the *more varied* the ways in which it can respond to changes in its market environment, such as in customers, suppliers, competitors, or politics. At the same time it will be all the more difficult and demanding to keep the system under control, and ensure that of the multitude of actions theoretically possible the most appropriate or even optimal one will be initiated.

A good analogy can be found in the game of chess: at the beginning and at the end of a game the number of possible moves is clearly limited. Once the game is in progress, each of the players has countless options for responding to the opponent's moves. This is what makes the game so interesting: no two chess games are the same. At the same time, it is what makes the game difficult and demanding.

In contrast to the business world, a chess game has the advantage of being completely transparent to both players. Each is able to watch everything happening on the board. All pieces are known, and there are clear and unmistakable rules for how they are allowed to be moved – that is, their specific variety. The variety of each *individual* chess piece is limited – pawns have the least, queens the greatest. But the *game as a whole* and as a system has an enormous degree of variety. The number of possible moves in a game of chess is 10^{155}. For those less interested in mathematics: this is a 10 with 155 zeroes. For comparison: the number of stars in our galaxy is estimated at 10^{11}.

Management – Control of High-Variety Systems

Certain analogies between chess and business are quite obvious. It is not without reason that we speak of "players" and "rules of the game". On second thought, however, the comparison is inadequate. The business world is by far more complex than the game of chess. In business neither the elements nor the rules are set. Both can permanently change – and they do, usually without those involved being appropriately informed. Even with the best of market research it is impossible to ascertain beyond doubt what stage the "game" is currently in, which player has made what move, what significance and impact that move has, and so on. Almost invariably, those involved operate on no more than probabilities and assumptions. Often it is not even clear *which* "game" is being played. Much the same may be said of the company itself: except in the simplest of cases it is usually rather difficult to determine the state of affairs at a company with sufficient precision and speed. Even all the advances in information sciences have done little to change this. Most of the time it is uncertain to predict what state of affairs a company will migrate to under the impact of all relevant factors. Most of the information available refers to mere probabilities. Large parts of it are uncertain. Everything is in constant flux. Moreover, not only is the behavioral variety of each "figure" much greater than in chess – it even cannot be precisely determined.

Hence, it is no exaggeration to say that even small business organizations are systems of astronomical variety. The technical term is *high-variety systems*. Consequently, the key question of management is: *how can a high-variety system be controlled?* That is why Stafford Beers statement is so important. I repeat: *"If cybernetics is the science of control, management is the profession of control – in a certain type of system."* From the perspective of system complexity, then, every manager is a cybernetician – a *kybernetes –*, a helmsman and navigator, whether he likes it or not, and whether he is or is not aware of it. Not everyone knows that there is a science helping managers to fulfil their tasks. And contrary to what most people think, it is not primarily business administration or economics. It is *cybernetics*.

It is the astronomical number of possible states that complex systems can theoretically produce, which makes the control and adjustment of these systems so difficult. How does *nature* solve this problem? Who or what controls, adjusts, and monitors its complex systems? The answer is both mundane and noteworthy: natural systems have *no* regulators because they regulate *themselves* – they have *no* organizers because they organize *themselves*. Two of nature's most important cybernetic principles are *self-regulation* and *self-organization*. They are *universal* architectural and functional regularities of nature.

As cybernetics is a science that cuts across disciplines, thus dealing with systems of *all kinds*, it is an obvious next step to seek these same basic principles in technical, economic, and social systems, and also to apply them in these fields. Take, for example, the automobile: owing to cybernetic advances in control engineering, the burden on the driver could be much alleviated. Many of the processes that previously had to be monitored and controlled by the person at the steering wheel can now be left to the vehicle's electronic control systems, such as ABS. In air traffic the effect is even more pronounced. Although pilots may not like to hear this, it is an open secret that today, thanks to modern auto-pilot machinery, flights can be a self-regulating process. Risks are no longer inherent in technology but in the human factor.

Nature's systems have self-regulation and self-organization *built into* their structures. There are no other natural systems. By contrast, in systems created by man, be they technical or social or mixed forms, self-regulation and self-organization do *not occur by themselves*. They must be "organized into them". Their design must deliberately be aligned with cybernetic function principles – it must be a so-called system design. Thus, the blueprint for the strategy of cybernetic management is this: *organize your company in such a way that it can organize and regulate itself as far as possible.*

If this is taken to heart, many apparent and much-discussed contradictions and errors can easily be solved. Of course, a sensible application of cybernetics to the field of management has never meant (contrary to what some contend) that those at the top should more or less retreat and leave the company to itself. The same is true for politics and the economy. Capable people have never considered "laisser faire" a viable solution for the management of business organizations, nor for the market economy or society as a whole. No-one has made this clearer than Friedrich A. von Hayek, in my opinion the best, sharpest and most precise thinker that liberalism has produced.

And while I am at it, I wish to correct another frequent error: no-one has ever proposed that *everything* could be organized so that it would organize itself. Cybernetics, understood correctly, is far more modest. It attempts to apply its principles if and when *possible*. Wherever that is not the case, it is obvious that other forms of control and regulation must be sought. Or it must be accepted that the system in question cannot be controlled – that it is *out of control*.

The Law of Requisite Variety

What I said in the last paragraph leads us straight to the central law of nature which was discovered in cybernetics: *the Law of Requisite Variety*. It was discovered by the British neuro-physiologist and cybernetician W. Ross Ashby, another great pioneer. In literature, the law he found is sometimes referred to as *"Ashby's Law"*.

When exactly he made his discovery is not entirely certain. His clearest formulation of the principle appeared in his book *An Introduction to Cybernetics*, which was published in 1956.[19] It goes as follows: *Only Variety can destroy Variety.*

A slight modifcation might faciliate the reader's understanding: *Only Variety can absorb Variety.* What does this mean? The extent to which a

19 London 1956, 5th Edition 1970, p. 207.

system can be controlled depends on that system's inherent complexity and on the complexity of the regulation mechanism available. As I said before, it is important to distinguish between "simple" and "complex". Simple systems can be controlled with *simple* means; complex systems require *complex* means.

Like almost all laws of nature, this is essentially evident. The law of gravity, for example, is obvious – so obvious, in fact, that we do not pay any attention to it. It is part of our world and we act accordingly. It goes without saying that the law of gravity did not come into this world with its discoverer. It took an Isaac Newton, however, to discover it, recognize its relevance, and enable its systematic application by man. Similar can be said of Ashby's Law.

To control a system, you need at least as much variety (or complexity) as the system itself comprises. The famous words of Jack Welch, the celebrated former CEO of General Electric, are very much to the point here: if the rate of change on the outside (of an organization) exceeds the rate of change on the inside, disaster looms. The statement proves Welch's sophisticated understanding of complex systems. He knew that complexity was the major future challenge for GE, if the company was to continue growing and remain manageable. "Requisite variety" means capability of adjustment and evolution, as prerequisites for sustainable healthy growth.

If – for whatever reason – there is a variety deficit, the system is *out* of control to that same extent. Here are some examples: it is impossible with only two commands to initiate three responses from a technical device. You cannot translate Shakespeare into another language if your English vocabulary spans 3,000 words. You cannot lead a complex business organization without an appropriate behavioral repertoire. To have a chance at winning, a soccer team needs to be at least as good as the opposing team. The same is true for armies, chess players, and competing companies. Is this trivial? Perhaps so. About as much as the fact that gravity causes objects to fall to the ground. From an *intellectual* perspective it may sound banal – but it is crucial for *succeeding* in a competitive business world.

Hence, the popular slogan "Keep it simple" clearly has its – albeit limited – justification. *If* things can be kept simple, control and regulation mechanisms can be simple as well. On the other hand, simple systems will never have higher capabilities. If the environment is complex, if customers keep getting more demanding and competitors keep getting better, a company needs to be able to develop *sufficient complexity* – or else it will not be able to respond properly.

Let me give you an example for this: from the perspective of cybernetics it was clear from the start that the orientation by one single parameter – shareholder value – which could be observed in the business world over recent years would imply a particularly risky limitation of variety. Altogether, the exclusive orientation by financial figures is too simplistic and reductionist. They are inappropriate means for the control of complex systems. This is evident from the problems piling up in business organizations due to a purely financial focus. These approaches harm the prosperity and vitality of companies and lead to a decrease in stability. In truth, this is not the way to create wealth and values – rather, it paves the ground for crises and collapse.

"Keep it simple" is only half the truth. It is effective where applicable. "Learn to cope with complexity" is the other half: the better an organization can cope with complexity, the greater the odds it will hold its own in an increasingly complex world.

New Role Models

When dealing with complexity we need to adopt new role models and search strategies. Back when Hans Ulrich developed the original St. Gallen Management Model, he already raised the question as to whether there is such a thing as basic sciences for management and what they might be. The hasty reply he received was: business administration. That, however, would have led to the very economic perspective that was to be overcome. Ulrich's assumption was a different one: he thought it could be the general systems theory (which was only just recognizable in sketchy outlines) and, above all, the cybernetics of complex systems. Incidentally, Peter F. Drucker had realized this as well. His comprehensive understanding of these interrelations is evident in both, his book *Landmarks of Tomorrow*[20] and his essay "Information, Communications, and Understanding"[21].

---

20 New York, 1947.
21 In: Drucker, Peter F., *Technology, Management and Society*, New York, 1958.

In my opinion, business administration is clearly suffering from stagnation and sterility when it comes to solving management problems. That discipline can hardly be expected to provide any new impulses. By contrast, truly interesting findings for the solution of complex problems, and in particular for the workings of complex systems, have emerged from biological sciences, brain research, and evolution theory – a fact increasingly recognized in technical disciplines as well.

One of the most interesting and probably most potent developments is bionics[22], the combination of biology and technology. Its basic principle is both simple and seminal: to solve a problem, you can either strain your brain or you can ask yourself whether nature might already have found a solution to a similar problem. Perhaps there will be some lesson to be learnt from it. After all, nature is a huge research lab with some four billion years of experience. Whatever has survived evolution's tough selection criteria might be able to teach us something as well.

Many of my suggestions on how to solve management problems are influenced by this school of thinking.[23]

---

22 Blüchel, Kurt G., *Bionik. Wie wir die geheimen Baupläne der Natur nutzen können,* Munich, 2005; and Blüchel, Kurt G./Malik, Fredmund: *Faszination Bionik. Die Intelligenz der Schöpfung,* Munich, 2006.

23 Malik, Fredmund, *Strategie des Managements komplexer Systeme,* Bern/Stuttgart, 1984, 9th edition 2006; and Gomez, Peter/Malik, Fredmund/Oeller, Karl-Heinz, *Systemmethodik: Grundlagen einer Methodik zur Erforschung und Gestaltung komplexer soziotechnischer Systeme,* 2 volumes, Bern/Stuttgart, 1975.

Chapter 3

Why Management Is Important

> "There are no underdeveloped countries;
> there are only undermanaged ones."
> *Peter F. Drucker*

Management is the most important organ of a functioning society. It is the key function of every society, community, or organization. No social system can exist and persist without management.

Management is the most important factor of competition. Management knowledge is the most important resource to achieve a competitive lead. This is true both for companies and individuals. Management enables people and organizations to have impact. Only management turns cleverness, intelligence, talent, and knowledge into what really counts: results.

Management Is the Most Important Societal Function

As I have often explained and argued before,[24] management is not just another societal function but – understood in its entirety – the most important one. Whether this is something to be appreciated or to be deplored, is a matter of opinion. The fact of the matter is that everything of importance in a society depends on the quality and professionalism of management.

Wherever an organization performs poorly, something is wrong with its management. In *public* this is usually perceived (or pretended) to be a failure of the individuals involved. In most cases, however, it is only a symp-

---

24 Exhaustively in: *Managing Performing Living*, Frankfurt am Main, 2006.

tom of deeper problems in the overall management system, the tools used, and the conceptual basis. This is particularly true for top management failure which, of course, gets plenty of media attention. It is generally made out to be a personal failure; other factors which are at least as important – such as management philosophies, perceptions, strategies, tools, and so on – are hardly mentioned. And even if it was a case of personal failure, there would still be the question as to what kind of recruiting and promotion system would permit a failure to get to the very top of a large, high-profile organization.

In one way or the other, everything important in modern society depends on the quality of execution of the management profession. Wealth, productivity, innovativeness, the use of societal resources, the population's state of health and level of education all depend on management and managers – whatever their actual titles may be.

Management is the most important factor of economic competition. All but a few competitive factors of economic location theory have become meaningless. Resource availability, transport connections, population numbers, and most politico-economic theories are of minor significance. Speaking of good or bad industries is pointless. There are only well-managed and poorly managed companies. If in a given country and in a given industry all companies face more or less identical conditions, and if some of them flourish and others are in difficulties, it cannot be due to the industry or to politics but must be owed to the management of those companies.

Management is also the most important function for globalization. Globalization must be more than Americanization, and it must be more than a legal black hole where the law of the strongest prevails. Globalization, if it is to work and do more good than harm, requires managed institutions.

Management Is the Social Code of the Ability to Master Life

A recent development claims management to be the key to performance and success (possibly even happiness) for individuals as well.[25] The knowl-

25 On this subject, see also the deliberations of Krieg, Walter, and Stadelmann,

edge that has been imparted since the 17th century, when compulsory schooling started, now finds its 21st century equivalent and complement in management knowledge. Within a rather short period – over the past twenty years – the institutions that used to determine, shape, and support lives have lost so much of their power and impact that they are about to become meaningless to mankind.

People no longer join large corporations in the hope of spending their entire working lives there. Companies that used to make such promises, and derive advantages from it, have ceased to do so because nobody can guarantee anything these days. Unions are about to lose significance, even if their rhetoric prevails. The state is withdrawing from all areas, not as a deliberate policy but because the organization forms and managements of social systems prove unable to solve the problems at hand. Lack of money is only a side effect, and a welcome excuse for deeper problems. The churches' influence on people's life conduct is being put to the test. And there is not much to indicate they are regaining their potency. Similar conclusions can be drawn for every kind of social compound.

For the first time, man is on his own. Maybe that is the reason why there is so much talk of networking. Everybody must strive to become fit for society, to make themselves socially useful wherever schools fail to do so. People, in particular young people, are forced to manage their lives for themselves. That does not simply happen – it must be learnt.

Even today, schooling and education are no longer enough. No-one is paid for smartness any more, only for what he or she does with it – for the results. Those knowing more about management than others may not have a career or success guarantee, but they have the best prerequisites for it. Conversely, a lack of management knowledge is almost a guarantee for failure. Management, the transformation of education into results, is the key to personal success. In analogy to the genetic code of viability, it is the social code of the ability to master life.

Peter in: Krieg, Walter/Galler, Klaus/Stadelmann, Peter (eds.), *Richtiges und gutes Management: vom System zur Praxis*, Bern/Stuttgart/Vienna, 2004, p. 323 et seq., and p. 115 et seq.

Chapter 4

Right Management Is Universally Valid

"When the shoe fits
the foot is forgotten."
Indian proverb

There is only one kind of management one needs to know: right manage-ment.[26] In this chapter, I suggest two differentiations which may appear banal at first but have enormous implications. They solve two major problems and eliminate a great deal of confusion. They render numerous education programs superfluous at once, thus saving time, costs, and stress.

Two Differentiations so Far Overlooked

Firstly, I differentiate between right and wrong management: secondly, I distinguish good from bad management. Differentiating between right and wrong refers to *effectiveness*. Differentiating between good and bad refers to *efficiency*. Other kinds of management are not required.

Right and wrong, good and bad have nothing to do with morals; rather, in this book they always imply impact and purposeful functionality; both terms are non-judgmental. It will become clearer at a later point, however, that I am not making a case for non-judgmental management or non-judg-mental management theory.

---

26 See also the relevant passages in Krieg, Walter/Galler, Klaus/Stadelmann, Peter (eds.), *Richtiges und gutes Management: vom System zur Praxis*, Bern/Stuttgart/ Vienna, 2004.

The most important consequence is that there is only one kind of management to be learnt: right and good management. Learning it just once, but correctly, and continuing to perfect it – that is the most reliable, the fastest and shortest way to effectiveness and success.

Effectiveness

		Right	Wrong
Efficiency	**Good**	Right management, done properly, leads to effectiveness and efficiency.	Wrong management can be done well; someone does the wrong things but does them perfectly – a superb path leading straight into disaster.
	Bad	Right management can be done poorly, which is a pity because it causes a loss in efficiency, but still better than doing wrong management well.	No comment required.

Once these two distinctions are comprehended, a third distinction will suggest itself. Everything else contained in text books, curricula, training programs and congress agendas – and which, above all, makes the cash tills ring – has nothing to do with management but with its *application* to different situations.

When right management is applied to what is known, it is *operational management*. When it is applied to what is yet unknown, it is *innovation management*. Hence, to manage new things we do not need any *other* kind of management. It is the same, only we need to master it much better. It comprises the same tasks, tools, and principles. Our masterly command of it, however, must be better.

The situation is comparable to a climber's first ascent. While with known routes we can use existing information and the experience gathered in earlier climbs, enabling us to plan the route quite well, in first ascents we know virtually nothing – the route is new. That is no reason, however, to use different ropes, ice axes, or crampons, nor to climb in a different way. What it does take is perfect command of one's tools, belaying techniques, and so on; in short, it takes an outstanding climber in excellent physical condition. It is not a *different* kind of climbing – it is climbing at another *difficulty level*.

Another example is driving. As such, it always remains the same once you have learnt it. There is a difference, however, in whether you drive through the city in low traffic or during Friday afternoon rush hour. The actual components of driving – braking, changing gears, accelerating, steering – remain the same. It is the conditions that make the difference: they involve difficulties, rush, stress, and risk.

A Solution to Time-Honored Pseudo-Problems

Much too quickly and unthinkingly, people speak of different kinds of management when actually referring to different issues. That does not help to improve management, nor to resolve the issues at hand – the error, thus, is twofold.

Distinguishing between management on the one hand and its application to concrete situations on the other, enables us to resolve a whole series of pseudo-management problems at once. As far as I can tell, this differentiation is not made by anyone so far. Yet it is crucial to avoid confusion.

As soon as the differentiation suggested here is adopted, the result is clarity, making it evident that this is how all other "kinds of management" can become superfluous.

Most of the much-discussed kinds of management, such as international, multicultural and global, virtual, or network management will then lose their power to impress. They shrink to their normal size, no longer justifying a particular kind of management training.

Of course there are international or global organizations, but there is no such thing as international or global management. The factual context is different but the elements of correct management remain the same. It goes without saying that someone about to be sent to China will have to familiarize himself with the country's particularities, its history and culture, its typical manners, customs and habits. The same, however, is true for tourists seriously interested in the country they intend to travel to; it is not exclusively required of managers.

Management is either right or wrong, good or bad, capable or incapable – it is not national or international, mono- or multi-cultural. The fact that managers in an international organization need to speak foreign languages and should be able to deal with foreign currencies, perhaps different measuring units, too, is not even worth mentioning: it is self-evident, and it has nothing to do with management.

Everybody Makes Their Own Mistakes

With these differentiations, I believe I can solve another problem that has been rattling around in management theory for years.

Wrong or *bad* management occurs in countless varieties. Right and good management is identical everywhere. It does not depend on nationality or culture, nor does it depend on the kind of organization, its size, or its field of activity. *Right management is universal and invariant.*

Note that I am not saying management in general is universal and invariant. I am not speaking of management as such, but of right management. This is the crucial point that has largely been neglected so far.

Right management is just as independent of nations or cultures as is sport. For instance, golf – if played correctly – is played the same way everywhere, as is tennis or chess. Of course there are many ways to play golf badly, which is what most people do, but only one way to play it correctly.

My hypothesis on universality has often met with harsh, sometimes even aggressive reactions. The belief that management depends on culture and similar factors seems so deeply rooted that people obviously fail to think and observe. It is ridiculous, so they argue, to say that Italians manage the same way as Germans do, given that they are so different, more temperamental, louder, gesticulating ... Yes, they are all that – if you like to nurture prejudice. There are also very soft-spoken, distinguished Italians, in particular in business. But that is not even what is essential.

The important thing is to differentiate between the What and the How, and, of course, between right and wrong. What gesticulating Italians do when managing the right way is exactly the same as what non-gesticulating Germans do when doing it right. In both countries we find well-managed organizations with clear goals, well-managed and excellently prepared meetings, and effective monitoring processes. Meetings in Italy may be more temperamental (which is not the case, by the way); they are still prepared and managed well.

Business Model and Management Are Different Things

What I said in the last paragraph does not imply – to prevent another potential misunderstanding – that every company cannot achieve its business success in different ways. On the very contrary: the variety of business models and strategies is a key prerequisite to business success, as I will show in the chapter on strategy. Hence, I am not proposing that all business organizations have to act the same way to be successful. Yet, however different their business models may be – the *management* approach of successful organizations is the same everywhere.

An effective automotive manufacturer producing high-end luxury limousines is not managed differently from an effective automotive company producing low-cost, small cars. Their products, production processes, strategies and so on are probably as different as can be; yet in both cases, the same kind of right and good management will be required for success.

The same applies mutatis mutandis to all countries and cultures. It has always been an element of good science to differentiate between appearances and reality. The fact that in business administration and management theory mere legends were allowed to exist for so long raises questions as to the level of their scientific nature, or at least their understanding of scientific approaches.

Also, the rules of managerial impact and professionalism are the same everywhere, just like the rules of grammar. Right and good English is the same around the world, as there is only one way to speak English correctly and well. The proof lies in the very fact that, apart from certain educated circles, English is spoken incorrectly and with poor style and pronunciation almost everywhere in the world. That, however, would never lead an Anglicist (or, in the example above, a golf pro) to speak of intercultural or multicultural English (or golf).

Important and Unpleasant Consequences

Taking account of these facts will have far-reaching consequences. Firstly, it leads us out of the jungle of ubiquitous *management kinds* and *management fashions*. It leads to transparency and clarity, and differentiates right from wrong. Secondly, it will bring enormous relief for company employees and their occupational training; thirdly, it will enable considerable time and cost savings for companies.

As I said before: it is no longer necessary to learn a new kind of management – mostly with bloated, allegedly new requirements – every few years; instead, management is learnt only once, but correctly and well. In short: professionally. It can then be applied to different fields.

The differentiations I am proposing here also have other, partly not very popular implications: much of the empirical research we see today will become superfluous. At present, countless research projects investigate how managers actually behave, broken down by types of organization, industries, countries, and cultures. There are endless research opportunities in this. What can they teach us? Well, mainly that everyone makes his or her own particular mistakes. They do not, however, tell us anything about what would be right – only how great the need for training actually is.

Another consequence, quite understandably not very popular among those concerned, would be the elimination of professorial chairs and of study facilities focusing on international and/or multicultural management and the like. The greatest impact, however, would concern the organizations themselves, their training programs and corporate universities, where much would have to be eliminated and most ot the programs would have to be redesigned. Also, a number of jobs would become redundant in those fields, which would benefit the quality of management training. Nobody would have to lose their jobs, though, as the need for right and good management is enormous.

The Courage to Be Normative

Right management requires the courage to accept normativity. The so-called empirical sciences abhor this like the plague. As far as management is concerned, there is no reason to avoid normativity – just as there isn't in engineering or jurisprudence, for example.[27] What we have here is some-

---

27 For those familiar with my other writings, and with the fact that I accept Karl Popper's scientific teachings, let me point out that there are no contradictions here. In this context I recommend the work of Hans Albert who, like no other, has brought clarity into the practice of scientific application.

thing that the prevailing empirical concept of science is struggling to accept, as it still clings to an outdated and misguided ideal of rationality. Paradox as it may seem, we could almost speak of an "empirical normativism" in this context (if the term as such was not so clumsy). It is a functionality defined by its purpose. Hans Albert deserves the credit for having solved all corresponding philosophical questions, both exhaustively and, in my view, very satisfactorily.[28]

Of course an engineer needs to ask what the proper engineering of a bridge, a paper machine, or an airplane involves. Depending on the situation, there may be certain variations, but the laws of function, material, and statics ultimately determine what is right or wrong. A Ferrari engineer will not have to be persuaded of the need to build a Formula I race car correctly. Also, we know from bionics that nature itself is highly normative in its blueprints and constructions: this – and only this – is how the wings of a dragonfly must look, how a salmon must spawn, and how a deer must act when in rut. Whatever fails to comply will die out.

Remember the proverb at the beginning of this chapter: correct management, if done well (that is, professionally) is not felt – just like a shoe that fits perfectly. It fulfills its function so well that you do not notice it. All the frictions brought on by wrong management will disappear – and so will all the fusses, in particular those caused by fashion trends.

---

28 See, inter alia, Albert, Hans, *Traktat über rationale Praxis*, Tübigen, 1986, as well as his numerous other writings on related topics.

Part II

Effectiveness: Managing People – Managing a Business

Chapter 5

Managing People: The Standard Model of Right and Good Management

In this chapter I will present the model of right management, managerial effectiveness, or effective leadership. The terms are interchangeable. The model has proven useful in the education of and consulting to tens of thousands of managers. It is a part of the original St. Gallen Management Model (see, above all, the first and last chapter of the new edition of *Managing Performing Living*).

Logic of the Model

I am picking up the basic idea of *Managing Performing Living* here, which is that management should be viewed as a profession. As I pointed out in the book, every profession is characterized by four elements:

- The tasks to be fulfilled
- The tools to be employed
- The basic principles determining quality and impact
- The responsibility for the consequences of one's occupation.

The first two elements are indispensable prerequisites for effectiveness and competence, not only for managers but for *anybody* wishing to be effective. In confining myself to the technical elements, I am not implying that management does not have other, further reaching facets. However, it is advisable to *start* with the professional dimension, and with professionalism in the sense of craftsmanship. If necessary, one can always build on that later. In other words, let us not take the second step before the first.

What should be mentioned beforehand is that there is hardly any consensus in management theory. As a matter of fact, it cannot even be considered one singular discipline, such as physics or chemistry, as everything is arbitrary. Everybody is free to invent his or her own management theory, and most people do just that. It is not fashionable to build on what others have developed; continuity is not a criterion.

In management theory, to this date there has been no such thing as a systematic, critical debate leading to consensus and progress – contrary to other disciplines where this is a matter of course. I do not wish to leave readers in the dark about this.

The following ideas and suggestions, thus, do not represent the usual schools of thought. While there is some consensus regarding the tasks of managers (along with a host of greatly differing views), there is hardly any consensus regarding the respective principles and tools. Thus, what I am presenting here are mainly my own findings from thirty years of cooperation with managers of all levels, almost all industries, and all company sizes. These are the things that, according to my experience as a practitioner, have proven most effective.

In other words, while the blessings of consent from academic circles are lacking (which, by the way, are not worth much in terms of validation) there are very valid reasons to contend that no-one can be effective and competent unless he or she has command of the principles, tasks, and tools discussed here. Let me remind you once more that I always speak of management with explixit regard to impact and professional competence. It does not matter whether a manager strives to be popular, clever, or modern – what matters is effectiveness.

At this point I do want to add a word of caution. Whenever you mention a task or tool to managers, the answers you will typically get are, "yes, right", "heard that one before", "forget it". I recommend some restraint here. Even if something has been *heard* often, that does not necessarily mean it is unequivocally clear. The key is to look at what is actually *meant*. The concepts as such may be known. Their content – which is what matters most – may not be.

In the following graph I have visualized the main elements of the management profession, including the logic required for the interaction among these elements. Figure 2 shows five concentric circles which are divided in five segments in the upper half and seven segments in the lower half. The inner circle represents the *responsibility* of managers as a regulative, ethical postulate. Due to the numerous scandals of the past years, the discussion on business, corporate, and management ethics has flared up again since the mid-1990s. It is an old topic which keeps emerging. In my view, to this date the discussion has not produced much in the way of new insights. Ultimately it will be crucial to effectively entrench managers' responsibility, and it is my firm belief that the only uncompromising solution to the problem will be a new, effective regulation of their *liability* – not only for violating professional diligence duties, but also for *entrepreneurial failure*.

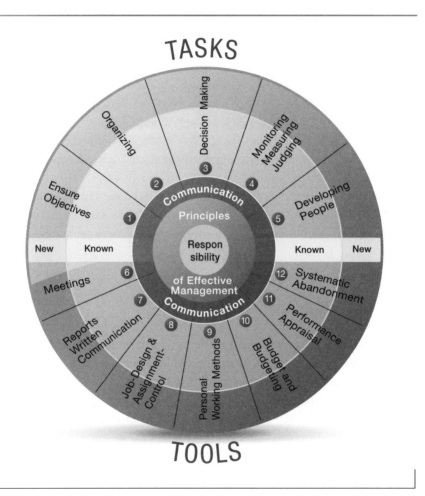

Figure 2: Standard model of Managerial Effectiveness

Further, the inner core – second circle – also comprises the six principles of effective management. They define the quality required in fulfilling tasks and using tools. The principles are another, very powerful subsystem of the total cybernetics of right management which, rather than defining what managers are like or should be like, determines how they must act.

Communication – third circle – is the medium through which these things are propagated, especially in a knowledge society. Communication has developed into a permanent topic, yet there is still little substance. The breakthrough advances that also stem from cybernetics are still largely unknown. One exception is the Syntegration® method by Stafford Beer[29] which is beginning to gain wider acceptance: it is a communication process which is optimized in a mathematically provable manner. It allows establishing consensus on complex issues across the largest possible number of people within the shortest possible period of time, demonstrably making optimal use of everyone's knowledge. Successes to date, achieved in more than three hundred cases, are very compelling.

In the upper semicircle we see the five essential management *tasks*, in the lower semicircle the seven management *tools* I consider most important.

I am using the two outer rings – note they have the same contents – to distinguish the management of the *known* from the management of the *new*, or operational management from innovation management.

What Every Manager Needs

The choice of tasks, tools and principles is determined by one question: what do *all* managers need at *minimum*, *everywhere* and at *all times*? Hence, the model contains everything that can be *generalized* across areas, industries, and managemenet levels.

This is why the model can be used in *all* organizations, why it is universal. No organization can function any other way. In some instances more elements might have to be added, due to the specifics of the *individual* organization's purposes. At minimum, however, it is always the same five tasks, seven tools, and six principles which determine the effectiveness of people and organizations. And there is yet another aspect to the model's universality: not only can it be used *in* all institutions; it can also be ap-

---

29 Beer, Stafford, *Beyond Dispute*, Chichester, 1994.

plied *to* all institutions. The reason is that I do not define in detail how the tasks should be interpreted. For instance, goals can be the personal goals of an individual wishing to be effective; they can also be the goals of a whole corporation. Likewise, the task of organizing can mean both, organizing one's personal environment or organizing an entire institution. The same is true in analogy for all other tasks and generally for all elements in the model.[30]

The Tasks

1. Providing Objectives

Without objectives there is no management, even if from time to time it comes into vogue to deny this. I am explicitly saying "providing objectives", not "agreeing on objectives" or "setting goals". Whether you agree on them or set them depends on the situation. It should not be a dogma. The task as such is to ensure there are goals, and that they are clear and precise.

2. Organizing

Managers must organize their fields of responsibility themselves, including both structures and processes. Whether they use expert help is of secondary importance. In some instances it will be useful. Still, it remains their task to provide a reasonable, functioning organization, and they are responsible for that. This is one of the vital tasks of management

3. Making Decisions

Making decision does not make you a manager (infants, ants, and even electronic fuel injection systems make decisions), but if you do not make decisions you are not a manager – whatever your rank or status. As we have seen, making decisions is not the only management task (although

---

30 I will keep the following descriptions as brief as possible. For more detailed explanations, please refer to *Managing Performing Living: Effective Management for a New Era*. Frankfurt am Main/New York, 2006.

some say it is) but it is still the most critical one. In decisions, everything is tied together and "put in a nutshell", so to speak.

4. Monitoring, Measuring, Judging

Monitoring is often considered outdated, and some authors even recommend dispensing with it. I do not agree with that. Monitoring is one of management's most essential tasks. You only need to choose between different kinds of monitoring. You can monitor in a way that will destroy all motivation, or you can do it so that this will not happen. In any case there should be no discussion about the necessity of monitoring.

The basis of supervision is measuring and judging. Wherever something can be measured, it should be. As this is not always possible in a stricter sense, judging and evaluating are part of monitoring. In this context, the issue of the evaluator's subjectivity is often emphasized. It is not as serious an issue as is often said, though. There would be a problem if it were pure arbitrariness; that, however, can be prevented.

5. Developing People

Finally there is the task of developing people. Note that I am saying "people", not "employees". All management tasks are important, but promoting people should have first priority – not the least because most managers find this task harder to fulfil than others.

Developing people is not the same as motivating them. There is hardly even a connection between the two, although they are frequently confused. Developing people means, first and foremost, not trying to change them but taking them as they are and trying to make the best of their potential. It means using their strengths and making their weaknesses meaningless – not by eliminating them (something that is hardly ever accomplished) but by putting people in positions where their weaknesses are irrelevant. It does not matter when a mountain guide is tone-deaf, or a violin soloist terrified of heights.

What About All the Other Tasks?

The list of management tasks proposed here may appear incomplete to some, and whoever wishes to amend it should do so if it seems useful. My point here is the minimum required, not the maximum possible. It is my view that management *cannot* function and will not produce results, if the five tasks described are not accomplished – except perhaps for a short while, thanks to fortunate coincidences and conditions that cannot be expected to stay that way.

I recommend restraint in adding more tasks. In most cases this will only complicate things further, and not much will be gained. In recent years, for instance, it was often said that the task of management was to "enable" or "empower" people. In my opinion that does not imply any real progress. Both are part of developing and supporting people; both are associated with the correct handling of goals and with sensible organizing principles.

Another example of a supposedly new management task is the proposition that managers must instil "enthusiasm" in those reporting to them. That may be a nice and romantic idea but it has little to do with management effectiveness. Firstly, most things to be done in a company are rather trivial. You would need to have a rather unique disposition to develop enthusiasm daily for writing invoices, financial controlling, or developing a business plan. Even innovation is usually only inspirational at the beginning; as soon as the realities of it emerge they will require hard work rather than enthusiasm. Secondly, enthusiasm is only seldom (if at all) required in companies. What matters is effectiveness and productivity, endurance and stamina, diligence and carefulness.

Even innovation is not a management task of its own, in my opinion, although it is doubtlessly a *corporate* task. When it comes to innovations you need goals, you need to organize, make decisions, etcetera. The list of tasks is long enough, no further additions required. Something else is much more important: in the case of innovations, these managerial tasks must be executed with particular *perfection* and *precision*. That is what causes most of the difficulties. Some special tips will be included in the chapter on innovation and change.

What will probably surprise many readers the most, however, is that two things are not listed here which are regularly mentioned in the context of managerial tasks: *motivating* and *communicating*. I have left them out very deliberately – not because they are unimportant but because they form part of another logical *category* distinct from the tasks I have described.

Communication can be better understood if you do not regard it as a task but as a medium through which tasks are executed. Just like money is a medium for business organizations, or a vehicle for their work, so are information and communication (which, of course, differ from each other). Communication is no end in itself. It is always *about* something – about goals, about decision options, about budgets. It is not a management task to simply communicate.

Motivation, on the other hand, is an issue still largely unresolved. The deeper you look into it, the more difficulties and ambiguities will emerge. It seems to me the issue of motivation is a bit like quicksand – on the surface everything seems in order; once you get deeper into it, however, you no longer have a fixed point to hold on to.

So long as we do not have more and better information about motivation, I suggest treating it not like a management task in the stricter sense but as an *outcome* of competently executing the five tasks described here. Perhaps we should try to do without the verb "motivate" altogether. The longer I think about it, the greater my doubts as to whether it is possible at all to motivate other people. Fortunately, there are people who are perfectly able to motivate themselves. Maybe that is even true for most, provided they are not hindered. Then there are quite a few who replace motivation with a sense of duty. That is quite a lot in itself, and in most cases it will take people farther than they would have thought. Of course it is possible to demotivate people, but that does not mean the opposite is possible as well.

If the management tasks described in this chapter are executed carefully, with due diligence and competence, there is usually no need to worry about people's motivation – at least I think this is true for a sufficient number of people. As for those still lacking motivation, I suggest not losing too much time with them. Perhaps they will be better off looking for another job.

The Tools of a Manager

Before I deal with this issue in my seminars, I often ask participants what they consider to be the tools of a manager. Invariably they list a series of highly complicated things, such as capital cost calculation, discounted cash-flow analysis, network planning techniques, market research, regression analysis, and so on; of course the computer is mentioned as well.

All these are tools – but tools for specialists, not general management tools. Every business organization needs people with good command of all kinds of capital cost calculation and cash-flow analysis. However, not every manager needs those things, least of all on a daily basis.

What, then, are the tools every manager needs and requires every day? What are the things he or she should use as tools? I will name seven: meetings, reports, job design and assignment control, personal working method, budgets and budgeting, performance evaluation, and systematic abandonment of the obsolete.

1. Meetings

Almost every manager spends plenty of time in meetings of different kinds. Even if a deliberate effort is made to minimize the duration of meetings, they will always require a major share of a manager's time. It is therefore in one's own interest, in the other participants' and in the company's interest to do one's utmost to ensure productive and efficient meetings – meetings that produce results. The key to that is preparation and follow-up.

2. Reports

In using this term I refer to all kinds of written materials, whether on paper or on the Web. This includes business correspondence, offers and tenders, messages, memorandums, file notes, and minutes of meetings. While the spoken word prevails in meetings, so does the written word in reports, along with images and graphs. Even if paper was to be completely replaced by electronic media some day – which will not happen too soon – that would do nothing to change the importance of written communication. This is why managers need to use reports (in the broadest sense) as tools if they aim for effectiveness.

3. Job Design and Assignment Control

In any organization, people work in jobs or positions. Regardless of whether an organization is flat or steep, functional, divisional, or matrix-based, whether it is tightly controlled or a loosely knit network – there will always be positions and jobs. And they must be designed – their architecture and logic must be right. Business organizations spend a lot of money on product design – and rightly so – but less so on job design. This is a serious mistake, and one of the main sources of deficits in performance and productivity. It is also one of the most frequent reasons for a lack in motivation. Careful job design will become all the more important, the more fluid jobs are becomig due to the influence of information sciences, and the more networkers, teleworkers, and in particular brainworkers we have.

Another topic closely linked to job design is assignment control. If a job is the static element, the assignment is one of the sources of an organization's dynamics.

4. Personal Working Method

Nothing characterizes effective people better than a set of well-thought-out working methods – and at the same time, there is hardly anything at the start of a professional career that depends so much on chance. Yet the working methods of effective and ineffective people are as different as day and night. Contrary to popular opinion, this is true also – and particularly so – for creative people, as anyone studying their biographies will find. The best knowledge, the highest intelligence, and the greatest talent lie idle if they fail to be transformed into results through a methodical working approach. That does not mean that all effective people have the same working method – quite the contrary. But all of them work methodically and systematically.

5. Budget and Budgeting

Artists and Freelancers may not need a budget, although many have one – at least a time budget. It is a definite fact, however, that every manager needs a budget and at least rudimentary budgeting skills. The budget is one of the most important tools of integration and control in an organization. In a sense, it represents the steering wheel, accelerator, clutch, and brake – all in one.

6. Performance Appraisal

Managers must enable people to perform and bear responsibility for the performance delivered. Hence they also need to evaluate performance. Not to achieve absolute objectivity – which is impossible anyway – but to exclude gross arbitrariness. It can be quite easy, as can be all the other tools mentioned here. Mind you, I am not advocating the grotesquely complex evaluation systems used by many organizations, especially large corporations. These systems are disliked by most managers – and for good reasons, in my view. They use these systems because they have to, not because they are convinced of their merits. On the other hand, few managers would entirely disapprove of performance evaluations as such. They are aware that without them we could not even speak of performance – much less of progress.

7. Systematic Abandonment of the Obsolete

Every organism has processes for the systematic disposal of waste products and toxins. The analogous is needed by every organization and every manager. They need a continuous process, initiated from within, of systematic revitalization and regeneration. There is a simple tool that does the trick – I call it the "sysematic abandonment". Only when this tool is missing or has become blunt will there be a need for harsh measures such as the Overhead Value Analysis. One of the most important and simplest methods to keep organizations slim, young, and energetic, is to *"stop doing the wrong things"* – which translates into abandonment of the obsolete.

Principles

The third defining characteristic of a profession is principles. The purpose of management principles in an institution is to ensure a certain – from a functional point of view a desired –, behavior of managers, in line with the requirements of the institution itself and of the people in it. Principles are all the more important the greater the division of responsibilities (in operational processes and in management), the higher the degree of decentralization, and, consequently, the greater the number of persons involved in overall management and required to act in a coordinated manner.

The content of an organization's management principles will obviously depend on its value system, which, in turn, depends on the organization's basic understanding of management. It includes issues ranging from leadership style and motivation to morals and ethics.

In practice there is a great variety of management principles with different names and widely varying content. Moreover, in documents entitled "management principles" we often find combinations of elements describing much more than principles, and which could also be categorized as "management tasks" or "management tools". The spectrum of variations is further broadened by the fact that to this date science has not produced an authoritative management theory, not even a terminology that would meet with general consensus.

The principles I am proposing in the following paragraphs, to provide a basis for the definition of management principles, follow two criteria which must be observed in any kind of organization: one is the effectiveness of management actions, the other is the quality of execution of management work. Hence they can be considered the foundation of professionalism in management. They determine how management tasks should be executed and how management tools should be employed. They are at the core of managerial effectiveness. I suggest considering them the essence of any viable corporate culture.

Being or Doing?

For much too long and to this very day, management theoreticians have been searching for the ideal type of the good manager. The key to success is usually assumed to lie in certain characteristics, skills, and personality structures.

Yet if the numerous analyses conducted in this context have proven one thing, it is the fact that the ideal type only exists on paper. Successful and effective managers are as different as humans can be. Some are extremely analytical, calculating, and systematic – others spontaneous, intuitive, and erratic. Some have extraordinary intelligence, others are rather average in this respect. Some are downright workaholics, others almost lazy. Some are open-minded, outgoing, and extroverted, others rather tight-lipped, even shy and withdrawn.

Effectiveness and success, however, are hardly correlated with factors like these. The essential thing is not how people are but how they act; not being but doing is what matters. Effective people – and this is true in particular for managers – let their actions be guided by a set of principles, irrespective of their personality traits or characteristics.

Whatever they do, why they do it and where: they align their actions with some rules. I will single out six of them here. It seems that the key to management success lies in these rules, rather than in characteristics, and this is why I propose them as a basis for and core to the formulation of management principles. There may be good reasons in the individual case for expanding and amending them.

1. Focus on Results

A consistent pattern in the way competent managers think and act is their focus on results. This is what they are primarily – sometimes exclusively – interested in. Everything else is of secondary interest to them, or of no interest at all. In some instances this strict focus on outcomes can even take on pathological dimensions. Still – it is the results that count for them.

A results focus is not something that comes naturally to most people. Even if we assume that all people in all organizations work hard every day, that does not mean they achieve results. Otherwise it would not be necessary to resort to approaches such as "management by objectives".

Every experienced manager knows how difficult it is to focus people on targets and results. People are not born output-oriented; most are input-oriented. A majority of them will focus on the effort, work, and expenditure required, rather than on performance and output.

Focusing on outputs instead of inputs is not very difficult, as long as an individual delivers a performance largely by him- or herself, or in a small group, as in those cases there will be a visible and tangible relation between the effort made and the result achieved. By contrast, in the world of organizations, and particularly in large organizations, it is more difficult to maintain an output focus because the relation between effort and result is much less noticeable, sometimes even non-existent. The work of staff employees, development engineers, researchers in the pharmaceutical industry, HR developers, and the like will often take several years to produce visible results, hence it is humanly understandable that they often focus more on the input side.

It takes a continuous, systematic effort to achieve a results focus, which is why this principle needs to be firmly embedded in an organization's management principles. At the end of the day, results are the only and decisive assessment criterion for managers and their effectiveness. What really matters is neither the work someone has put in nor the endeavors and efforts he or she has made, but solely the results achieved.

2. Contribution to the Whole

Of course it is not enough to just achieve results, period. They must be the right results. While it certainly differs from one company to the next what those right results may be, all of them can only be determined if from time to time we look away from our immediate area of responsibility, from our field of specialization, and fix our gaze on the big picture. The key question is: "What can I do to make a substantial contribution to the whole?"

Regardless of all the lip service paid – the strive for a wholistic view, the effort to regard an organization as an entity, is much less common than it should be in a highly complex business world. The greater the division of labor and the more specialization we have, the higher the risk that we lose our sense of the overall purpose, and that the results we achieve will no longer be related to that purpose. As a result, deliberate coordination and permanent intervention in the inner fabric of an organization are becoming increasingly important, which, in turn, implies the need for centralistic management – even if none of those involved really want it.

The only way to avoid it is to keep asking again and again how each individual can contribute to the whole: this is the basis of what is usually referred to as self-regulation, self-coordination, or self-organization in institutions. These organizational skills do not flow from some kind of mystical force, nor are they achieved with computer systems; they are simply the result of many people subordinating their actions to the whole, driven by a deep understanding of the greater purpose.

At the same time, this is the only way to turn specialists into near generalists. You can hardly ask a specialist to study more specialty fields in addition to her own, but you can ask her to or even make her see that specialty in relation to the whole, and integrate herself into the totality.

The larger an organization, the greater the difficulty in answering the question of individuals' contributions. Finding clear, comprehensible and compelling answers to this question, both for themselves and their reports, is one of the crucial tasks of managers. This very question enables a person to take the step from efficiency to effectiveness: from the ability to do things right to the ability to do the right things, as Peter Drucker[31] so poignantly put it.

It was with reason that Drucker suggested the question of individuals' contribution become a central criterion for the very definition of the term "manager". Outward characteristics like rank and status, income, prestige, title, and number of subordinates are of little use in identifying the persons performing (or who should perform) the function of manager in a modern sense, a sense appropriate for today's societal structure.

Of all the different definitions of "manager" and "management", the best is probably that which emphasizes the individual's responsibility for a contribution to the whole and makes it a central criterion. What matters is not power but a certain function. It is the function which is responsible for the productive use of resources in the broadest sense, the function that can create the conditions under which all the forces available within its sphere of influence will deliver an overall performance which is more than the sum of its parts, and which represents an essential contribution to the overall institution's functioning and purpose fulfillment.

"Responsibility for delivering a contribution" is the only perspective permitting the correct fulfillment of the tasks of a manager. A consistent focus on this perspective enables all available resources to be deployed efficiently and, in particular, effectively (that is to say, for the right things) under continually changing conditions.

Only this focus on the individual's contribution to the overal institution – as vague and insufficient as this criterion may seem – offers the chance to identify the right goals at all levels of the organization, adequately deploy resources, find suitable measures for assessing results, and build trust and justice. Hence, the key questions to be asked over and over again are: "What exactly is my contribution to the whole?", "What exactly is my people's contribution to the whole / what should it be?"

Simple and convenient answers to these questions can always be found. Good managers distinguish themselves from mediocre and non-managers by applying high standards with regard to the quality of their answers, and by never being satisfied with one answer only. A thorough analysis of the contribution to be made will always reveal a series of problems. It of-

---

31 See, inter alia, Drucker, Peter F., *Management – Tasks, Responsibilities, Practices*, London, 1973, p. 17 et seq.

ten shows the goal of the overall institution to be anything but clear enough for determining the contributions of individual divisions, departments, and so on in a meaningful way. In many cases it will take plenty of consideration and discussion with staff members, colleagues, and superiors to finally arrive at an answer.

One thing, however, will invariably prove true: rendering a contribution to a complex institution requires, above all, the art of balancing, weighing, and integrating. The question about one's contribution never has a one-dimensional answer. There are always several dimensions to be considered and integrated, trade-offs to be made, and strengths to be combined with weaknesses. Here, again, a good manager will learn to live with the ambiguities and inherent uncertainties of a real situation, and he or she will not assume pseudo-clarity and pseudo-certainty where there is none.

3. Concentration on a Few Things

If you focus on results and on your contribution to the whole, you will quickly find that you cannot do that in many different areas. You will need to concentrate on just a few. No-one can be permanently successful in many fields. As Drucker rightly says, "if there is a 'secret' to effectiveness it is concentration. Effective executives do first things first and they do one thing at a time."[32]

The significance of this principle is not diminished by the fact that managers have to deal with dozens of different issues day in, day out. Management, like hardly any other profession, is permanently exposed to the danger of fragmentation and dissipation of forces. This, however, is precisely what further increases the need to concentrate on a selected few things; it is the reason why concentration is required to achieve results. You can busy yourself with hundreds of things, but you can only achieve excellent results in a few. The principle of concentration almost automatically leads to the right priorities and to professionalism.

This will be particularly important for the brainworker, for that fastest-growing group of people in our organizations which has begun to replace those doing physical work. Result-oriented brainwork requires long, undisturbed stretches of time. Every interruption will prolong the overall

---

32 Drucker, Peter F., *The Effective Executive*, New York, 1966.

working time by the time required for mental readjustment, for "picking up the thread" again.

In the past hundred years we have succeeded in making manual work so productive that the classical industrial worker will become "extinct". In ten to twenty years, he will have a share of employment comparable to that of farm workers today, about 3 to 5 percent. Even today, brainwork contributes a by far greater share of the overall performance, and the key to productivity of brainwork will be relentless concentration on a few focal areas.

4. Utilizing Strengths

So far, we have discussed three pillars of managerial effectiveness: a focus on results, a clear understanding of the individual's contribution to the whole, and concentration on a few things. They must be amended by a fourth principle following from the fact that people do not have a uniform potential for achievement. Among other things, their individuality is expressed in greatly differing strengths and weaknesses.

Almost all organizations are under high and increasing performance pressure. In many areas, top performance is expected. So how can we expect people to meet these expectations, considering that millions of people working in organizations are basically ordinary people, far from being able to deliver top performances every day?

There is only one way to resolve this contradiction – the permanent demand for top performance on the one hand, the availability of only ordinary people on the other: we must build on existing strengths. Performance can only be expected to the extent that the design of tasks permits a maximum of people to deliver their contributions exactly where they have their natural talents and strengths.

The fourth pillar of good management, thus, is to ask oneself without prejudice: what can I really do better than others? Where are my true strengths? Managers have the additional task to ask this question not only for themselves, but also for their people. There is probably nobody – or hardly anybody – who only has strengths. Everyone has both, strengths and weaknesses, and the more pronounced the strengths of a person are, the greater usually their weaknesses.

No-one will expect, neither of himself nor of others, to see optimal performance and excellent results where a person's greatest weaknesses lie. Perhaps it is possible for a while, but it would be inhuman to demand it permanently. It is not inhuman, however, to demand high performance in fields where someone has his strengths. What is more, it often turns out that in those fields performance does not even have to be demanded: it is delivered voluntarily because many people find it easier to produce results in fields where they have strengths.

5. Trust[33]

Trust is another element crucial for the effectiveness of organizations, their performance potential and, consequently, the distinction between good and bad management. Over and over again we observe managers who are obviously making every mistake in the book – but still have managed to achieve an excellent situation in their division or unit. On the other hand, there are those going strictly by the book and doing everything correctly – but who are nevertheless struggling with a crisis or permanent difficulties. Why is that so?

Almost invariably it is because the first type of manager has won the trust of his people, peers, and superiors. If and when someone succeeds in building a trust base there will also be a robust management situation. It must be robust against all the management mistakes happening every day. Most managers make mistakes – unintentionally, and mostly without realizing it. It simply happens in the rush of day-to-day business.

The key point, however, is not whether or not mistakes are made but how serious they are. Only a sound and solid trust base can cushion such mistakes. While employees will suffer frustration and occasionally anger, ultimately they will know they can rely on their boss. The same is true for colleagues.

Quite remarkably, there is much literature on motivation but hardly anything about trust. Trust in organizational environments is among the topics least researched – much in contrast to its significance in practice. Good managers act according to the principle "when in doubt, what matters most is mutual trust, rather than the much-discussed motivation". They will therefore do anything to build trust, and avoid anything that could undermine it.

---

33 See also Linda Pelzmann in: Krieg, Walter/Galler, Klaus/Stadelmann, Peter (eds.), *Richtiges und gutes Management: vom System zur Praxis*, Bern/Stuttgart/Vienna, 2004.

Although we do not know much about trust yet, it is quite obvious that it is no psychological category. Good feelings, good interpersonal relations, the "chemistry" between people and the "same wavelength" may be good and important, but they are mere side-effects of trust. Ultimately, trust equals reliability and calculability. People need to be able to know where they stand with their superiors and co-workers. Integrity of character seems crucial – meaning what you say, and practicing what you preach.

6. Positive Thinking

Good managers think positively and constructively. They force themselves to do so if need be. They are neither naïve optimists nor do they rely on miracles, but in the course of their lives they have learned that even in dark clouds you need to look for the silver linings. That does not mean they are permanently successful; they know, however, that negative attitudes and expectations will stand in the way of success, while positive ones will give it a chance.

The ability to control one's thinking, and thus one's attitudes and expectations, is important in two respects: it leads from a problem focus to the exploiting of opportunities, and from external motivation to self-motivation.

Every day, managers are called upon to solve dozens of problems, iron out difficulties, and clear roadblocks out of the way. That in itself is not managerial performance or success. Rather, performance and success can be expected only if chances and opportunities are seized, and that requires positive thinking. "What are the chances inherent in this problem, and how could we turn it into a productive opportunity?" This is the question good managers should keep asking.

The same positive thinking causes good managers not to wait until they are motivated by someone or something, but to motivate themselves. Even if an assessment of the situation reveals that it is bad, they still ask themselves: now what can I do for something to change?

All of the above could be considered faith healing, wishful thinking, or mysticism – if we did not have the impressive findings of psychology on the so-called Pygmalion Effect, or the phenomenon of self-fulfilling prophecies. The mere anticipation of an effect can cause that very effect to happen; at the very least it will increase the likelihood of its occurrence. This may not hold true in the world of scientists. It is certainly true in the world of communication.

Quality of Management

As mentioned at the beginning of this chapter, the principles suggested here determine the quality of execution of management tasks. Contrary to personal traits, they can be recognized in someone's behavior, and derived from it.

In individual cases there may be additional elements resulting from the specifics of an industry; perhaps also from the structural conditions of an organization, its history, or its purpose. It is, however, advisable to be sparing with amendments.

As I have pointed out, these principles form the core of corporate culture or – in less posh terms than have become fashionable in management circles – of good, competent, and effective management. They do that in two respects: firstly, more than these six principles will not be required in most cases; without them there can be no good management, nor can there be a viable corporate culture sustainable even in times of trouble. Secondly – and more importantly – without these principles it will be impossible to manage an organization successfully in the long run, irrespective of any other elements one might consider necessary.

In both cases, the aspect of sustainability is important. Of course it cannot be ruled out completely that, under otherwise favorable conditions, it may be possible to momentarily disregard or neglect one or several of these principles and permit them to erode without there being any major repercussions – at least for the short term. Long-term consequences, however, will invariably be negative.

The six principles must be viewed and adhered to in their entirety. They are not interchangeable, there are no trade-offs. They form a set of behavioral rules, the purpose of which is to establish effective, professional management.

Moreover, these principles exclude a number of unnecessary and superfluous "theories". Hence they also provide a basis for a certain economy of the mind, for it is neither possible nor really necessary to read and learn everything that has been said and written about management. The decision on what to observe and what to disregard requires criteria. The principles for effective management provide standards for a critical appraisal of management theories.

Obviously they can also be learnt. They are easy to understand, though not always easy to follow. But it is possible to internalize them, and learn to apply them. To a certain extent they replace managerial talent; wherever talent exists, they facilitate its full utilization.

Expansion of the Model

It is important to note that great restraint must be exerted in expanding the model.[34] It does not take a genius to draw up long lists of perceived management tasks and tools. The art lies in restraining oneself to what is truly essential and what can be generalized.

It is one of the greatest deficits of today's management scene that new lists keep being drawn up which are entirely arbitrary at heart and do not follow any compelling or even discernable logic. If in individual cases there are good reasons to add an item to the list of management tasks, such as planning, that is indeed possible. I would place it between the first and the second task, that is to say, between "providing goals" and "organizing". The circular shape of the graph permits it without breaking the logic. In general, however, I prefer to consider "planning" a part of "providing objectives".

Management Tasks and Operational Tasks: A Much-Neglected Distinction

Management tasks must be clearly distinguished from operational tasks. Due to the fact that management is often confused with business administration or economics, the two types of tasks are hardly differentiated. The widespread opinion that management is mainly, or exclusively, somethng that concerns business enterprises further adds to the confusion.

Tasks like procurement, logistics, production, marketing, distribution, accounting, finance, personnel, and so on are clearly *subject-specific, op-*

---

34 For the relevant argumentation, see my book *Managing Performing Living.*

erational tasks of a typical manufacturing business. Their execution requires other skills and experiences than their *management* does. A person can be an excellent financial expert, and at the same time a lousy manager. Likewise, even the best manager can be a complete layman in financial issues, for instance because he has his subject-specific competencies in marketing or personnel. Even the best and most seasoned managers cannot solve every subject-specific task, hence they cannot lead just any organization, as some people are fond of believing.

The nature of operational tasks depends on the kind of institution to be managed. It can differ greatly even among business organizations. In banks and insurance, logistics is of minor or sometimes no importance; in manufacturing companies it is usually crucial. Service providers seldom have research departments in the stricter sense. In pharmaceutical companies research is one of the central tasks; yet it is very different from research in automotive companies.

Marketing in a branded luxury food company is something entirely different from marketing in plant engineering, in the steel industry, or in durables. It is different in a fashion company, and yet another thing in a commercial discounter.

As a general rule, it takes highly specialized and very different subject-specific skills, specialized methods, and different kinds of expertise to execute subject-specific tasks.

Management tasks, by contrast, remain the same throughout. I have pointed it out before and will repeat it again: management is the transformation of resources into results. Every task requires management, in order for the subject-specific knowledge (the resource) to produce results – to *become effective*. Historically, operational tasks and management tasks were closely linked, often inseparably and indistinguishably. Craftsmen of earlier times did not make that distinction. In their vocational training they usually learned both, subject-specific skills and the methods to transfer them into results.

The more vocational training and practical application fall apart, the more important it is to acquire the transformational or effective knowledge – or, in other words, to learn management.

For instance, marketing must be given the right goals. This requires both management skills and marketing skills. Marketing must be organized, marketing decisions must be made, marketing activities must be controlled, and marketing staff must be developed and supported. It always takes both types of skills and experience, from marketing and from management. This is equally true for all other operational tasks. The following graph illustrates this in a general manner.

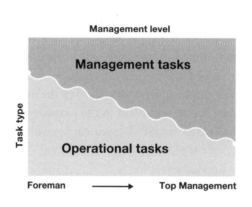

Figure 3: Distinction of operational and management tasks

What is shown here is the distinction (not: the separation) of the two kinds of tasks – operational and management tasks. The sinuous line implies that the distinction is not always sharp, and that both kinds of tasks often overlap – for instance, the subject-specific tasks of human resource management and the management task of developing and promoting people. Transitions are also fluid when it comes to strategic questions, structural issues, and issues of corporate culture, which, however, does not diminish but rather increase the importance of said distinction.

In addition, it turns out that there must be *both* kinds of tasks at *all* levels – from the production foreman to top manager. A foreman has plenty of operational tasks and a small, but not insignificant share of management tasks. With a top executive it is the other way round. As will be discussed in the chapter on top management, it is highly advisable also for top managers to take on one or two subject-specific tasks, instead of focusing on management alone, as otherwise they will gradually lose track of reality.

Specifics of Application

Operational tasks are not identical in all institutions but differ according to their respective purpose. Up to now I have used the typical business functions of *commercial* organizations for clarification. There are other operational tasks in other institutions and organizations. Hospitals, schools and universities, opera houses and symphonic orchestras, government agencies and political parties each have their particular operational tasks. The execution of these tasks requires *management*, and the management tasks involved are the same as in a business organization.

The differences often emphasized with regard to the management of different institutions, thus, are not inherent in the management tasks as such but in the operational tasks required from each institution. This is expressed in figure 4, where typical specifics of different organizations have been entered into the previous graph.

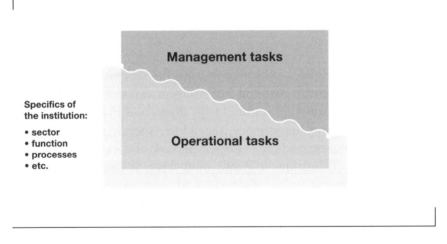

Figure 4: Application specifics of institutions

The specifics of operational tasks depend on the institution in question, the industry (if it is a business enterprise), its functions and processes, and also on the situation the particular institution is in. For instance, when a previously public institution is privatized or when a clinic adopts a specialization, there will be new and different operational tasks as a consequence of that change.

These differences are only indirectly related to management; they result from factual and operational aspects. Yet they must be observed in executing management tasks. This, again, is an application problem.

An additional step is required to clarify the application specifics of management. For instance, there is a difference in managing experienced or inexperienced people, elder persons or younger ones, people with a higher or lower educational level. Another factor concerns the living conditions of the people to be managed: it should be self-evident that managers care about their people's health. Likewise, it is important to respect cultural and religious values and customs.

We could simply speak of cultural idiosyncrasies. That, however, would cause confusion with corporate culture. Corporate culture really has nothing to do with these things, as they represent the particulars of individual situations rather than general characteristics of the organization. I therefore prefer the term "application specifics", resulting from the situation at hand, or "situation specifics", relating to the execution of management tasks in the individual case.

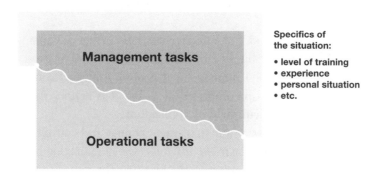

Figure 5: Application specifics of management

These situations can change quickly, which is why they should not be considered questions of corporate culture. The interplay of both aspects discussed is depicted in the following graph:

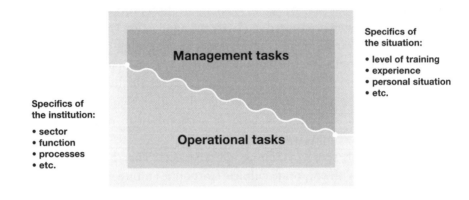

Figure 6: Overview of the specifics of application

Five Fields of Application in Practice

The Standard Model of Effectiveness has further advantages. The following graph shows the five immediate fields of application. As I have explained in chapter 1, management is often understood to mean managing people. That is also comprised in it, but it is neither the most important nor the most difficult field of application.

In three decades as a management trainer and consultant, I have hardly ever been told that the main difficulty was in managing people. This observation is in sharp contrast to the fact that the issue of managing people is the topic that dominates both literature and management training. The best employees are those who do not need a boss. They will soon be one of the most important elements in functioning organizations.

Compared to the people in an organization, the remaining elements of the overall management network are much more difficult to manage because managers lack the authority to direct them.

At the same time, however, managing those other components is also more important, as success is much more dependent on those factors than it is on the management of one's people. With regard to significance and level of difficulty, there is a clear ranking order:

- Managing oneself
- Managing the boss
- Managing the outside world (subsidiaries, customers etc.)
- Managing the peers
- Managing subordinates.

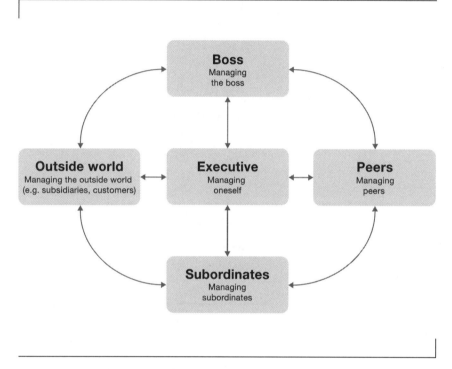

Figure 7: Fields of application for management

Mentally, we add the circular Standard Management Model to each component shown in figure 7. The resulting effects of interaction lead to an enormous self-organization capability for the organization which cannot be accomplished any other way.[35] The standard model of effective man-

---

35 See also *m.o.m.*® *Malik on Management Letters* Nos. 3/95 and 5/95 on the management of bosses and colleagues.

agement comprises the very rules that, if adhered to by the key executives in an organization, will lead to the emergence of a so-called spontaneous or self-generating order[36] or, in other words, to an efficiency-enhancing self-organization.

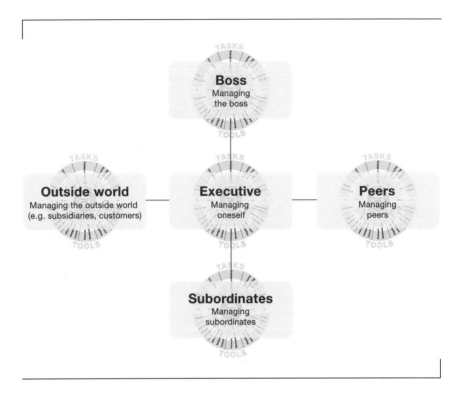

Figure 8: The Standard Model of Effective Management, applied to all fields

Note that not all managers of an organization have to explicitly manage in accordance with this model although it is preferable. It is sufficient if a critical number of them do. Usually they are the opinion leaders, hardly more than about 30 percent of all executives.

Apart from the creation of true self-organization, numerous perceived management problems will not only be resolved but entirely dissolved, because they are essentially pseudo-problems. One of them is the eternal

36 See also *m.o.m.*® *Malik on Management Letter* 9/04 on self-organization in management.

problem of motivation; another is corporate culture: no need to worry about it if you observe this model. Its application will bring to light what are probably the most important parts of the right culture: performance, effectiveness, and accountability. We could also say that effective management is the right corporate culture.

Chapter 6

Managing a Business: The Integrated Management System (IMS®)

As mentioned before, my standard model is not only valid at the level of individuals or groups of people; it also applies to entire institutions and their essential elements. This can be achieved in one single step: in figure 7, the term "outside world" is replaced by "institution" and the standard model is then applied.

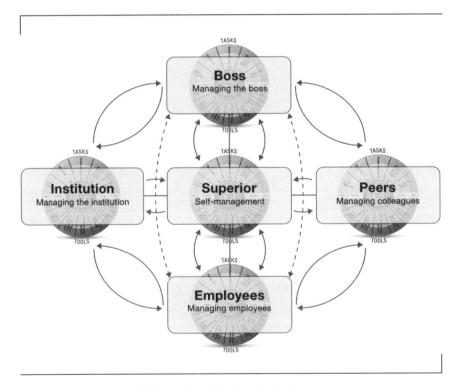

Figure 9: "Outside world" is replaced by "institution".

It is advisable, though, to use a special concept at this level to facilitate the transfer and application of the model. The right and effective management of an entire institution requires a wider frame of reference beyond the standard model, a "map" as it were, which facilitates practical orientation in introducing and using a wholistic management system. In the early 1970s, the first comprehensive, wholistic management model[37] known in the German-speaking region was developed in St. Gallen, Switzerland. To my knowledge it is the only one worldwide. Between 1975 and 1980 I have tested this model in practice and dynamized it. It was first published in 1981 within the series "Die Orientierung" by Schweizerische Volksbank.[38] Together, the Standard Model of Effectiveness and the Integrated Management System (IMS®) can be applied to over 90 percent of all areas of application. Additions may be required for special situations; it is indispensable, however, to properly observe the underlying logic.

The Integrated Management System (IMS®) I am presenting here can be applied to all kinds of organizations and implemented immediately. It is suitable for commercial and non-profit, government and non-government organizations.

The elements of this management system are the same for all organizations, in line with its universality; only some terms need to be adapted to the use of language outside the business world.

On first view, the IMS® appears complex, which it is in a certain way, and which it must be for reasons of cybernetics. As with any cybernetic system, however, it is surprisingly easy to capture its complexity.

Experience shows that managers quickly learn to deal with this orientation grid. It helps them to recognize interrelations clearly and to sort individual elements and tools. They learn to understand the function of parts within the whole, and the function of the whole as derived from that of its parts, as is typical of a landscape and in line with systemic thinking in its true sense.

---

37 See Ulrich, Hans/Krieg, Walter, *Das St. Galler Management-Modell*, 1972; republished in: Ulrich, Hans, *Gesammelte Schriften*, Vol. 2, Bern/Stuttgart/Vienna, 2001. This model is based on Ulrich, Hans, *Die Unternehmung als produktives soziales System*, 1968; republished in: Ulrich, Hans, *Gesammelte Schriften*, Vol. 1, Bern/Stuttgart/Vienna, 2001.
38 Malik, Fredmund, "Management-Systeme", in the series *Die Orientierung*, No. 78, ed. Schweiz. Volksbank, Bern, 1981.

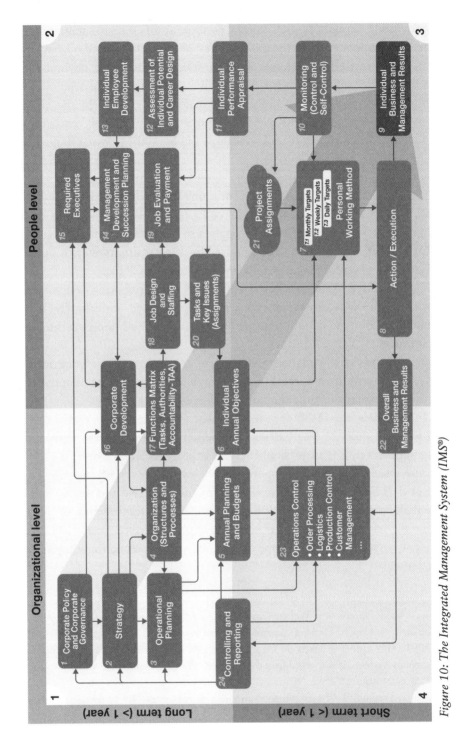

Figure 10: The Integrated Management System (IMS®)

Function of the IMS®: From Corporate Purpos to Results

A system must be understood and designed from the perspective of its functions. The function of the IMS® is precisely defined: *management* of a *"result-producing unit" (RPU)"* The IMS® comprises all elements *required and sufficient* for the management of an RPU – that is to say, everything necessary for designing, leading and developing it. In essence this means: *using right and good management to make the transition from corporate purpose to results.*

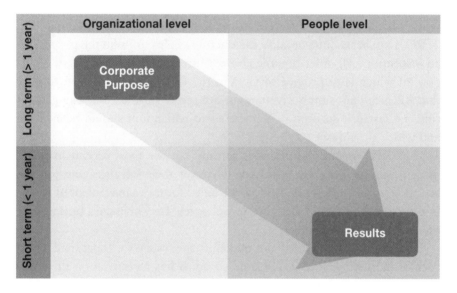

Figure 11: Management of a result-producing unit (RPU)

The Result-Producing Unit as a Basic Element of Management

What is a result-producing unit (RPU)? It is an organizational unit which can produce an economic result and could basically set up a balance sheet. The decisive point is not whether a balance sheet is produced or not. In the commercial sector the most descriptive term is "business", hence "managing a business".

Both in practice and in theory, there are no consistent terms so far to be used for such units. The criterion "basic ability to issue a balance sheet", however, should be sufficiently clear despite the multitude of terms.

Above all, an RPU is a whole independent enterprise, irrespective of its legal form. Besides, RPUs can also be subsidiaries, divisions, strategic business units, market centers, performance centers, profit centers, and result-producing centers. In short, it is all the units where economic results come about, units with a "bottom line". They are the units crucial to economic performance, hence their management – in terms of both process and people – has central significance.

This is precisely why I am using the term RPU to emphasize what these units, which carry very different names in practice, have in common.

RPUs are basic units because their activity helps to fulfill the purpose of an institution. All other organic elements are ancillary functions, the purpose of which is to provide services to the RPUs. It is important to note that RPUs are not simply given. Some are rather obvious, but as a general rule, a conscious decision is required as to which unit should be an RPU and which should not.

Thus RPU managers hold not the only but the most crucial management positions in an organization, whatever their job titles and job descriptions. They need to be especially trained for the management of RPUs. In principle their task is the same at each level: They manage a business, or the analogon of a business.

The IMS® is not intended as a management system for functional areas, such as marketing, R & D, HR, and so on. It has an impact on them but can only be applied to them with modifications.

Dimensions of Integration

The integration of parts (elements, components) to form a whole must follow a certain logic and comprises several dimensions. In the case of the IMS®, a multidimensional integration could be accomplished in a rather simple manner: *business- and people-related*, *short- and long-term*, *static* and *dynamic* components are integrated. Moreover, all elements of this management system are depicted with their *mutual effects on each other*, with their most important input and output relations.

Some of the components are highly complex subsystems themselves, such as corporate policy and the individual stages of corporate planning. Some of them are simple and can be introduced immediately. Occasionally additional aids can be required, such as templates, manuals, and so on; in most cases, however, everything is computerized.

In the context of the Integrated Management System (IMS®), the size of a company is of secondary importance. In essence, every organization needs the same management instruments. Size and – much more importantly – complexity determine the degree of detail to which the individual components are shaped. In a large and complex corporation, for example, an elaborate strategy is likely to be needed, while in a small firm with a rather simple setup only a set of basic strategic decisions will be required, which will often not even be documented. A metaphor might be helpful here: in a small Cessna aircraft you only need a few simple instruments for its typical purposes of usage, while an intercontinental flight requires appropriately sophisticated avionics.

Overview

Corporate policy and corporate governance define the purpose of a business enterprise. If understood correctly and designed appropriately, they form a power center for the overall institution, as does an engine for a motor vehicle. What ultimately matters, however, is not the horsepower but how much of it you can put on the road, how much is transformed into output. It is the same with a management system: it is not corporate policies, governance or strategy which are decisive but what is actually implemented – that is, results.

A car needs plenty of complicated technology to get its engine power on the road, irrespective of road and weather conditions. Its transmission, power shaft and joint, underbody and wheels must be perfectly matched and finely adjusted to serve that purpose. Under certain conditions, the four-wheel drive and speed regulator, the differential lock, and several sophisticated electronic control systems may be needed in addition. Similar is true of management.

Figure 12 provides an overview of its most important components.

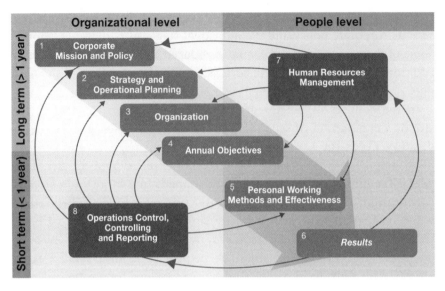

Figure 12: Overview of the Integrated Management System (IMS®)

Logic and Elements of the IMS®

In the following description of the Integrated Management System (IMS®) a certain degree of detail cannot be avoided. For a cursory first reading you may wish to skip the following four paragraphs and settle for the graphic overview.

The IMS® has a precise logic represented by its coordinates. Its graph contains a *vertical* and a *horizontal* axis. To the left of the *vertical* axis we find management elements primarily referring to the *organization as a whole*, those referring to *individual employees* are situated to the right. The *horizontal* axis allows us to differentiate by *time horizons*. The elements situated above the horizontal axis refer to periods *longer than a year*, those below the axis refer to periods of *less than a year*, that is, to the current fiscal year.

This coordinate system divides the graph in four fields, which are numbered clockwise from 1 to 4. They differ in terms of factual content and timeframe. The individual components are numbered from 1 to 24.

The first coordinate field contains components operating in a timeframe of more than a year and refers to the company as a whole – the subsystems of *Corporate Policy and Corporate Governance* (1), of *Strategy* (2) and of *Operational Planning* (3) which determine the company's positioning and direction.

Figure 13: Field 1: Long-term and company-related

The time horizons of these elements have deliberately been left open because they can only be defined for the individual case, as they depend on the actual line of business and its timing. Time horizons in the automotive industry will differ from those in the fashion or software industry.

In practice, corporate policy and strategy can often be considered one single element. In companies with several different business units, however, they need to be distinguished, with corporate policy comprising all aspects of joint relevance for all units. Corporate policy also includes corporate governance and leadership elements such as guiding principles and the mission statement.

Furthermore, this coordinate field includes the *Organization (Structures and Processes)* (4). They are influenced by the strategy, in line with the fundamental principle of structure following strategy, not vice versa. From here there are several links to coordinate fields 2 and 4: on the one hand, all outputs must ultimately concern the individual employee, on the other hand they must be implemented in the short-term field.

Implementation of the organization, as shown in field 2 – the people-related field with a longer time horizon – is achieved via a *Functions Matrix* (17). It is positioned precisely on the axis because it is an element referring to both the overall organization and the individual. The corporate strategy results in requirements for the organization's longer-term development, which, however, also depends on corporate policy and on inputs from management development and succession planning.

The elements in field 1 are somewhat static by nature in that they develop gradually over time. Their outputs, however, need to be implemented in systems operating with short and very short timeframes, which are therefore much more *dynamic*. This is achieved by transforming operational planning into *Annual Planning and Budgets* (5), and there, into the *Individual Annual Objectives* (6) of each job holder.

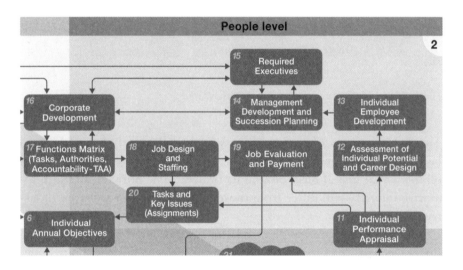

Figure 14: Field 2: Long-term and people-related

The annual objectives are positioned in the very center of the coordinate system, as they represent a key element of effective management. They form the crucial tool for *synchronizing* different time cycles of the company, as well as the two reference variables "company" and "individual".

I use Peter Drucker's famous term "Management by Objectives" (and Self-Control) (MbO), which he created back in 1954, when I talk about managing by individual – i.e. personalized – annual objectives. It is necessary to make a conscious decision on how to use the term MbO because in every institution there are different kinds of objectives with different time horizons and degrees of specificity. In English there are several terms to express this: aims, objectives, goals, and targets have different meanings. In many other languages these distinctions are less clear or totally absent.

Starting from the Functions Matrix, the actual individualization of the organization structure is accomplished via the *Job Design and Staffing* (18); that is, from abstract structures we get to the individual job and the person holding it. The *Job Evaluation (and Payment)* (19) indicates the particular job's relative position within the overall fabric of jobs, and within the compensation system. The job design determines the tasks of its holder and, in general, certain key issues inherent in the job, its holder, or the annual performance assessment, which result from the particular situation. These *Tasks and Key Issues – the Assignments* (20) –, together with the targets from annual planning relevant to the particular job and the budget, form the inputs required to define the *Individual Annual Objectives* (6) for the job holder.

Another element positioned on the time axis is *Individual Performance Appraisal* (11), for which inputs are obtained from individual performance as well as from management results via monitoring. Performance appraisal provides inputs for (Job Evaluation and) *Payment* (19) – within the framework of the particular company's compensation structure –, for the *Assessment of Individual Potential and Career Design* (12), as well as for the above-discussed key issues of the individual job.

Based on the assessment of individual potential, measures for *Individual Employee Development* (13) are determined which, in turn, constitute essential elements of the overall *Management Development and Succession Planning* (14). The latter is determined by the *Required Executives* (15) which, in turn, results from the strategy in coordinate field 1.

In the short-term, people-related field, we find all the elements which in the original St. Gallen Management Model are categorized as "management methods". This field is about translating annual objectives into concrete management action, and thus into concrete *Individual Business and Management Results* (9) – the very results that the company's customers pay for and which serve its corporate purpose.

A crucial issue here is the *Personal Working Method* (7). It comprises the translation of annual objectives into shorter-term targets (which must be met in the course of the fiscal year) in order to directly monitor people's behavior and/or task execution. These are the short-term work plans, including *Monthly, Weekly, and Daily Targets* (7.1, 7.2, 7.3) which provide the input required for individual actions. In some cases not all of these plans will be required. Actual requirements depend on the characteristics of the individual job and the annual objectives defined. In addition, people's behavior is greatly influenced by the compensation design, which needs no further explanation.

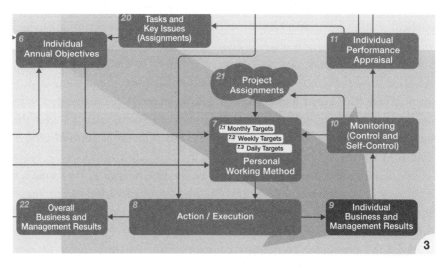

Figure 15: Field 3: People-related and short-term

These components transform the annual objectives into tangible targets and guidelines, influenced by the continually changing conditions that result from people related individual *Monitoring* (10) and from the operative systems shown in field 4. In element 10 we find the term *Self-control* in parentheses. As mentioned before, Drucker has always used the two principles, Management by Objectives and Self-Control, in combination. The basic idea is to enable as many people as possible to monitor and manage themselves, which depends on two factors: clear targets, and sufficient information on the extent to which the targets have been fulfilled. Nevertheless, I also hold on to the principle of monitoring, as it is necessary from time to time to check whether employees monitor themselves, which will not necessarily be the case.

Another input are short-term *Project Assignments* (21), given by the respective superior subject to the particular situation. Rather than large, cross-divisional projects requiring specific planning, this refers to the numerous small projects which constantly have to be carried out in organizations, and which do not require any network plans or similar, but simply a set of technical tools and aids such as project plans, scheduling and cost control.

By means of these situational assignments, annual objectives are constantly adjusted to the change in external conditions. This element is important because annual objectives can only take account of the information available at the moment they are defined, which is normally around year-end. External conditions, however, may change dramatically in the months to follow, which may call for immediate action. In other words, it is important to avoid the impression that annual objectives will not change throughout the fiscal year.

It is of crucial importance that the components contained in field 3 work well. It is no exaggeration to say that they ultimately determine how *efficiently* a business organization operates. If the implementation of that field fails, all other parts of a management system will remain without effect.

Considering that in most companies the potential for major streamlining and improved productivity is no longer found in manufacturing itself but in administrative and management functions, these elements of management systems are not paid nearly sufficient attention in practice.

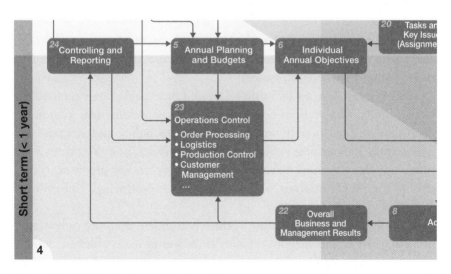

Figure 16: Field 4: Business-related and short-term

In field 4, we return to the business-related sphere, this time with a short-term focus. Dominating components here are the systems of *Operations Control* (23), which derive their inputs from operational planning and annual planning and translate them into targets for the short-term work plans of individuals in field 3.

As illustrated by the examples given, operative systems regulate the processes of the company. From the results summarized and aggregated in this area in accordance with different criteria – the *Overall Business and Management Results* (22) –, control and monitoring inputs are directly passed both to the operative systems and to *Controlling and Reporting* (24), from which they will be returned to the short-term field, or the longer-term elements of field 1, after appropriate evaluation.

As I said in the beginning, these management elements and their concerted interaction are enough to manage a result-producing unit. There is no need to have more; less would be too little. These elements are necessary and sufficient.

What Else Must Be Considered...

Environment

An occasional objection is that the IMS® does not take account of the environment in which the company operates, and therefore represents a closed rather than an open system.

This argument can easily be invalidated. I have deliberately omitted environmental considerations because, firstly, there is consensus among experts that any reasonably conceived corporate policy and strategy will have to take the business environment into consideration. You cannot develop a strategy without having achieved clarity on key premises. Here I refer to the SWOT analysis, a widely known concept, which constitutes a part of strategy development.

Secondly, and more importantly, the environment does not only matter to a company at the corporate policy stage but at many different points. At each of them there will be different environment-related aspects to be considered. The business environment plays a role in operational planning, in budgeting, in defining annual objectives, in the personal working methods – basically always. All managing activities must be aligned with the relevant environmental aspects in a logically compelling way. It would not make much sense, therefore, to overload a graph with them.

Operational Tasks

Another frequent point of criticism is that this model does not explicitly mention important management tasks like marketing, research and development, finance, personnel, and so on. The explanation is obvious if you have read chapter 1. What is mistaken for management tasks are really the operational tasks required in a certain type of institution: the function-spezific business enterprise. Even in a generalized case, where tasks of every institution are concerned, they represent operational rather than management tasks. Therefore they do not belong in a model of a management system.

Emergent Properties

The most important and productive question is aimed at something entirely different: where in this model do we find elements like communication, motivation, culture, learning, and so forth? The answer pertains to the fine art of management: these elements belong to another category than those listed in the IMS®; they cannot directly be influenced in terms of making, creating, bringing about. They are what in biology is called "emergent properties", and can be considered one of that discipline's greatest discoveries. All complex systems have such properties, hence so do institutions and management systems. They are *systemic* properties. Emergent properties result from the coaction of elements, representing new phenomena which previously did not exist and were not included in the individual acting elements.

Two examples: awareness, motivation, and learning are not found in man the same way as are bones, organs, and nerve cells, although the human being is aware, motivated, and learning. In a motor vehicle we will find cylinders, valves, and a transmission, but we will not find horsepower, although the car does have horsepower which can even be measured. The

concerted coaction of certain elements produces other, categorially different elements.

The way we develop, plan, control, etcetera, a strategy brings about
communication, motivation, and culture. Any other way of looking at it
will produce serious confusion and misunderstandings – as always happens when logical-categorial distinctions are ignored.

Introduction of the IMS®

The IMS® is a system of closed loops, and in its entirety it forms a closed
loop by itself. An explanation of the system can therefore start at any
point. This is the advantage of circular structures and systems: a straight
line, as opposed to a circle, has a logically imperative beginning and end,
even if both are positioned in infinity.

The important point, then, is not where to begin. That depends on the
given situation and purpose. What is important is that, no matter where
you begin, you go through the whole circle without systematically neglect-
ing any of its elements.

This has major advantages for the practical introduction of the IMS®.
There is no need to begin with corporate policy and strategy, just because
they are numbered 1 and 2. You start wherever your organization's development needs are greatest, where "the shoe pinches the most". Often it
will be right and appropriate to start with strategy. In many cases, however – more than is commonly assumed – the most pressing point will be
the working methods of a boss and his or her people: this is a point where
enormous deficits are found almost everywhere and immediate, visible
progress is possible at the same time. Another good point to begin with is
the field of *Individual Annual Objectives* as a starting point for Management by Objectives (and Self-Control).

Wherever one starts, depending on the stage of development an institution is in, the key is to have connectable elements – elements that are compatible with, and can be linked to, the subsequent development steps. This,
precisely, is achieved by using the IMS® and the consistent terms and meanings which were also typical of the first St. Gallen Management Model.

Both models – the Standard Model of Effectiveness and the Integrated
Management System (IMS®) – are basically sufficient to solve virtually any
management problem and manage any kind of institution successfully.

As I have repeatedly stated, formal elements and mere terminology are not enough. There are too many, often contradictory meanings. The linchpin of right and good management is content. "Strategy", for instance, could be understood to mean a lot of different things, even if the term had already been defined within the IMS® context (which it has not).

My book *Managing Performing Living* explains what the Standard Model of Effectiveness is all about. The contents of all other elements of the IMS®, as far as they pertain to general management, will be dealt with in the next section of this book and in the remaining volumes of this series. Let us now proceed to yet another perspective on the elements of the IMS®: I will now discuss them in a modified context, primarily focusing on what they really mean.

Part III

The General Management Functions

Chapter 7

The Basic Model of General Management

To demonstrate what general management should be, I use the basic model shown in the following graph. It has proved to be the most comprehensible and useful concept, as it provides an overview of all essential elements and their interaction. It is a wholistic model setting limits to both, the idea of a noncommittal wholism and the reductionism that was taken to extremes over the past years and reached its peak in the shareholder value principle.

The term "general management" in my definition comprises all elements and sets of tasks which are common to all institutions, and which every kind of organization needs in order to function. As such, they also represent the areas where all managers, including specialists, need basic skills. Executives aiming for a career in general management – that is to say, generalists – need comprehensive and detailed knowledge about these subjects. I believe that this also solves latent contradictions between specialists and generalists. Generalists need to specialize as well – but in other fields than specialists do. They specialize in totalities, in the institution as a whole, and most specifically – in line with the definition of management – on shaping, guiding, and developing complex, productive, social systems.

Slogans such as "specialists know more and more about less and less; generalists know less and less about more and more" are good for a joke. They are not really to the point, though. It serves nobody's interests to belittle these things sarcastically, or play off one side against the other. We need both, specialists and generalists. In the manner suggested here, we can rather precisely define who should know (and be able to do) what, which is also important for training purposes.

Things are quite straightforward at the general management level: every institution operates in an *environment* in which its purpose must be fulfilled. External conditions must be analyzed and understood, as otherwise it will be impossible to fulfill the business purpose.

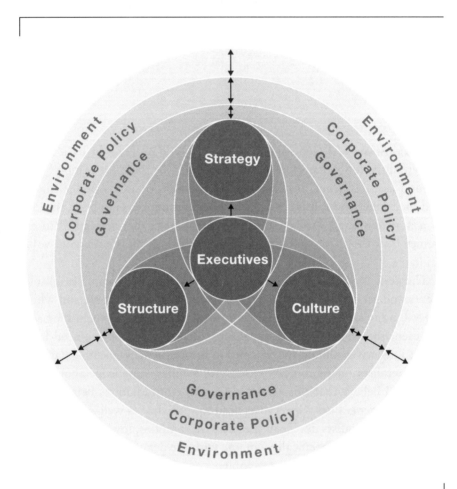

Figure 17: General Management Model

Every institution needs to make its *governance* decisions depending on its environment. They comprise the basic definition of purpose and the over-arching values and rules which are to govern all activities, as well as the relations with key elements of the environment.

Another thing to be defined is *strategy*. Decisions must be taken which will determine the institution's positioning in its respective environment, its field of activity, and the overriding objectives, means, and measures required to fulfill corporate purpose. I am using the term "strategy" in a broad sense, also including goal-setting. Depending on the individual institution, the word "strategy" will be more or less fitting and might have to be adapted; the function it describes, however, is always required.

Further, every institution needs a viable, robust *structure* which, most importantly, must remain functional under any condition that can realistically be assumed. The structure determines the institution's functionality and viability. It should make it easy for people to fulfil their tasks successfully.

The next level of general management is *culture*. It must be aimed at performance, accountability, and effectiveness, and it must be tolerable for people. Treating culture as a special subject does not contradict my above comments on the so-called emergent properties. The fact that culture is emergent does not mean it cannot be described with regard to its content.

At the center of the graph we see the *executives* who have to make their specific contributions to the design and implementation of strategy, structure, and culture. Their actions are guided by the Standard Model of Managerial Effectiveness, as shown in the right-hand part of the graph.

Elements that are not integral parts of general management, but universally existent, are certain subject-specific or functional areas. They exist in every institution, from a business organization to an opera house.

Every institution has recipients of service. As there are fewer and fewer monopolies, more and more units can be service recipients – or *customers*. Consequently there are also competitors, and thus a market. Every institution therefore needs to have a certain basic knowledge of customers, market, and marketing. Every institution needs *people* to deliver its services and to function. We therefore find an HR function in each. All institutions have in common a need for *money*, so they also need a finance department, and all incur *costs*, so they need a controlling unit. Finally, we have *data* in each of them, which calls for a certain basic knowledge of information sciences.

Managers need a minimum of skills in these fields. They do not need to be specialists – they could not specialize in all of these fields. But they should understand them enough to be well-respected discussion partners for specialists rather than being at their mercy.

Chapter 8

The Organization's Environment

"The system always kicks back."[39]

Management must have its point of reference in the very environment where the institution needs to function. If you do not understand your organization's environment you will not stand a chance of practicing right management. Neither will you be able to adapt to that environment, nor to shape it according to your organization's needs. "Environment" is often understood to be limited to ecological issues. That, however, would not be sufficient for the management of societal institutions.

An individual institution cannot dominate its environment. History has shown that no organization – however powerful in its time – could prevail over its environmental conditions, and in particular over the changes in it, in the long run. Even the largest and most powerful organizations were not able to permanently shape their environment so as to provide favorable conditions for them, even if they enjoyed monopolistic rights.

Reasons lie in the complexity discussed above, and in the constant change owed to the relentless progression of self-organization The environment is a textbook example of why managers absolutely need to concern themselves with complexity, as well as with complex systems and their regularities. Even those firmly believing in the "keep it simple" principle will have to accept sooner or later that that slogan does not apply to the environment of a business or any other organization.

---

39 Gall, John, Systemantics: How Systems Work and Especially How They Fail, New York, 1975, p. 23.

Model Categories for the Environment

When I talk about "environment" here I refer to anything of importance, or potentially important, for the institution as such – irrespective of whether this is generally known or not, whether it can be known or not. Two seemingly contradictory aspects must be considered: firstly, there are basic limits to the knowledge one can have about one's environment, implying some clearly defined requirements to management; yet, secondly, it is possible to know more – and above all, more important things – than most managers would think, and more than what is found in most organizations.

The following graph contains the essential components of a company's environment, structured under two perspectives: the company's (suppliers, investors, media, etc.) and the functional perspective (spheres of the environment). This graph was developed for the first version of the St. Gallen

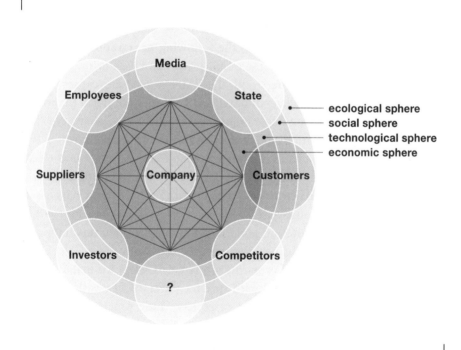

Figure 18: Components of an organization's environment

Management Model and has since proved its validity and usefulness. It explicitly includes what some pseudo-reformers of the shareholder-value principle now consider to be the latest progress in the field: the stakeholder approach. As we will see later on, it was already conventional wisdom back then. In management, the same wheels (even useless ones) are reinvented every few years because most people simply do not have a clue about the standard of knowledge.

I have introduced two changes to the original version: firstly, I added the media which have much greater importance today than they used to. Secondly, I highlighted the customers to distinguish them from other stakeholder groups. Customers are doubtless one element in an organization's environment, but they are not *stakeholders*, as I will show in the chapter on corporate governance.[40]

Understanding Economic Aspects

The above graphs demonstrate the multidimensionality to be considered in every environmental analysis. In the following paragraphs I will focus on some of the most important *economic* aspects which in my view are largely unknown or misunderstood. They are immediate causes of the prevalence of wrong management practices. This does not mean that other environmental categories are less important – rather to the contrary. They will be discussed at length in the respective volume of the book series.

Ultimately, all environmental influences manifest themselves in the economic sphere. This is true for all companies, even if for some organizations it may be limited to the expenses required to achieve their purpose as well as the financial resources available for it. Whether we like it or not, it is a fact. Therefore, a profound understanding of economic functions and interrelations must be at the heart of right management.

The prevailing theories of economy are largely useless for managing an organization. They mainly deal with specific questions, use rather incomprehensible language, and in most cases have little practical relevance.

---

40 See my book *Effective Top Managemet*, Weinheim, 2006 and several other publications, in particular my monthly *m.o.m.*® *Malik on Management Letters*.

Even the underlying assumptions have little in common with the reality of management. Some are downright and dangerously misleading.

Examples include the much-propagated neo-liberal ideas and the New Wealth theory so popular in the United States. It is just as faulty as the New Economy "theory" was back then. We are left with amazement. How could such nonsense ever be adopted, even advocated with dogmatic fervor, by nearly all economists, media, consultants, and many managers? I have opposed them from the very beginning.

Neoliberal Misconceptions

Neoliberalism, which emerged and came into vogue after the collapse of communism, is a travesty of liberalism. A unique chance was wasted: the chance of convincing the world of the merits of a truly liberal economic and societal system. The protagonists of neoliberalism do not miss a chance to tell everyone about the beauty of their ideology. What they actually do is spread delusions, ideas that no true liberal has ever vindicated, thus creating disappointment and a new anti-business attitude in the population.

I am being very frank about this precisely because I am a firm proponent of a free enterprise economy and because I am in favor of using the market as a coordinating mechanism, wherever it functions or can be made to function.

Instead of admitting to these errors and correcting them, as true liberals would, the discussion fatally resembles the rearguard battles of neomarxism. As a result, the theory loses all power of persuasion. Its proponents will achieve the exact opposite of what they are aiming for: they will pave the way for a revitalization of socialist ideas, as is already happening in many countries.

Whereas during the Second World War, politics was (mis)perceived to be the universal remedy, now it is the economy. Neoliberalism has led to an economization of society – a very simplistic, reductionist form of economization, as I will explain later. True liberalism, however, is not an economic but a societal theory. At its core are not economic factors, least of all financial ones such as profit. True liberalism is a theory on society, and its chief value is individual freedom. The great liberal economists would not have accepted today's version of neoliberalism, with shareholder value and value creation as central themes. Nor would they have spoken of deregulation, because they knew very well that the highest liberal value, individual freedom, cannot be achieved without rules. They would have resorted to "re-regulation", for their goal would have been to replace the wrong rules with right ones, rather than doing away with rules as such.

It was this profound understanding of a well-functioning free society from which liberal thinkers such as Friedrich von Hayek, Ludwig von Mises, Wilhelm Röpke, and long before them the Scottish moral philosophers, deduced what functions the business sector had to fulfill in such a society, and what criteria should consequently guide the handling of economic affairs. This thought has completely been lost to the proponents of neoliberal positions, in particular to most officers of trade associations and most business lobbyists. Also, what business people and managers have to say about neoliberalism rarely reveals much expertise.

The starting point must be society, not business. Without a functional society there can be no functional economy and thus no functional economic institutions. In a decayed society there may be much wheeling and dealing but no corporate management. In my experience most people understand this fairly well.

One of the things often described badly and incorrectly is the market. We are incessantly told what a great and beneficial thing the free market economy is. Those telling us so are either talking from a privileged position or have not really understood the principle. None of the true liberal economists, least of all Friedrich von Hayek, believed the market to be a good solution – or even a possible solution – to all economic and societal coordination and regulation problems. On the contrary, they consistently worked from the insight that the market is a poor solution, always pointing out that all other solutions known are even worse, and often they went in search of better ones. That has given them credibility and authority.

Anyone claiming that a market can create a maximum of growth and national product is wrong. Friedrich von Hayek, in my view the sharpest of all liberal thinkers, put it very clearly: *"Of course the so-called 'maximum' we can achieve in this (market-driven) manner cannot be defined as a sum of certain quantities of goods ..."*[41]

---

41 Friedrich A. von Hayek demonstrates this in "Adam Smith's Message in Today's Language" in *New Studies in Philosophy, Politics, Economics and the History of Ideas,* London, 1978, S. 267 et seq

Whoever fails to see the deficiencies of the market runs the risk firstly of overexerting it, secondly of blocking the search for better solutions wherever they could exist, and thirdly of further increasing the widespread ignorance of economic issues. A case in point is the view that the market effectively corrects the errors in the management of large corporations.

It is simply naive of neoliberals to maintain that the market will "take care of everything". As indispensable as the market may be, neoliberalism overvalues its potential. The market does not bring about economic performance, it does not even prevent mistakes, it only punishes them. Also, it does not correct mistakes in the usual sense of the word, it merely brings in the undertaker after the patient has died. These methods are too crude for modern society. Therefore, right and good management is required not only to manage organizations well, but also to compensate for the inherent systemic shortcomings of the market. I will explain this in greater detail later.

Another misperception: no true liberal has ever demanded egoism as neoliberals do. It is nothing but a myth that Adam Smith has advocated it.[42] Liberalism is not based on human egoism, and it does not depend on it to work. On the contrary, it is the only system explicitly giving people the freedom to behave exactly as they wish, and pursuing exactly the goals they choose. True liberals, however, uphold something that has often been mistaken: that *within the order recommended by them, including the legal system, even those behaviors considered most harmful, will ultimately turn out to be to the benefit of society.*[43] Or, to put it in simpler terms: liberalism is a system in which bad people can do least harm.

True liberalism does not call for profit either, let alone profit maximization, not even profit orientation. Market economy and capitalism are not defined through profit at all but through liquidity: whoever is able to pay the bill at maturity will remain in the game. Creditors do not care where the funds come from.

Finally, one last misunderstanding: true liberalism does not demand we subordinate all our goals to the economy. No one has put this more clearly

---

42 *"The worst of all the multitude did something for the common good"*, Bernard Mandeville, quoted according to F. A. von Hayek, *New Studies*, p. 251.

43 *Hayek, Friedrich A. von, Der Weg zur Knechtschaft*, (first published in 1944) Munich, 1971, p. 120, with reference to L. Robbins, and 30 years later in *Law, Legislation and Liberty*, Volume II, *"The Mirage of Social Justice"*, Chicago, 1976, p. 113.

than Friedrich von Hayek: ultimately, all goals are of a non-economic nature. "The ultimate goals which rational beings seek to attain through their actions are never of an economic nature. Strictly speaking, there is no 'economic motive' but only economic factors conditioning our striving for other ends." What in ordinary language is misleadingly called the "economic motive" merely refers to the desire for general opportunity, the desire for power to achieve unspecified ends."[44] We could probably turn many influential opponents into proponents of a free economic system if we ceased to demand they subordinate everything to pure economic reason, which justifiably meets with rational and emotional reluctance. What liberalism does demand is that each and everyone be responsible for their actions. That principle must apply to managers as well.

New Economic Understanding Needed?

The answer is Yes. Not only are many neoliberal positions highly questionable. The entire understanding of economic prevailing today is fundamentally wrong, with very few exceptions. For instance, it is still very much based on the barter principle, although to this date nobody has been able to furnish evidence of the existence of a barter economy for any period of history.

My following remarks are oriented by the views of Gunnar Heinsohn and Otto Steiger, who made a very strong case in demonstrating that for all intents and purposes what we currently have is not a theory on economics[45]; so far it is only a theory on the productive use of assets. Whereas real economic activity requires ownership, not for its use but for its value as a collateral.[46]

---

44 Heinsohn, Gunnar/Steiger, Otto, Eigentum, Zins und Geld: ungelöste Rätsel der Wirtschaftswissenschaft, Marburg, 2nd edition 2002 (1st edition, Reinbek b. Hamburg, 1996).

45 See also the masterly depictions by Otto Steiger "Eigentum und Recht und Freiheit" and by Gunnar Heinsohn "Warum gibt es Märkte?", both in: Krieg, Walter/Galler, Klaus/Stadelmann, Peter (eds.), Richtiges und gutes Management: vom System zur Praxis, Bern/Stuttgart/Vienna, 2004.

46 See Heinsohn, Gunnar, Privateigentum, Patriarchat und Geldwirtschaft, Frankfurt, 1984.

Want or Must?
Debt Pressure as a Driver of Economic Activity

Every day we are faced with smart theories about business and economics. Most are outdated before long, or in conflict with other expert statements. To keep a cool head amid the swirl of contradictory comments and suggestions, it is useful to keep in mind a few basic truths of economics.

Why does man work? Why is there such a thing as economic activity? Why is it done in a certain way? And why was it clear and noticable from the very start that the talk about the New Economy was just that: idle talk?

Psychological Reasons?

Working and economic activity are commonly explained with certain forms of human striving and wanting: man – so we are told – wishes to satisfy certain needs. As a consumer, man strives for benefit or the fulfilment of wishes. As an entrepreneur, man wishes to achieve profit or growth, or both. As an employee, man works because he or she was motivated. As a manager, man feels called upon to be innovative. Obviously, then, psychological elements must be considered the drivers of economic activities.

Not only does this sound plausible, it is established theory. But is it really true? Do subjective elements of wanting, wishing, and aspiring account for the pressures in the economic system? Why, then, do we not face up to those pressures instead of evading them? The answer usually given is, because of competition. Can that be the whole truth?

Economic Activity is Driven by Constraint

One aspect is often disregarded or underestimated: a major reason why people work and why companies do business is not because they wish to work or do business, but because they have to. They act under constraint.

Where does this constraint come from? It follows from the simple fact that people and companies have undertaken *obligations* which have been defined with regard to scope and time, and which they are *forced* to fulfill. Or, put in simpler terms: they have liabilities. The constraint they face is a result of debt agreements they have previously concluded, and any failure to fulfill those contracts will lead to compulsory orders, seizures, and ultimately bankruptcy. Not too long ago we used to have bonded labor.

Part of the debt obligations is undertaken *voluntarily*, and could thus have been prevented. The respective purchasing acts, such as installment or credit card purchases, could have been postponed. Once these obligations have been generated, though, they take their grim effects in that their fulfillment is compulsory, and it exceeds the obligation originally entered into in that it includes the interest agreed.

Involuntary Obligations and Compulsory Supererogation

By far the larger part of debt contracts, however, is concluded involuntarily. All productions and all the work must be *prefinanced*. There will not be buyers before something has been produced, or salaries before the work has been completed. Producing something before buyers are found means that loans must be taken out. Waiting for the salary to arrive at the end of the month means having to incur debts, which today is done by using a credit card, the modern (and much more expensive) equivalent of what used to be running up a bill at the corner store. Prefinancing leads to compulsory debt contracts, and thus to additional costs in the form of interest rates.

People are not only buyers and sellers, consumers and producers, employees and employers, as economic theories would make us believe. Above all, they are debtors and creditors. No matter what the aim, intention, or motivation – a debtor is forced to generate not only the loan itself, delivering a performance which he otherwise might not have delivered; in addition, he needs to perform in excess of that, to the extent that the interest incurred can be covered. This cause of economic rush and pressure is rarely mentioned – which is remarkable, in particular as we have the highest debt, both in absolute and relative terms, that ever existed at a global level. This driver of economic activity is totally independent of psychological motives and other aims, wishes or intentions.

The sum of all contractual obligations, multiplied with the respective interest rate, equals the sum of the minimum economic performance required to prevent ruin. This is the *cause of growth* in the business sector, the cause of rush, stress, and anxiety – and at the same time, of performance, productivity, and innovation. This cause is entirely independent of psychological motives. Of course, psychological elements like greed or a relentless pursuit of profit may aggravate the situation.

If successful performance cannot be achieved the debt must be liquidated. If debtors fail to pay, creditors must write off the bad debts. The fact that there will previously be a legal seizure of assets, bringing the debtor down to subsistence level, usually does not help either party.

Economic growth is a consequence of debt previously incurred. If it decreases or even turns negative there will be less national product and income, but not only that: a much more dangerous effect, although rarely considered, is the resulting need for value adjustment in companies' balance sheets.

Thus, the market is not only the place where supply and demand meet. It is also – and primarily – the place where manufacturers in debt attempt to raise what they need in order to cover their debt: money. This phenomenon could be observed in all cases where illusions of an infallible financial system have collapsed.

The problem is not in people's exaggerated standards of consumption. They can lower those standards, in particular those concerning everyday needs, and they will when they have to. What they cannot lower is the debt previously incurred and which relentlessly grows due to compounded interest, irrespective of how people do economically.

It does not matter whether a company (or the persons representing it) is or wants to be more productive – financial obligations are *objective* obligations, and so are the respective interest burdens.

The Circle Is Incomplete

The immediate cost of production flows back to the market in the form of operating cost. Thus, production seemingly creates its own purchasing power and demand. It is *seemingly* so because every production and, generally speaking, every economic activity needs to be *pre*financed as explained before. From a macroeconomic perspective, however, the money (or capital) needed for prefinancing can *never be existent*. In other words, the economy as a whole is permanently in debt.

Double-entry bookkeeping – the business administration viewpoint that is occasionally used to explain economic phenomena – is dangerously misleading in this case. The costs of prefinancing, risks and profits are calculated and booked but do not actually exist in the supply and demand cycle. They appear to exist as economic realities; in truth, however, they are a fiction of accountancy. Invariably and exclusively these costs can only be covered by running in debt. What this implies is that production cannot – and never could – create its own demand, as maintained by the common theories.

As I said before, the legal obligations taken on voluntarily and involuntarily and the interest loads associated with them are the crucial drivers of dynamics and pressures.

These considerations are based on the so-called debitistic economic view which, to my knowledge, was first developed by *Gunnar Heinsohn*[47] and subsequently refined by him and his colleage *Otto Steiger*[48] as well as by *Paul C. Martin*[49]. This implies a series of consequences:

Money, from this perspective, is debt made circulatable. This applies to all its manifestations. With banknotes it is easy to see: they are the issuing banks' I.O.U.s.

Hence, the much-claimed dynamics of the monetary economy do not result from economic policies but from the contractual obligations taken on voluntarily or involuntarily, and the irrevocable liability for loan redemption and interest payment.

Contrary to what many theories claim, the cause of economic development, its direction and dynamics is not something located in the future – more profits, more wealth, and so on – but something in the past: the debt obligations previously undertaken.

Consequently, money creation does not primarily occur in the banking system but in people's individual purchasing acts. Purchasing as such does not require any payment (or money, for that matter), but crediting, albeit the banking system makes it much easier to achieve crediting and turn debt into something that can be circulated. In conjunction with the state as

---

47 Heinsohn, Gunnar/Steiger, Otto, *Eigentum, Zins und Geld*, Marburg, 2nd edition, 2002 (1st edition Reinbek b. Hamburg, 1996).

48 Martin, Paul C., *Der Kapitalismus – ein System, das funktioniert*, Munich, 1986.

49 *See m.o.m.® Malik on Management Letter* 3/94, p. 56 et seq. on the leverage of loans, as this is essential to the understanding of economic processes and interrelations.

seemingly infallible debtor, possible consequences include *excesses of debt accumulation* as well as economic *boom periods* leading to periods of *deflation* and *depression*, which will be virtually inevitable once the will or ability to incur additional debt (beyond what has already been accumulated) is no longer there. A current, and quite dramatic example has been provided by the Japanese economy since 1990. What has been happening there for the past 15 years is only understandable from the perspective outlined. Causes of the current developments lie in the excesses of the 1980s. The U.S. economy is likely to take a similar course, if not worse.

Expansion and Depression

Monetary economy, then, does not only have immanent dynamics in terms of expansion but also its opposite: the immanent danger of *shrinkage* and *depression*. Every dollar of debt in a balance sheet is countered with a dollar in receivables in another balance sheet, and vice versa. In some instances this debt will grow to become *excessive* debt, with the consequence that it turns *irrecoverable* or bad for the creditor. Usually this will happen when interest can no longer be earned but must be financed by incurring more debt. Results are the *compound interest effect* and, associated with it, the dynamics of debt perpetuation.

In a sense, there will still be growth – but it no longer results from economic performance but from book entries reflecting irrecoverable claims. For a while, the true nature of these claims can be veiled by what is – a bit too nobly – referred to as "securitization". In truth the risk of value adjustment is simply passed on to the next party, in line with the Greater Fool Theory. What it means is that receivables from certain groups of debtors – for instance, mortgage loans – are pooled, securitized at appropriate denominations, and traded on the exchange. In other words, debts are turned into securities. For some time the price may be cultivated, then it is left to the dynamics of supply and demand. As long as the price rises, everything seems to be okay. Everyone makes money, whether from capital gains or from having passed on the risk. Share price gains, however, are gains on paper. They can only be realized by finding a buyer for the securities in question, preferably at an even higher price. From a certain point on it will obviously have to be a fool, and he will have to find an even greater fool for the game to continue.

Sooner or later the process will be discontinued, as there will be no "greater fool" available and the possibilities of borrowing money will come to an end. Consequently, the economy is *forced to raise liquid funds* in order to be able to fulfill its debt obligations. As a result the real values will usually decrease, as their earlier price increases were largely due to the leverage effect of earlier crediting processes rather than economic performance and value creation.

This is the moment when additional payments and security will be required, as the underlying values – or the securities based on them, such as company shares or investment certificates – will no longer suffice to cover or securitize the obligations incurred. More and more debt obligations will fail; more and more bad debt must be written off; more and more businesses and individuals will fall into bankruptcy.

The lesson from all this is that in an economy there are no values, only prices. The value of an economic good is what the next buyer is willing to pay for it. If he pays more than the current owner has paid himself, the "value" has gone up; if he pays less, it has gone down – irrespective of what so-called evaluation methods might reveal. These methods, particularly popular in the 1990s, may be helpful as a reference for negotiation. They have nothing to do with true *value* because there is no such thing.

As a consequence of failing debt obligations – and this will come as a surprise to monetarists – the growth rates of money supply and credit demand decrease and may even turn negative, even if central bank policies remain unchanged and, in fact, even if there are massive cuts in interest rates.

Inflation and Deflation

Debt liquidation then sets in motion the process of *wealth destruction*, resulting not from inflation but from *deflation*. It is not the *purchasing power* of the money that is destroyed – that would be an effect of inflation. What is destroyed is the *money supply* available. In periods like this, liquidity is the most important good and the scarcest one as well. The money does not lose value, as it would with inflation – on the contrary, it *gains* value. However, there is less and less of it, as its *foundation* – the debt incurred earlier and made circulatable – now has to be liquidated.

Due to the simultaneous depreciation of underlying assets, the scope for taking out new loans decreases, too, since they require the underlying assets as collateral.

As this goes to show, the dynamics of economy play out on both sides, and with a force inexplicable by the usual theories, much less by the psychological categories mentioned in the beginning – a force hardly manageable by means of economic policy. It does not matter whether people pursue profits or not, whether they are greedy or not, whether they aim to satisfy their needs or not. All of that neither motivates nor explains their behavior. The real driver of their actions, and the *only* explanation for all these phenomena, is the *comercive effect of debt*. The momentum and inevitability of these processes will be all the more pronounced, the greater the state's share in debt accumulation: its possibilities for intervention and support will be limited by the fact that it has used up all its credit leeway – usually during the good times, in order to artificially create or maintain a certain level of wealth.

The Myth of the U.S. Economy's Superiority

Paricular attention is due to the state of the U.S. economy: not only is it considered the "locomotive" of the world economy, it is even deemed to be the role model par excellence. Here is where the key to global economic development lies: whoever misjudges the U.S. economy will hardly have a chance of judging other countries correctly.

How Good is the American Economy?[50]

According to what most people think, the American economy has recovered quickly after a surprisingly short recession in 2000 and 2001 and, as also stated by the then FED Chairman Alan Greenspan, demonstrated its *superiority*, *flexibility*, and *robustness*. This opinion is up-

---

50 The translation is based on the German original text from 2007. I decided to keep this chapter for the sake of indicating the historical genesis of my thinking.

held all across the media, be it newspapers, TV channels, or the internet.[51]

A majority consensus believes the U.S. economy to be sound, strong, and superior to all other economies. As a result it is often thought to be the benchmark for economic policy, and for management in all other nations. I consider this to be wrong and fatally misleading, for the following three reasons: *firstly*, as I have often demonstrated, the numbers published for the U.S. are *wrong*.[52] *Secondly* and astonighingly, the current situation is never compared to the course of earlier recessions and recoveries. If anyone did that they would see that the present recovery is alarmingly *weak*.[53] *Thirdly*, and most importantly, the U.S. economy suffers from fundamental structural deficiencies which have emerged over many years of misdirected developments, resulting from poor management and flawed economic policies. In economic mainstream debate they are either *ignored* or said to be *meaningless*, with reference being made to a "new paradigm". One noteworthy example was when former treasury secretary Paul O'Neill declared the U.S. foreign trade deficit to be "irrelevant". This is dangerous reality-blindness and a serious case of calculated optimism. I firmly believe that we are not witnessing a beginning economic recovery in the United States; instead the country will turn out to be a *focal point of pre-programmed crises*.

In sum, the U.S. economy is suffering from structural deficiencies giving an economist of European training plenty of reason to worry. The problems are: massively overvalued assets, greatest overall debt of the post-war period, credit-financed consumption of grotesque proportions, lowest savings, lowest net investment since World War II, rapidly increasing foreign debt, poor corporate balance sheets, lowest profitability of the post-war period, rapidly increasing unemployment, a monstrously leveraged financial system.

The facts are there. They cannot be denied; at the most their *relevance* can be questioned. This is exactly what numerous American economists

---

51 One of the notable exceptions is Robert Gordon of Northwestern University, Chicago, who for many years has been disproving the figures published, in particular with regard to productivity increases.

52 See, inter alia, appendix 1 of *Effective Top Management*, Weinheim, 2006, as well as the *m.o.m.*® *Malik on Management Letters* Nos. 2/04 and 3/04.

53 See *m.o.m.*® *Malik on Management Letter* 2/04.

do, simply by inventing a new paradigm: the so-called *asset-based, wealth-driven economy.*

Not only the U.S. economy as such is at an impasse; so is the U.S. economic theory defended by most.

In essence it is the same way of thinking that was already used way back to support the New Economy nonsense of the mid-1990s. Arguing that "this time things are different", the majority of economists negate any structural deficits of the American economy, quickly piecing together some pseudo-theory such as "jobless recovery", or declaring that the lack of savings is one of several "wealth effects".

The recovery of 2003 has led to another wave of absurd economic theories being propagated as the intellectual non-plus-ultra: it says that people simply need to consume excessively, even with shrinking incomes. The debts they need to incur do not matter because their shares and homes are constantly gaining value, thus providing an ever broader basis to borrow on.

That is what is meant by "asset-based, wealth-driven economy". If you don't act that way you are stupid; if you don't understand it you are ignorant. I declare I am both. This pseudo-theory is dominated by emotions, rhetorics, and unproven statements. The only thing lacking throughout is arguments.

This way of thinking has kept the U.S. economy from focusing on its real strengths, quickly correcting the mistakes of the 1990s, and eliminating damages. On the contrary, it has given the economy the seemingly scientific legitimation for continuing on the trodden path. This is why, for instance, debt was not reduced but further increased during the recession. The policy adopted was "more of the same" – almost like trying to cure alcoholism with alcohol.

The American Wealth Theory and Its Errors

The "Wealth Theory", which originated around the mid-1980s, initially leads to a mixture of denial and pseudo-justification of speculation bubbles. It provided the FED with a welcome excuse for not having to intervene: a bubble, they said, could only be recognized in retrospect, never beforehand. Then, however, the theory leads into a dead end – the political pressure to keep producing new bubbles, lest the economy collapse.

Essentially the basic view underlying this theory is that it is the duty of the state, or of economic policy, to keep increasing the market value of assets. In the past, or so the theory goes, societies woud take a long time to prosper, because people first had to save their money so they could invest it later. Today the process can be abbreviated by continually raising the prices of assets so that people can borrow against them. This way they can easily take out loans, using the increased values as collateral. They can use the borrowed funds to consume, or to purchase additional assets which again rise in value. Consequently, the overriding goal of economic policy must be growth through value creation. The growth of the real economy – of the production of goods and services – is not a goal of economic policy under this theory, or a secondary one at best.

This, in essence, is the kind of thinking common among U.S. economists, politicians and, almost limitless, among business managers. It is a seemingly plausible justification of shareholder-value and value creation strategies, and of the excesses that will inevitably result from them.

Its errors are easy to recognize. Firstly, it is a free ticket, even a request for unlimited debt accumulation. It can work on two conditions only: permanently low interest rates, and a stock exchange that never goes down and does not require any major corrections. In fact, it is a time bomb: even the slightest stock price fluctuations can trigger veritable disasters, as we have witnessed already.

Secondly, it is a justification for unlimited consumption, which in the U.S. is almost considered a patriotic duty. The general perception is that it is the consumer who keeps the economy rolling, even if companies cease to invest. Debt is not a problem per se; it depends on what you do with your loans. In the case of the U.S., the excessive consumption resulting from that view deprives companies of the funds they need to make investments. Individual savings are no longer necessary, as people have continually increasing assets at their disposal and seem capable of limitless consumption without any harm. This is how the theory justifies the lack of *savings* in the United States; at the same time, however, the disastrously low *investment rate* is overlooked.

Thirdly, the approach may enable wealth on an individual basis, but it will not do so for the population as a whole, as new buyers will have to pay the higher prices. Those who started buying very early may have gotten rich by now, but those buying at today's prices will have to pay all the more. Another point to be considered is that gains are only achieved on paper. In order to realize them one must sell. Whenever many people attempt to do that, prices will drop and in some instances even collapse.

This is a typical example of a failure to consider the micro and macro view of economics. What may be favorable, even necessary in the individual case, can turn out to be very harmful for the economy as a whole, which in turn can have repercussions on the individual case. One example: if an individual company cuts jobs to save cost, this is an economically reasonable measure. If all companies do that, the outcome will not be a sound economy but recession. The micro-macro problem is something that makes it difficult for many people – particularly entrepreneurs and managers – to understand the economic system as a whole.

The Theory of Wealth Creation is based on the belief that stock exchanges will continue to go up, without any setbacks to speak of, or that – if a bubble bursts – there will always be another speculation bubble in another sector of the economy which will create new values to borrow against: after the stock bubble it will be the bonds bubble, and most recently it was the U.S. housing bubble, accompanied by a rescheduling of loans and credit expansion.

According to this view it would be wrong to combat the different bubbles; on the contrary, they must be artificially created if they do not emerge by themselves. As mentioned before, throughout the 1990s the former FED Chairman Alan Greenspan claimed – thus justifying the FED's inactivity – that a speculative bubble could not be antipicated, only recognized with hindsights. This is all the more amazing as classical economists had provided a clear definition of economic bubbles. There are two kinds that need to be distinguished: the first is an asset bubble. It means that the prices of a certain asset (such as shares) are driven up by excessive borrowing, to the point where there can no longer be a reasonable correlation with the returns that asset can yield. Cases in point include the overvaluation excesses and the low dividend returns. They were discernible early on.

The second kind of bubble affects the entire economy, not only submarkets: a "bubble economy" emerges. This happens when excessive credit expansion leads to excessive expenses and further borrowing. The question is what will happen with these credits and where demand will flow. In the case of Japan it was the real estate and stock speculation some twenty years ago which led to the deflationary recession we are still witnessing today. In the United States it is the same, *plus* a consumer spending frenzy. That, too, can be recognized early on.

The fact of the matter is: this peculiar Theory of Wealth Creation leads to the continued impoverishment of growing parts of the population. It leads to excesses and illusions, and it enables neither the creation of income nor the enhancement of productive capacities in an economy. The structural problems of the United States bear witness to this.

False and Genuine Wealth

Wealth does not arise from the increase of stock and real estate prices. Wealth arises – and that is a general consensus among economists – from the creation of *productive capital*: factories, equipment, infrastructure, know-how, education. The *price increase* of assets was never paid much attention in economic theory, except as a warning sign. All economists, much as they may have disagreed on other points, realized that wealth can only result from *investments*. Investments can only be made with funds not used for consumption – in other words, funds that are *saved*. Investment expenses create the *income* that enables people to purchase the assets that are produced with the money invested.

Wealth creation through investments leads to an increase in jobs and employment. This, in turn, increases demand. In addition to investments there must be an appropriate amount of savings. In a healthy economy, credit expansion is limited by savings.

The numerous positive effects of true wealth creation have no equivalent in the American Wealth Theory. Wealth creation through increasing *market valuation* can only be realized through additional borrowing, or the sale of assets. This requires finding someone who is able to afford that higher price, and who will actually pay it. In other words, all there will be is a *relocation of assets*, not a true economic income effect.

An Alternative Scenario

Everywhere a silver lining appears to show on the economic horizon. In Europe – with the exception of Germany – a moderate but increasing optimism is spreading. Asia is booming, and in the U.S. the general mood is even better than it was in early 2000, shortly before the great collapse of the stock exchanges.[54] Most mood indicators are approaching their historical high points, some have even reached an all-time high. The center of force is thought to be the American economy, which is expected to provide the crucial momentum.

Perhaps things will happen as expected; that would be wonderful. Perhaps things will take another turn. Realistic management does not rely on forecasts – no one can really predict the future – but on scenarios. It does not rely on majority opinions either. An old stock exchange wisdom says that the public mood is always at a peak when stock prices begin to turn. An alternative scenario would comprise elements like these: a high likelihood that the worldwide stock exchange recovery has come to an end, because contrary to common opinion we are having a strong bear market rally rather than a new bull market. This would mean that the next major move will be downwards, and deeper than most would imagine. Contrary to popular opinion, we would also have to expect a price drop in real estate and precious metals, and in general a drop in commodity prices.

Rather than growth and a latent danger of inflation, such a scenario would imply shrinkage and deflation. We would have to expect increasing interest rates, as the options for issue banks would be considered insufficient in the face of scores of failed debt obligations.

In this scenario, the U.S. would not be the center of an economic upturn but the cradle of inevitable crises. The reasons, as mentioned before, are: massively overvalued assets, both stock and real estate; the highest aggregate debt ever, relative to the national product; the lowest profitability, lowest savings, and lowest net investment of the post-war period; and a financial system that has been leveraged to the limit.

Things would further be complicated by the fact that since 1997 consumption has been accounting for almost 90 percent of the U.S. national product, compared to what would be a healthy rate of 60 to 70 percent. The current theory of "wealth-driven spending" would have to be countered with the argument that wealth does not arise from speculative value creation but from real net investment, financed by savings at appropriate rates.

---

54 On the phenomenon of mass psychology manifested here, and the associated danger of panic reactions, see Linda Pelzmann in: *m.o.m.*® *Malik on Management Letters* 11/02 and 2/03.

An enormous public and foreign trade deficit would have to be analyzed in detail. The conclusion would be that a sinking dollar can only marginally reduce that deficit because America has very little to offer in the way of export goods: a few airplanes, semiconductors, some financial services, all adding up to some 100 billion dollars – compared to a deficit in excess of 500 billion.

One would then have to think about what would happen if the U.S. had to pay for its energy imports, with a total volume of 100 million dollar, at least partially in euros rather than dollars, perhaps even in Yuan before long. At that point, the thought might cross one's mind that this very danger may have been the true reason for the U.S. aggression in Iraq: not the oil as such but oil paid in dollars. Saddam wanted euros rather than dollars. Other oil suppliers, too, do not feel like gradually being disappropriated. The scenario would further entail Russia invoicing its energy supplies in euros, which would be the true reason why the Russian government laid its hands on the Yukos group – not because it wishes to reinstate state-owned businesses. One would then realize that the truly exciting event of the millennium has never been celebrated – for the first time in history there is an alternative to the dollar as the world's lead currency – and one would anticipate the next war to be waged with currencies rather than weapons.

This alternative scenario would further show that, compared to the five post-war recessions, the present recovery of the U.S. economy has been the weakest so far, despite the most comprehensive supporting measures ever in terms of tax reliefs, public expenditure, and low interest rates.

America's high growth rates would have to be depicted in the same manner as for any other economy. They would then have to be divided by four, as they have always been annualized and therefore stated too high. Consequently – to mention only the most drastic example – there would have been no reason to celebrate the exorbitant growth rate of 8.2 percent, which was reported for the 3rd quarter of 2003 and considered the definite turnaround from recession to a new economic boom: this same rate would have to be reduced to 2.05 percent. Another factor to be corrected would be the volume of IT investments, which in the statistics has been artificially blown up to several (up to 10) times its actual figure by using so-called "hedonic pricing". As a result, that same 3rd quarter which was presented to the world with so much fanfare would come off with little more than 1 percent. One would come to realize that for the past ten years the growth of the U.S. economy would have to be corrected down by at least 2 percentage points, leaving it scarcely above European levels. One would then have to ask how it could happen that the U.S. economy has been considered a role model, whereas Europe, and in particular Germany, was perceived to have been run down economically.

Chapter 9

Corporate Policy and Corporate Governance

> "The Nature of the Trap is
> a Function of the Nature of the Trapped."
> *Geoffrey Vickers, management thinker*[55]

In this chapter I will show what Corporate Governance must be, contrary to conventional wisdom, and that its main purpose is not to make shareholders rich but to ensure that an organization is managed properly and well.[56] It can therefore not be restricted to legal questions, as is often attempted.

I have discussed my views on corporate governance, which I have published throughout the 1990s, with thousands of managers in training seminars. The stock market boom, the New Economy, and the alleged superiority of the U.S. economy have not eradicated my doubts regarding the much-propagated "ultimative new truths". I have always considered them wrong.

Corporate governance has been the central theme of the past 15 years. The resulting form of corporate governance which is being practiced has caused one of the most harmful developments in economic history. It has almost replaced any reasonable concepts of proper economic activity and management. The nonsensical neoliberal economic theories, as discussed, have been topped with nonsensical management philosophies.

---

55 Vickers, Geoffrey, *Freedom in a Rocking Boat*, Harmondsworth, 1970, p. 15.

56 Regarding the contents of the entire chapter, see my book *Die richtige Corporate Governance*, 3rd edition, Frankfurt, 2002 (English version expected for 2010), as well as several issues of the *m.o.m.® Malik on Management Letters*, where I have explained the misguided developments in this field, which I feel are rather evident. The 3/94 issue, for instance, contains my most important hypotheses on that issue.

The absurd theories which have come into the world along with the corporate governance debate – shareholder value, value creation, stakeholder approach – are detrimental to the economy, and thus to society as a whole. The kinds of information that have taken the center of attention, along with these disastrous theories – namely, purely financial assessments, key figures from accountants and analysts, and the pseudo-information of the stock exchange crowd – are impractical for the management of a company. They may be useful for other purposes; for those who have to manage an organization they are systematically misleading.

My criticism of the shareholder-focused corporate governance – let me say this clearly to prevent misunderstandings – is not related to profits; much to the contrary. It is, however, my strong opinion that companies not oriented by shareholder value considerations will usually achieve higher profits and, more importantly, healthier and more sustainable profits.

Not one excellent company worldwide is managed in line with the shareholder value doctrine. Most people do not realize this, which is a result of systematic (self-)deception by appearances, media reports, and management rhetoric. Even the fiercest opponents of shareholder value temporarily had to succumb to the terror exerted by financial analysis and the media; besides, they knew how to use skillful rhetoric to take advantage of the mass hysteria.

This is a particularly instructive example of the uncritical adoption of U.S. American theories on economics and management, and of their detrimental effects. It is almost eerie to see how there are extremely successful U.S. managers who have never been followers of the shareholder doctrine, but who in Europe are considered its high priests.

One example is Jack Welch, the legendary former CEO of General Electric, who is praised for the right reasons but for the wrong things. GE's success has little to do with shareholder orientation, although Welch, a master of rhetoric, often gave a different impression. The true reasons for the success of the company were rooted in its market and HR strategies which Mr. Welch had introduced four years before Alfred Rappaport's book on shareholder value had even been published. GE's increase in market capitalization virtually fell into Welch's lap because his decisive changes to the corporate strategy happened to coincide with history's greatest stock market boom. His strategies would have been right either way, and would have made the company great. If there had been a secular bear market GE's share price would not have benefited. There is no systematic connection between the management of a company and its stock price. This may sound absurd to many but it can easily be proved.

Investor icon Warren Buffett is an outspoken opponent of the shareholder value principle, and in general of the entire finance-dominated management scene of our time. The annual reports of his holding Berkshire Hathaway, which are freely accessible on the internet, are prime examples of right and good management.

Mind you, I would never question the sincere intentions behind the corporate governance debate. It just goes to show once again that the road to hell is paved with good intentions.

The debate that has been carried on for over ten years, in part with a dogmatism of medieval proportions, has led to the opposite of what had been intended: to the most scandalous frauds ever against shareholders, to wealth destruction of hitherto unknown proportions, to the most poorly managed companies, to the greatest enrichment of managers, regardless of the results they had achieved, to the shiftiest of balance sheet manipulations, and to the worst kind of white-collar crime. In response to that, the most monstrous sets of regulations in history were created in the era (and under the label) of deregulation. Shareholder value and value creation have caused one of the most disastrous trends in the economy, a misallocation of resources, anti-innovation and anti-investment attitudes, and the systematic deception of corporate management. Nobody wanted this but it is reality. It goes to prove that complex systems cannot be managed with simple means.

The potential reforms that have been discussed in recent years, as a result of gradually growing insight, such as the stakeholder approach or corporate social responsibility, would only replace one evil with another.

I am placing corporate governance in direct connection with corporate policy because it must be seen from the perspective of corporate management. Popular opinion is misleading in its belief that corporate governance refers exclusively or primarily to the question of how the legal balance of power between the different entities of a corporation should be defined. Even if we wanted to – the subject cannot be restricted to this one question, as the answer will inevitably have massive repercussions on the entire management of the company, in particular on the design of its corporate policy and strategy. This follows from the Cadbury Committee's original definition dated 1992: *"Corporate Governance is the system by which companies are directed and controlled."*

To me this seems to be the only useful way to understand it: a definition that will not lead the management of a company astray, or permit it to go astray under the pretense of legitimacy.

One of the main reasons why the corporate governance discussion has developed in a wrong and harmful direction is that it has predominantly been in the hands of corporate lawyers and finance people. Hardly anyone with general management expertise has had a part in it. With all due respect to the expertise of lawyers and finance people: corporate management is not their forte.

Two other points of view, for which I am quoting Böckli and Witt in lieu of several others, are much more reductionist and one-sided, which involves the risk of causing massive errors and – even worse – of legitimating them.

"Corporate Governance is the sum of all guidelines oriented by shareholder interests, aimed at achieving a sound balance of leaderhip and control at a company's top management level while preserving the ability to make decisions and maintaining efficiency "[57]

Here, governance is exclusively oriented by shareholder interests, thus codifying the shareholder value approach.

"The term 'corporate governance' refers to the organization of leadership and control of a company with the objective of balancing interests between the different stakeholder groups."[58]

This third point of view is centered around the stakeholder approach.

Errors of Corporate Governance

Corporate governance, as it has emerged since the early 1990s until today, is a monstrosity that has caused the greatest material and immaterial dam-

---

57 Böckli, Peter, *Corporate Governance: Swiss Code of Best Practice.* Economiesuisse, 2002, p. 5. (English translation by the author).

58 Witt, Peter, "Corporate Governance" in: Peter-Jürgen Jost (Hrsg.), *Die Prinzipal-Agenten-Theorie in der Betriebswirtschaftslehre*, Stuttgart, 2001, p. 85 (English translation by the author).

ages in economic history. More will follow as soon as stock prices drop again.

The approach is based on the uncritically adopted view that a company must be managed in the interest of shareholders and shareholder value, that value creation is the right strategy, that the stock price is the measure of all things, and that financial analysts know how to determine the value of a company. As a result, corporate management has degenerated into a primitive form of profit maximization which is harmful to companies, and in extreme cases even into sheer cash moving maneuvers, in part with criminal methods. These developments were system-immanent and not due to individual misconduct. The disastrous development is not a question of morals or ethics either; rather, it is a logical consequence of the system-immanent faulty logic in the understanding of economic institutions and corporate purposes.

There was no corrective element.[59] Precisely where a particular extent of rationality is alleged and expected – in business –, a decisive element of rational thinking has been lacking over the past years: institutionalized criticism. Science has largely failed here. Nothing critical could be expected from the U.S. as all the nonsense was invented there. But the majority of German-speaking business economists did not voice a critical opinion either. On the contrary, they eagerly helped legitimize and propagate the new "theories". There were a few scientists who did express some criticism, but they belonged to a small minority which was drowned out with partly very unfair means. Instead of building a strong case, the proponents established dogmas. Critics were ignored, ridiculed and branded as "dinosaurs", unable to grasp the naively acclaimed new paradigm of the New Economy with the shareholder approach as its core element – or else they were combated. There was no other "argument" in favor of the blessings of the New Economy, apart from the claim that "this time things are different", but this one was recited like a mantra and defended with religious fervor. The false doctrines originated in the late 1980s in the U.S.; in Europe they were adopted with some delay, starting in the mid-1990s, in an uncritical and partly naïve manner.

---

59 The propagation of the shareholder value approach and the New Economy nonsense have all the traits of mass hysteria or mania; see also Linda Pelzmann in: *m.o.m.*® *Malik on Management Letter* No. 11/02.

Shareholder-Value: Flawed Logic

In the minds of a generation of young managers, journalists, analysts, consultants, management trainers, and scientists – or at least the vast majority of them –, the shareholder value theory and, the value creation strategies based on it, were firmly implanted as the seemingly only and logically compelling kind of corporate governance.

Naturally – because they had not experienced anything else – they interpreted everything in the context of the stock exchange bull market, and were apparently unaware that they knew only *half* of the stock market reality: the *pleasant* half. These people have yet to know a bear market; they have no idea how brutal it can be, how long it can take, how deeply prices can plunge, and that historically there has always, *without exception*, been a downturn following an upturn, pushing prices back down to where they were before the upturn, or lower. They have not learnt anything else but shareholder value and market capitalization. They are not aware of any alternatives. They do not know why this theory even came up in the late 1980s, from what situation and historical development it resulted. Therefore they consider this theory to be the only conceivable truth – and they defend it with dogmatic persistence.

The shareholder value theory, however, is far from being the *only* theory. It was only the newest one for this generation – and it is the worst that was ever conceived. It is therefore likely to be the most short-lived, too, albeit with very serious consequences. *Peter Drucker* voiced his doubts back in the early 1990s, and has repeated them several times since. My own skepticism has been documented since 1994 in several pulications.[60]

Misleading and Dangerous

As I have explained above, I consider the shareholder value theory to be wrong and misleading, in some points even dangerous, since strict abidance by it has serious negative consequences for the economy and society. What we often hear in discussions, now that the damages are obvious, is that the shareholder value concept has only been misunderstood. This is

---

60 Inter alia, in *Effective Top Management*, Weinheim, 2006, as well as Nos. 7/94 et seq. of the *m.o.m.*® *Malik on Management Letters*.

not the problem. The concept has not been misunderstood – it is simply wrong – an unsuitable reference variable for sustainable entrepreneurial and managerial activity. It is the opposite of what it pretends to be. It is destructive for capital, adverse to investment and innovation, and it leads to a misallocation of resources. Ultimately, it is neither to the benefit of shareholders (let alone pension funds) nor to that of management, least of all to the benefit of a functional organization, since – contrary to what is frequently said – it does not lead to higher revenues and profitability, which would be very desirable, but to a purely monetary orientation and a focus on cash. Moreoever, it causes deep rifts in society, fierce battles between social fractions, and a loss of credibility for the leaders.

This, in itself, is not necessarily a compelling reason for managers and supervisory bodies to dismiss shareholder value as a guiding principle. The crucial point is that we are not dealing with laws of nature here. In a free society, everyone is free to choose one or the other theory, even a wrong one. It would be wise, however, to make one's choice in full awareness of the implications of a theory, and in the light of available alternatives.

One of the inevitable and dangerous consequences of the shareholder orientation is the temptation, even the pressure on managers to do anything to make the company look profitable, in particular when it is not. This includes pampering the public with profit expectations; showing pro forma profits when there are no real ones; touching up balance sheets wherever possible, even manipulating them; and pouring out all reserves to the stock market, or using it for price cultivation (not least with an eye to the stock options programs for managers), in order not to belie the expectations one has carefully nurtured.

This phenomenon was *bound* to result from the shareholder value theory; it does not belong in the category of occasional mishaps and individual failures, as is often believed. It is system-immanent. All the sublime appeals to morals and ethics which are now conjured up as a solution provide no escape from the malaise. What we are dealing with here is a veritable *error in the system's architecture* rather than individual moral-ethical lapses. Among other things this is obvious from the fact that even the group that was long considered the most noble caste of the commercial sector – the accountants – became accomplices to criminal machinations; not to speak of the corruption in investment banking, asset management, broking – in short, the entire Wall Street industry. The fact that U.S. top managers were required to certify under oath to the accuracy of their balance sheets can hardly be considered an act of capitalist self-purification – it is the declared bankruptcy of an inept system.

Wrong Question

The root cause of this development lies in a wrongly asked question: in whose interest should a company be managed? From that point, a seemingly logical and plausible path leads to the shareholder. But appearances are deceptive. This answer is neither logical nor compelling, nor – as was pointed out before – is it the only possible answer. As a matter of fact, it can only appear plausible under certain, rather rare conditions.

These conditions were most clearly prevalent in the United States at the end of the 1980s, whereas in most other countries they did not exist at all, or only in rudimentary forms, and could only be implemented artificially and temporarily to date. Prime examples include the Southeast Asian "Tiger Countries", which for a while were propagated to represent the economic future per se, as well as some Latin American countries which collapsed precisely because of these artificially created conditions – namely, a financial bubble based on excessive borrowing.

Another example of rare special conditions, which was not visible for a long time but gained all the more significance after 2000, is the fact that the shareholder theory can only appear reasonable, even the only theory possible, in times of rising stock prices – which was also the case in the U.S., specifically since 1982. This date seems unknown to most people who started stock market investing in the 1990s and who believe in causal relations with economic prosperity and business performance, partly based on grotesque pseudo-theories about the rationality of capital markets and their superior wisdom in assessing the value of companies.

Together with the New Economy illusion this ultimately led to a temporary speculative mass mania, as happens and has happened in economic history every 60 to 70 years – intervals long enough to forget the bitter experiences of the past, shrug off the lessons learnt, and say, *"this time things are different"*. It is absurd to assume that stock markets will keep going up. This very absurdity has determined all thoughts and actions – and it is equally absurd to base corporate governance on it. Although it was wrong before, the whole futility of this view will become increasingly visible as the bear market progresses.

Wrong Context

The shareholder concept appears most plausible in the context of publicly owned corporations with international activities, *if and as long as their stock is going up.* However, it is, *firstly,* only the appearance of plausibility and not real logic; *secondly,* major corporations are not representative of the economy; they only attract the greatest media interest. Large corporations account for a relatively small share of economic power in all countries. Only rarely do they contribute more than one-third of the economic value added, or one-third of employment. Corporations are important, but they are not typical for what happens in the business sector.

The same applies to another segment which, ten years after the invention of shareholder value, almost hypnotically attracted the attention of the masses: the start-up businesses in the internet and e-business sector. They, too, are not representative of the economy, not even of a New Economy, which was propagated the louder the less people understood about the nature of economics.

In all countries, around two-thirds of the economic output is produced by small and medium-sized businesses, and they account for the same share of employment. For these businesses shareholder value is not only useless, even with lots of well-intentioned adaptations; it also shows its misleading and detrimental effects quickly and immediately. This is why the concept has not found widespread acceptance here, which, however, has always been the cause of condescending criticism by zeitgeist proponents.

The term "small and mid-sized businesses" is a bit misleading here. It is not a matter of small and mid-sized organizations but of organizations managed in an entrepreneurial manner, and they include companies of all sizes. In this segment we find firms that are managed extremely well and which, more often than the public and "experts" are aware of, are world market leaders in their fields. In lieu of many others based in German-speaking countries I will only name the following few: Hilti in Liechtenstein, Swarowski and Rauch in Austria, Logitech and Schindler in Switzerland, as well as Boehringer Ingelheim, Stihl, Würth, Miele, and Otto in Germany.

There were precious few reports about companies of this kind at the times of boom and bluff. Large corporations and dot.com firms took front and center of media attention. The most important and best segment was practically blanked out. As a result, the public gradually adopted a dangerously distorted impression of economic activities. Major corporations, let alone dot.coms, are anything but typical of economies.

Contrary to a widespread erroneous belief, entrepreneurial management in the sense referred to here is possible everywhere and any time, irrespective of size, industry, legal form, and financing sources, regardless even of whether a company is listed on the exchange, as impressively demonstrated by companies such as Porsche, BMW, and Nestlé.

The Stakeholder Approach – a Pseudo-Solution

Thus, even for the wrongly posed question there would have been several possible answers, and it was owed to very specific circumstances that the shareholder theory found enough receptiveness to become the only answer that seemed plausible. It is an irony of history that now, in the wake of the balance sheet scandals, the first dogmatic proponents of the shareholder theory – having come to realize that something must be wrong with their doctrine – are now initiating its great "reform", which in essence is a mutation to the stakeholder theory. Apparently its advocates fail to see (or do not know) that it is just another, earlier, and equally wrong variant of the same thing, and that it was the very failure of the stakeholder concept which led to the accidental plausibility and receptivity of the shareholder concept.

As shareholders and shareholder value are losing persuasive power as a frame of reference for right corporate management, there is a growing suspicion that it may have been these very concepts and the resulting management, assessment, and evaluation practices which caused the formation of those bubbles and their disastrous effects. But instead of stepping back to rethink the whole subject carefully, another deception was quickly created. Instead of the shareholder we now have the stakeholder.

It is true, the argument goes, that a company should not be managed in the interest of *one* group only – the shareholders; rather, several stakeholder groups must be considered. This term, however, holds several grave errors:

The stakeholder concept is anything but an effective reform of shareholder value thinking. On the contrary, history has shown that it leads to even worse errors in company management.

Historically, the stakeholder approach was the *precendent* of the shareholder approach. As early as in 1952, it was *General Electric CEO Ralph Cordiner's* answer to the question: *who does the top management of a public corporation respond to?* As right and as important as this question may have been, Cordiner's answer to it was wrong. The stakeholder approach has failed, and its failure was the very origin of the (allegedly better) shareholder approach. Its creator, *Alfred Rappaport*, thought it could be used to make "lazy" managers get a move on.

Low returns, Rappaport opined, should no longer be excused by saying that management had to consider the interests of all stakeholders, not only those of one single group, the shareholders. As he and several others realized clearly and correctly, a management body having (or pretending) to answer to all stakeholder groups will actually have no responsibility at all. They can whitewash all their actions on the pretext of having to consider one or the other group's interests, just as it suits them at the given moment. Today it may be the interests of employees and unions – tomorrow those of suppliers, the public, of science, the government, and so forth. Poor corporate performance will always have its justification.

Not that the stakeholder approach would have prevented good management: there were excellently managed companies at that time. General Electric was one of them. But poor management could always be excused with seemingly plausible arguments, and bad managers had means and ways to shirk all accountability.

A management theory centering around *stakeholders*, no matter how many and how they be defined, will inevitably put the organization *at the mercy of the changing balance of power* among these same stakeholder groups. As a result there can no longer be any meaningful standards for management performance. The consequences are devastating, as past examples have shown. Just think of the *British* industry, which was in the unions' stranglehold and almost suffered its demise; or of the *Italian* business sector, mired in political corruption for decades; or of the decline of state-owned enterprises in the 1970s and 1980s in *Austria*, where all kinds of management nonsense were tolerated in the interest of the government parties.

Rappaport's alleged improvement was, in fact, an improvement for the worse. This was unmistakably clear from the excesses and debacles of the late 1990s. There is only one way to manage an institution properly: the institution *itself* must take front and center. Consequently, management must be oriented by the organization's *potential and competitiveness*. We have sufficiently clear standards for that purpose, against which all top management activities can be aligned and assessed.[61]

Of cource, what is good for an institution is not equally good for all its stakeholders – but it enables the *greatest possible* number of legitimate interests to be satisfied. After all, a badly managed institution cannot satisfy any interests at all.

Employment, another Pseudo-Solution

Arguing against shareholder and stakeholder value does not necessarily – as is often contended – imply a bias for job creation and for holding on to obsolete welfare state structures. Although demanding more jobs will always get you brownie points with many people, no matter what the political situation – which is tempting not only to politicians but also to entrepreneurs, top managers, and trade union officials –, it can certainly not be a solution. This becomes particularly obvious when you focus on the organization itself, *its ability to function and to perform.*

The Right Solution

It is a company's job to deliver an economic service to the market. This is not some nondescript metaphysical concept; the meaning is straight forward: value to the customers. The company meets its obligation to society by achieving customer satisfaction, not by meeting some specially designed social responsibilities.[62]

If it takes a large workforce to satisfy customers, this may please the unions; if, however, the purpose of a company can only be fulfilled by reducing its headcount, it must not be hindered from doing that. Customer satisfaction must be given priority over workforce interests.

---

61 See Malik, Fredmund, *Effective Top Management*, Weinheim, 2006, as well as the *Strategy* chapter in this book.

62 Peter F. Drucker has expressed this opinion as early as in 1955: "There is only one valid definition of business purpose: to create a customer." *The Practice of Management*, New York, 1954; new edition, 1982, p. 35. The validity of this view has remained unchanged; there has rarely been clearer evidence of this than during the aberrations of the 1990s.

This emphasis on customers regularly leads proponents of the stakeholder approach to claim that the customer was one of the stakeholders.

This is a serious mistake with regard to the logic of economic activity and management. As I have said in the chapter on business environment, customers are part of a company's environment but they are not a *stakeholder group*, and the reason is that they do not have any stakes in the *company*. They are interested in the *product*.[63] As important as suppliers may be – for customers, the company supplying the product is of secondary importance because they have a *choice*. As a matter of fact, in a market economy the term "customer" is only defined by his having a choice. A customer dissatisfied with the products or services of one company will purchase from another company next time. It is therefore utterly unrealistic to expect customer *loyalty*, even though every attempt should be made to achieve it. The fact of the matter is, however, that what appears to be loyalty is always the outcome of a *value consideration*. *Customers pay for the value they get.*

An objection frequently raised here is that customers have a proper interest in the continued existence of a company because they need and depend on suppliers. No doubt customers need suppliers, but in a functioning market economy there will always be several options. Every customer will have a vital interest in *not* depending on one supplier, as with a lack of options he will cease to be a customer in the true sense and become dependent on monopolies instead. As close, good and friendly as customer-supplier relations may be, their basis remains the value-related satisfaction of customers in combination with their options.

Remarkably often the economically ignorant reply is, if this was all true a company would have to give away its goods for free. That conclusion is wrong. The correct implication is that a company needs to achieve better market performance than any competitor could.

There is only one logic for good corporate management: *serving the customer better than the competitors can.*[64] Customer value and competi-

---

63 Similar reasons could be brought forward for employees – in particular high-ranking specialists – and for suppliers, which is why I consider the stakeholder approach to be fundamentally inept. Customers, however, always have more options than the other groups do.

64 Ironically enough, the chief witness is the very inventor of shareholder value, Alfred Rappaport himself: "Even the most persistent advocate of shareholder value understands that without customer value there can be no shareholder value. The source of a company's long-term cash flow is its satisfied customers."

tiveness are the only two *incorruptible* and *non-manipulable* frames of reference for the management of organizations. If you have satisfied customers you will always have financiers as well; unfortunately the opposite is not true, as countless dot.com examples have clearly shown. If we want to talk about value it must be customer value, not shareholder value, which corporate management must focus on. The strategy chapter will deal with what customer value is, how to quantify it and how to make it a cornerstone of a useful strategy.

Profit, thus, is not all that matters; other crucial factors are the quality of profit and its realization. Profit resulting from customer satisfaction is obviously something very different from profit gained through asset deals, let alone profits from manipulating balance sheets.

Whichever way you look at it – wrongly posed questions will never get a right answer. Not only must the question be posed at an earlier point, it must also refer to a very different logical issue: not to the *distribution* of the economic result but to its *creation*. Consequently it must be: *What is right company management?* and, proceeding from there: What is a strong, healthy, viable organization? What should the executive top management and its supervisory bodies do to create and maintain it? Obviously we have plenty of answers to that.[65]

Only the right management of companies will bring about economic results in the form of productive potential, be it factories or computers, bricks or bytes, in the form of products and services, national income and national product, wages, taxes, interest, and profits.

Once an economic result has been created it can be distributed. Only then does the key question of the shareholder approach – how much to distribute to whom – take on a meaning. Only then does it make sense to think about which of the different stakeholder groups, whatever their legitimization, should have what part of the economic result. Then there might even be good reasons to give priority to shareholders.

Rappaport, Alfred, *Creating Shareholder Value*, New York, 1998, p. 8; he then goes on to undermine his own insight with unsustainable arguments.

65 See the comprehensive writings of Peter F. Drucker; I have documented my view, which is largely consistent with it, in *Effective Top Management* as well as in numerous issues of my monthly management letter *m.o.m.® Malik on Management*. See also the essays by Aloys Gälweiler. Hans Ulrich has taken the same view in his work on the St. Gallen Management Model and System oriented Management Theory.

Over the years I have discussed these questions with numerous managers at all hierarchical levels. There was not one knock-down counterargument. Whenever entrepreneurs where present there was approval. Not one of them was managing his or her firm according to the shareholder value concept. Real entrepreneurs find that school of thought absurd, as they know very well, and experience every day, that only customers pay the bill – no-one else.

Value Creation – What For?

When talking about fads and errors I must not leave out the doctrine of value creation. In particular the idea that value creation must be the goal and purpose of a company, even its only goal and overriding purpose, is utterly wrong.

It is not a purpose of a company to have value. This can only be a goal for shareholders – specifically, if they are really not that interested in the company itself but in the papers documenting its equity ownership – its equities – and if they mistake company stock for companies. This is why in a company's articles of incorporation we never find a sentence like "the purpose of the company shall be to have value". The articles specify other purposes, such as "trading goods of all kinds" or "conducting banking business" or "manufacturing software".

Let me repeat once more: the business purpose of a company must be to be *competitive* in a given field – which is something entirely different from being valuable. A company is competitive if it does whatever it is the customer pays for better than other companies. We could therefore say, as mentioned before, that the purpose of a company is to create satisfied customers. Neither the creation of jobs nor the creation of shareholder value can be the purpose of a company. It must be focused on creating customer value.

At this point I would like to highlight a very telling responce: The publication of this concept in a renowned German business paper provoked a public reply by a German professor of business administration. In an attempt to prove that shareholder value and customer value were essentially the same, he demonstrated how to quantify customer value, and how this will lead to an increase in shareholder value. It seems he had not understood what this is all about: not value *of* the customer – to the company, that is – but value *to* the customer ...

There is no causal relationship between the value of a company – no matter how it is determined – and its competitiveness. I have often said it, and now the stock market is proven the point even to the most stubborn skeptics: it is impossible to draw conclusions – either negative or positive – from the price of a stock to the competitiveness and performance of the company.[66] The only things to conclude from it are the naiveté, greed, and fear of its investors. There may be a relation the other way round, but not necessarily so. The causal relation between competitiveness and stock price is not stringent, as the valuation excesses of recent years have impressively shown.

Unlike shareholders, customers do not pay for the value of a company but for the value of its goods and services. This is not a value *of* the company, nor to the company. It is a value *to* the customer. Customers will pay for what is valuable to them – and only to them – and it is only for this reason that they buy at all. It does not matter to them one bit whether this purchase will or will not increase the value of the company. So if you want to operate with value creation, the goal must be to create value to the customer.

The value of a business is only significant to people wishing to buy or sell the business as such. For the economic activity of that company the question of company value is entirely irrelevant – what matters is the issue of performance and competitiveness, which arises anew every day.

At this point we should call to mind that the concept of shareholder value and its quantification were not developed for the purpose of *acting on behalf* of companies – that is, for *managing* them – but for dealing *in* companies, and a major driver of this was the surging M & A wave of the mid- to late 1980s.

Obviously enough, what we have here is the mistaking of the *shareholder* purpose with the *company* purpose, and the highly questionable equating of one with the other. Also, what today is referred to as "investor" is dangerously confused with what we mean by "entrepreneur", including the entrepreneurial manager. The interests and logic of both are profoundly different, which is easily recognizable from the fact that every entrepreneur must be an investor but only few investors are entrepre-

---

66 Owing to the effects of stock option programs, people are gradually beginning to realize this.

neurs.[67] The interests of an entrepreneur are, at least during his lifetime, so much in line with those of his company that it is not necessary (and would even border on hairsplitting) to make a distinction. What we are witnessing now is something entirely different: the performance targets of today's shareholders (commonly equated with entrepreneurs) – and in particular those of funds managers – have very little in common with the performance a company needs.

Entrepreneur or Investor?

Every entrepreneur is an investor. But is every investor an entrepreneur? As a result of developments at the stock exchanges and financial markets, an important distinction – between the entrepreneur-shareholder and the investor-shareholder – is neglected. And while ownership in a company and ownership in company shares is established by the same kind of document and there may be no difference in legal terms, the economic difference could not be greater. Some believe that a new form of capitalism has been invented. Whatever one may think of it, so far only half the truth has been considered, and only half has been important. It will not take long, however, until the second half will have to be faced up to. It is something which the big capitalists of all eras have experienced: "If you can't sell you have to care."

The investor operates temporarily; he is interested in his papers as long as they yield returns. Entrepreneurial activity, however, is long-term by design.

The investor-shareholder *gives up in the face of trouble* – he sells – and if he is smart he will have structured his investments so that he can get rid of them quickly, for example by focusing on liquid markets where even large volumes can be sold at decent prices. The entrepreneur-shareholder responds differently when trouble looms: he fights. He *cares*. The "why", is not important; what matters is that he does it. This one may fight be-

---

67 It would have been better not to adopt the term "investor" in German; then it would have been clear that investors are "*Anleger*" but not "*Unternehmer*". This way, another fashion – the adoption of anglicisms – has contributed to erroneous developments. There is a tendency to use bad translations of English terms, or the terms themselves, in German.

cause he *cannot* sell; to another, his company may be more than just a money machine – it may be his life's work or even that of generations before him. A third may fight because she never wants to go into employment again. Whatever the reason – she fights.

An investor is interested in one resource – money – and seeks to maximize it. The entrepreneurial task, however, stretches across several resources. It is defined that way – by the combination of resources, which must be balanced as creatively, innovatively, and productively as possible.

The investor-shareholder is only interested in the financial result of a business. Anything else does not have to concern him, except as an indicator of what papers to buy. The entrepreneur-shareholder also cares about the financial result; however, he is bound to care about the company's performance and capabilities as well, even if he does not always like it and will often find it hard to do. He has no choice.

An investor needs the stock exchange. Without it he could not pursue his investment objectives; he would have to mutate into an entrepreneur. The entrepreneur, however, *can do without the stock exchange*. With or without stock markets, there are always entrepreneurs – as important as the markets may be in many respects. There were entrepreneurs long before there were stock exchanges, even banks, and there were entrepreneurs when stock markets and banks collapsed and were temporarily closed.

The shareholder-value-type investor only exists in bull markets. He can only obtain the shareholder value he seeks (and is promised) during times of continued upturn. He is a good-weather phenomenon. During a depression he will actively destroy value because he will only be able to make profits on the short side. The deeper the stock prices plunge, the better his puts and his short-sales will perform. For instance, in Japan it was almost impossible for investors after 1990 to make profits on the long side, while on the short side they could. The worse off the Japanese companies were, the greater the gains of short operators. It is inherent in their function that they are interested in destroying value.

Entrepreneurs create value precisely *in these situations*, as we can clearly see in Southeast Asia and Japan, but also in Latin America. In economic terms, an entrepreneur is an "all-weather" type. He does not only work in good times when it all comes easily, but also when things go badly – and even more and even harder then, not because he is a "hero" but because he does not have a choice.

The Magic of Indicators

Fixating on financial ratios is the vogue. A considerable percentage of executives seem to believe that a knowledge of mainstream financial indicators will qualify them for managing a company. A dangerous error!

As long as only EBIT was used to measure performance, the risk of faulty management was limited. Yet that ratio was also misused.

In our consulting practice at Malik Management we have used EBIT in strategy consulting since 1984; so it was not all that new when it came into fashion in the mid-1990s. Of course, before the bubble years it was never used or recommended for managing a company. This indicator was used exclusively for comparing companies with one another. As each company has another financial and tax situation, it was necessary to use a gross instead of a net profit figure to achieve meaningful performance comparisons. Interest and taxes had to be eliminated from the economic result.

EBIT originated from the so-called *PIMS* (Profit Impact of Market Strategy) program, which in the 1960s was developed by *General Electric* to judge and compare the performance of individual divisions. Of course it was always clear that a true economic result will have to be *after* interest and taxes, and that dividends could only be considered after that.

Under the influence of shareholder thinking, what had been invented for purposes of comparison turned into a management benchmark. It was the first step toward wrong management. The next steps were predestined and inevitable: EBITD, EBITDA, and so on – all of them financial ratios from the world of finance experts, accountants, and investment bankers, and of no use for the management of a company.

All financial indicators are highly problematical for management because they fall short of essential management issues. From what has meanwhile become a rather large pool of indicators available, only one is suitable for management purposes: EAE – *Earnings After Everything*. Only after all necessary provisions have been made and reserves have been built up to help the company through bad times, can we speak of *real*, bottom-line results.

The true origin of these unfortunate developments was the confusion of perspectives and management purposes with those of investors and their consultants. At the same time it was a confusion of real economic corporate purposes with *financial* investor purposes.

Wrong Understanding of Profit

After years of debate over the term "profit" – first among practitioners, then among scientists, then among consultants, accountants, and investment bankers – one would think that it is now unequivocally clear what profit is. Lamentably this is not so.

We may know better than before how profit expectations can be created and manipulated, but the term as such is still hardly understood and therefore often misused. The more a manager speaks of profit, the more skepticism will be advisable, and the more we will need to find out what he is really talking about, in particular when he is talking about *profit optimum or profit maximum.*

For the management of a company the idea of a profit maximum is downright useless. The contrary is helpful: the profit minimum – the question as to how much a company needs to earn to stay in business. Not for the capital service of today, mind you, but for staying in business in the future. The goal is not to do without the term "profit" or without profit as such. The profit minimum, in this definition, will often exceed what most would accept as profit maximum.

For a truly professional management we should even go one step further and stop using to term "profit" altogether. There are no real profits, if you think about it, only costs. There are two kinds: the costs of today's business, and the costs required to stay in business tomorrow.

The costs of the first kind are known to us because we have them in the books. The costs of the second kind are unknown to us; there can be no book entries because there are no vouchers. Yet they are just as real as the costs we know. If we cannot pay the costs of the second type, our company will not have a future. As long as we speak of costs only, there can hardly be any major management mistakes. An overly narrow understanding of profit, however, has always been the beginning of a company's decline.

Functioning Corporate Governance – Because the Market Reacts Too Late

The market may have been a place of effective control and correction, back in the times when a company's collapse had no major repercussions

– companies were small, their radius of action was narrow and chain reactions were rare and had their limits. It is no longer so.

It is often forgotten that the market – as important as it may be – does not suffice to bring about economic performance, let alone societal performance. This statement is not a concession to anti-market views – much to the contrary. Some people are dissatisfied with the market and with market-economic solutions because they disagree with certain results of market-economic processes, such as income distribution or performance pressure. That is not my argument.

There are other reasons for being dissatisfied with the market: firstly, it is too slow; secondly, it does not have an anticipatory effect but works only after the fact; thirdly, at its core it does not have a conducive but only a punishing influence.

The market does not tell us where and how resources should be employed, only where and when they should have been deployed. When this signal comes from the market it is too late, in particular for large corporations. Even the fastest company has its "dead time", as the delay between a signal and its effect in a system is called in cybernetics and control engineering. Large companies are slow by nature and have long lead times for investments and innovation. Once certain decisions have been made, such as, for instance, the development of a widebody aircraft, they cannot be corrected for decades – no matter what the market signals may say.

The market as such does not induce anything positive, and it does not prevent any mistakes. All it does is punish them – but only *after* they have happened, which is too late. In particular the proponents of market-economic solutions should realize that. Whenever economists and finance people, brimming with the smugness of infallible experts, say that faulty developments will be corrected by the market (as they regularly do), it is evident they do not know much about the decision processes in a company. This is all the more serious as we have much more knowledge today of strategic decisions and the corresponding means of information than the signal effect of market prices. Going by market prices is almost as if ships, in times of satellite navigation, would still be navigated using the North Star as a compass.

This market deficiency can only be offset by an effective supervisory body, the board of directors. Almost like a twin to the market, its task is to ensure that the executive management of the company does its job well, and that mistakes are avoided rather than punished ex post. That is not only possible, it is necessary to prevent value destruction in the economy, as well as a new adversity to business dealings.

Business Mission: The Basis of Right Governance

One of the basic questions of coporate governance is how to determine the basic direction of the company – its corporate purpose, policy, and principles. This is equally valid for every institution, not only for commercial enterprises, so we should probably use a more general term and speak of institutional governance.

What should or must our business purpose be? What should it not be? With what business areas should or must we therefore concern ourselves – which ones should we avoid? These are questions of the governance type.

An appropriate term for defining this basic direction is business, organisational, or institutional mission.

Vision or Mission?

Visions as guidelines for management action and corporate strategy development are no longer as popular a topic in business writing as they used to be. However, even though the hype has abated, the concept of vision is still prominent in managers' thoughts and discussions. And it is still as *ambiguous* as it used to be.

I have never considered the vision concept to be useful. In my opinion it is a result of poor translations from English to other languages, but even in English the word has several meanings. It would have been appropriate at least to define the term precisely. That did not happen. Therefore we have as many definitions today as we have authors, and most of these definitions are rather wooly.

Certainly *terms and definitions* cannot be our chief concern, although they are important enough to be chosen carefully and deliberately. What matters much more is another question: How to distinguish a good vision from a bad one – a useful vision from a dangerous or misleading one? How can a vision that is suitable as a basis for entrepreneurial action be distinguished from daydreams resulting from economic and/or strategic ignorance?

There is no denying that these distinctions are important when economic resources are at stake, and even more so when human beings and their fates, their jobs, their incomes, and their future are involved. Yet I have never come across a discussion of these issues in all the literature on vision.

In view of the wooliness of its definitions and in particular the *arbitrariness* of its usage, what I prefer is the term "mission", and for corporate management purposes, the terms *"business mission"* or *"corporate mission"*. In more general terms we can speak of "institutional mission" or "organization mission".

The mission of a company is the fundamental *purpose* it was established to fulfill and against which all its actions and their results must be judged. In military organizations, for instance, these things are perfectly clear; every officer knows what a mission is; he is trained to put it in clear and unambiguous words, and he knows very well what items the description of a mission must entail. He also knows how to distinguish a meaningful mission from a meaningless one. The same is true in, say, space flight, where the term is used in the same sense.

Company Purpose and the Function of Profit

What is the purpose of a company? During a visit to Beijing I posed this question to several dozens of discussion partners. All of them responded without thinking: "To make money!" or "To make profit!"

No doubt companies need to make profit. But does this imply that making profit is their fundamental purpose? Does it imply that man's purpose in life is to eat and drink? It is impossible to stop people from seeing it that way and from acting accordingly. The implications are clear...

Companies do not "make" money. They make shoes, dress shirts, cars, bread, or computers. Not money. Even the monopolized printing business that prints banknotes does not "make" money.

Albeit, even these undisputable truths cannot keep anyone from thinking that a company's purpose is to make money or profit. Everyone is free to define the purpose as they like.

The belief that the purpose of a company is to make profit is as old as it is misleading. It is probably impossible to eradicate. Every few decades it emerges in a new guise, a new theory; at present it is the shareholder value concept which, in conjunction with neoliberalism, has led to the rise of an extraordinarily primitive profit maximization doctrine.

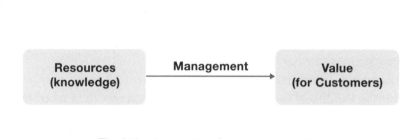

The following applies for the organizational
form of market-oriented corporations:
PROFIT IS THE TEST FOR THE RIGHTNESS
OF THE BUSINESS MISSION AND FOR ITS
EFFICIENT IMPLEMENTATION.

Figure 19: Purpose of the company

The crucial point, however, is not that everyone is basically free to define those things as he pleases; the decisive question is what definition is best for the management of a company.

What we are looking for, then, is the definition associated with the lowest likelihood of systematically wrong decisions, and/or the greatest probability of right decisions. If your actions are geared toward the customer you will make mistakes, too, but your decisions will be oriented by the right parameters. If you get your bearings from shareholders and the stock market, however, you can be certain to make systematically wrong decisions – decisions that will harm the company. That is true in particular when your shareholders, via pension funds, are the future retirees.

Management, and I repeat again, is about transforming resources into value. So far, the best organizational form to achieve this is the enterprise set up in accordance with market economy principles. Both, resources and value, are situated outside the company; hence there are no values or value creation within its boundaries – contrary to the theories of Michael Porter, which so often are adopted unquestioningly.[68] Inside the company there is only expenditure. The best research, the best production, the best marketing – they all cause nothing but expenses. Value is created only, and exclusively, where someone pays a bill – and that is at the customer level, outside the company.

The purpose of a company – and I have quoted *Drucker's* writings of 1954 before – is to *create satisfied customers*. Value to the customer is the purpose of a company, not value to the shareholder, not profit, and not options for managers.

What is the function of profit? Profit is a two-fold test: firstly, it is a test for the validity of the business mission – a test revealing whether the company is doing the right thing, a test for its effectiveness. Secondly, it is a test for whether the company is fulfilling its purpose correctly, that is, whether it is doing the right thing the right way – a test for its efficiency.

These are the functions of profit for the *management* of a company. For the company itself it has additional functions, such as being a source of capital and capital premiums – a topic we will pursue no further at this point.

Three Elements of a Business Mission

A useful business mission[69] comprises three elements. Hence, what one certainly does not want to begin with is the wording, least of all with finding a catchy, appealing slogan. The first things to be determined are the basic elements of the business mission. They must be made as clear as possible, and that requires thorough, usually time-consuming discussion. From what I have observed, this is one of the main reasons why managers are not so keen on developing a business or corporate mission. As long as one of the elements is missing, the job cannot be considered complete.

---

68 See Porter, Michael E., *Competitive Strategy – Techniques for Analyzing Industries and Competitors*, New York, 1980.

69 Regarding the following, see also Drucker, Peter F., "The Theory of the Business", in: Drucker, Peter F., *Managing in a time of great change*, New York, 1995, p. 21 et seq.

A business mission must provide answers to the following three questions. They *appear* to be simple, or even trite, as some people like to believe. Of cause there are always *easy* and *quick* answers. They are almost always *wrong* as well.

Anyone setting out to seek answers to these three questions with the sort of *seriousness* suited to the decisions to be based on them will realize that they are *difficult* questions, questions penetrating to the very heart of any organization. That, in fact, is what a business mission is about.

1. What does the market need? or: What does the customer pay us for?
2. What is our superiority based on? or: What can we do better than others?
3. Where does our strength come from? or: What do we believe in?

Need

The first question focuses our attention and discussion to the *outside*, to society, economy, and the markets. Not in a *general* sense, though, as that will often lead to inconsequential philosophical considerations, but *specifically* referring to the *customer*. Whatever one may think of shareholder value and its function in the management of a company, one thing is unquestionably true: a company that no longer has any customers will soon have no shareholders either, so shareholder value will become superfluous.

The seemingly innocuous question as to what the market needs leads to further questions which, almost invariably, are rather difficult to answer: *Who is our customer? Who ought to be? Who is not our customer? Why not?* Non-customers are regularly *overlooked*, often with disastrous consequences. A company holding 30 percent market share can certainly point to a splendid achievement. On the other hand, a 30 percent market share also means that there are 70 percent of the market it *does not* reach…! Why not?

The crucial point in defining the first element of a business mission is to look *outside* – to the reality of a company, the real opportunities and the real risks. Obviously this has always been important, but it is more so today than ever before. Spoilt by the enormous amount of information at their fingertips, managers today believe they are well-informed. What they usually know "everything" about is the inside of their own organizations, and what they generally know very little about is the world outside.

Strengths

The second element of every business mission is the question: *What are our strenghts? What can we do better than others, what is our superiority based on?* This question directs attention away from the world outside and onto the company, but always in *comparison* with others. Note that this is not simply a matter of looking inwards. Things are not as simple as that. It is a matter of *looking from the inside outwards and then inwards again.*

As a young consultant I was very proud when we had compiled an issue catalog discribing all the deficits of a client organization, along with appropriate steps to eliminate them, of course. I believed we had done a good job and were justified in submitting our invoice. It took some time until it dawned on me that that was the simpler and less important part of the job. Today I consider it my most important – and really my only – task as a consultant to help my clients determine their strengths, both of the people and of the organization. This is by far more difficult to do, but it is also more important.

What are we able to do? What are our real capabilities? And what can we do better – a little better – than others? Note that this is not about excellence, record-breaking competitive leads, or miracles of the kind so often showcased in business literature. Being a *little* better than others means a great deal, and every experienced manager knows that it takes all the strength available to maintain a small lead, let alone increase it. It is the same experience every athlete has to make.

Belief

Where does the strength come from that we need, as inviduals and organizations, to deliver performance beyond the routine, everyday business? What I am thinking of here is more than what is commonly understood by the word "motivation". It is the sort of strength that is needed when our "normal" motivation has been used up and we still have not reached our goal; when serious difficulties have to be overcome; when truly massive efforts are required, when the last reserves have to be mobilized.

History as a whole, and economic history in particular, have seen enough examples of this phenomenon when it was the mobilization of these last power reserves which – often in seemingly hopeless situations – tipped the balance. Some organizations may never need to go that far; so much the better. Then again they may get into a situation in which they need to demand the kind of commitment that is at the very limit of human capacity, far beyond anything imaginable in normal times.

In most cases the reasons for releasing such reserves are either existential threats or the *certainty* that the matter at hand is important enough to warrant this kind of commitment.

One of the core elements is what we call *corporate culture*. In fact, what can be found here are the very values which historically led to what used to be referred to as culture, in the narrower meaning of the word, before the term began being trivialized by management theory. In the light of this observation, I find most of the ongoing discussion on corporate culture to be remarkably superficial and stale.

The Interaction of the Elements

Clarifying each of the elements described is important enough. It should be obvious by now that this goes well beyond the state that has been reached in the debate on vision; and also, that it is the only way to achieve the sort of thoroughness and concreteness required to provide a justifiable and strong foundation for the far-reaching decisions regarding a company's strategy, structure, and culture.

Yet there is much more to be said. Only the interaction of the three elements will produce a *whole*. There are also three further elements that originate from the first three; they are what in system sciences is referred to as "emerging phenomena".

1. The Source of Value

The interaction of need and strengths creates *value*, in particular *customer value*. This is immediately clear once you think through the relationship between the two elements: where an existing need (or demand) is not met by a company's strengths there will be no value. Likewise, there will be no value when a company has capabilities for which there is no need. The creation of value, thus, requires both.

2. The Source of Self-Respect

The interaction of strengths and belief leads to things as important as pride in the company and its performance, as well as *self-respect* and *confidence*. People cannot be proud of something their company is incapable of, so there cannot be any belief in that ability.

3. The Source of Meaning

Finally, the interaction of belief and need creates what we might call *meaning* – not in some metaphysical-philosophical sense but in the very practical sense that *Viktor Frankl*[70], a man I very much esteem, assigned to the term.

It is the meaning to be found in devoting oneself to a matter or task. As already mentioned, this is something entirely different from the common idea of motivation. It could hardly be put in better words than those by *Nietzsche*, occasionally quoted by Frankl: *He who has a why to live can bear almost any how…*

Figure 20 shows the elements of a business mission and their interrelations. Analogous questions must be asked for all kinds of organizations – commercial enterprises, schools, hospitals, administrative agencies, cultural organizations – when it comes to defining the fundamental jobs they have to do. The questions are the same; the answers will be different.

Putting the business mission in concrete terms, translating it into objectives, thus preparing it for the different planning stages and finally its implementation, is done using the six central performance controls discussed in the next subchapter. A business mission will be all the *easier* to implement, the more it forces an organization to *concentrate its forces*. All successful organizations were established to serve one purpose only. As soon as you try to pursue several purposes at once, the results will be erosion,

---

70 See Frankl, Viktor E., *Der Mensch vor der Frage nach dem Sinn*, Munich. 1979, 3rd edition, 1982. I have summarized those parts of his theory which have particular relevance for management in the *m.o.m.® Malik on Management Letter* No.3/97.

mediocrity, and often demise. A business mission is all the more promising, the more it forces an organization to *distinguish itself* from others, the more it leads toward uniqueness. Copying others is a useful strategy only if you can do the same thing much better.

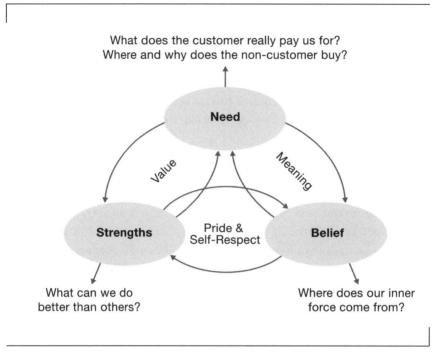

Figure 20: Elements of the business mission

In the sense explained here, the business mission is also a prerequisite and a basis for one of the still largely misunderstood elements of well-functioning organizations: the development of a promising brand and the pursuit of an effective branding strategy.

Stating the Business Mission

Mission development must not *start* with attempts at formulation – those should follow *after* careful consideration of all elements and interactions between them. And while the wording of a mission statement is certainly important, it does not need to take the form often aspired to: a *single* sentence, as brief and succinct as possible, both elegantly worded and, if possible, emotionally appealing. If it is accomplished, congratulations on a great job. However, only very few mission statements can be phrased that way, as only very few organizations' activities lend themselves to elegant wording.

That, however, is by far less important than many people think. In most cases two very different things are being *confused*: the desires and demands of marketing, advertising, and public relations, and the essence and logical dimensions of a company's activities. Hence, it is not a problem at all if a mission statement requires several sentences, and if these sentences do not come out quite as elegant or brillant or emotionally appealing as one might have hoped.

A well-thought-through business mission is not a *guarantee* for business success. The mere notion is absurd. There will never be a guarantee for success. Even the best of business missions can and will ultimately be overtaken by the events and changes in the market and in society, and will thus become outdated. Particularly dangerous are business missions that have proven to be right over long periods, such as 50 or 80 years or even more: it will take almost superhuman courage to challenge them.

So, success guarantees do not exist. Guarantees for *failure* do, and one of them is a business mission that is obviously wrong. It originates from a lack of understanding of what a business mission is and what it should be, and from replacing it with vague, modern sounding metaphysical figments that are presented to the world with a persuasive show of rhetoric.

The Six Central Performance Controls (CPCs) of a Healthy Company – the Real Balanced Scorecard

There are six key variables by which to assess a company's success. Only monitoring all of them over a prolonged period of time will permit a reasonable assessment of the state of a company. Together, these Central Performance Controls (CPCs) form the manager's "cockpit". They are also the key factors of any corporate strategy.

It is surprising how fast the term Balanced Scorecard was adopted by business organizations, although what its creators[71] have to offer is neither new nor a true solution. The timing was right, in that a counterweight to the reductionism of the shareholder value concept was provided. Not the shareholder value as such was challenged – it still appears in the Balanced Scorecard – but additional parameters to be observed were proposed. This suggestion is very welcome, although it is not new. During the 1960s and 1970s, the concept of a "balanced system of objectives" was standard in German-speaking business administration. Alas, the real problem always lay in determining its content. It was commonly acknowledged that several objectives were needed, but what should they be? Kaplan and Norton have not presented a solution to that – or at best a partial one which is not very good. Much better insights have been presented by Ulrich and Krieg when publishing the St. Gallen Management Model in 1972; and Peter Drucker always worked from content-related objectives. For the present purpose, I will use his suggestion as a reference.[72]

The first CPC is the company's *market position* in each of its lines of business. Unfortunately there is no one measurement which, in and by itself, would permit a sufficient depiction of market position. Usually "the" market share is referred to. But what is it? Is it defined geographically or by customer segment, by distribution channels or applications, by direct customers or end consumers? Is the market share of substituting products known? What about quality and customer value, market awareness and image? Every company needs to think for itself about what factors will adequately describe its market position, and develop mathematical indicators for it. Continuously improving the market position as a whole – not only market share – must be at the heart of every company's strategy. You can hardly go wrong with it.

The second CPC is *innovation performance*. Companies which cease to innovate are on the wrong track, and almost incorrigibly so. Typical – but not exclusive – indicators of innovation performance are *time to market, hit versus flop rate*, and the share of new products in overall sales. But internal innovation is important as well – the continued renewal of systems and processes, methods and practices, structures and technologies. As in the case of market position, every company needs to think through the

---

71 Kaplan, Robert S./Norton, David P., *The Balanced Scorecard*, HBS Press, 1996.
72 Drucker, Peter F., *Managing for the Future*, Oxford, 1992, chapter 33.

fields of innovation relevant to its individual situation, and develop and monitor appropriate measurements. Declining innovativeness is a serious warning signal. It is recognizable early on, long before its effects will show in any accounting tools. Continued renewal, therefore, must be a standard element of corporate strategy.

The third CPC is *productivity*, or rather: productivities. In the past it used to be sufficient in most cases to measure one kind of productivity – that of labor. Today we need at least three ratios: labor productivity, capital productivity, and productivity of time; and we would be well advised to begin looking into a fourth one: the productivity of knowledge – even if nobody can really tell what it is. Productivity ratios are only meaningful if expressed in value-added dimensions, i.e., as value added per employee (labor productivity), value added per monetary unit invested (capital productivity) and value added per unit of time. Not every business can permanently grow, but every business can keep getting better in terms of productivity. So far there are no limits to productivity that we know of.

The fourth CPC of success is the *attractiveness to the right people*. The key question is not how many people leave or join the company (i.e., the fluctuation rate) – but what kind of people they are. When good people begin to "leave ship" or when it gets more difficult to recruit good people, beware! When good people quit – no matter at what level – this must be considered a top-management issue. In most cases it will be impossible to hold them back, but if you conduct exit interviews with them – and provided you are seriously interested – you will be able to learn some truths you would never hear from any other source. Erosion effects in the workforce cannot be detected by accounting systems, no matter how sophisticated they may be, nor will they appear in any other data and information bases, nor on the internet or intranet.

The fifth CPC is *liquidity*. It is an old truth that a business can survive for a while without making profits, but without liquid resources it cannot. Profit increases at the expense of liquidity are dangerous; for instance, when payment periods are extended to increase margins. Most companies will do the right thing when in a profit squeeze – they will get rid of poorly performing businesses. In a liquidity squeeze, however, you will usually have to do the wrong thing: you will have to get rid of your best businesses because they can be sold quickly and at good prices.

The sixth CPC of success is the company's *profit requirement*, which can rarely be deduced from profit as such or, for that matter, from any of the financial ratios used in accounting. It is the answer to a question, not the result of calculations.

These six key parameters are also the shortest possible and most practical summary of the cornerstones of a proper strategy, the subject of the next chapter. If I had to condense these six points even further I would select the two factors which can be considered the supporting pillars of every business oganization: customer value and productivity.

The simplest possible strategy is: maximizing customer value and maximizing production efficiency. These two goals can never be wrong, and even if a company commits serious errors in other areas it will always remain on the healthy side.

Chapter 10

Strategy

> "The rules for our actions
> whenever we lack the knowledge."

If you make the wrong corporate governance decisions, you will never have the right strategy because you use misleading variables as a reference.

Corporate strategy has always been important, and developing a good strategy has always been difficult to do. After nearly thirty years of working in this field I have to say, however, that it is much *more difficult* today than it used to be.

This becomes most obvious from the trend gurus' books, which have never been more vague. These people do not seem to know what to write, which is probably why they act so secretively. The general uncertainty also shows in the bewilderment of many managers, which makes them listen to the trend gurus letting off hot air.

A good corporate strategy has *never been as important* as it is now, precisely *because* so many things are impossible to forecast, *because* trends are intransparent, and *because* we are going through a phase of fundamental change.

Fortunately we have reached a higher level of strategic skill and methodolgy compared to than in the past. A good strategy is independent of the possibility to make forecasts, or the accuracy of the data available. Strategic fix points may be dependent on the "climate" in which we operate; they cannot, however, be dependent on the "weather". These things can and *must* be known. Ignorance in that field is no longer excusable today, the way it would have been some 15 years ago.

An additional factor to be considered is that many *more* managers need these skills today than in the past. It is a consequence of decentralization, of the organic development of business units, the flattening of hierarchies, and the cutbacks in central staff departments. In the past, it was safe to assume that only top management, together with an appropriate staff department, needed strategic skills. Now *every* head of a decentralized business unit needs them, in particular if he or she carries profit responsibility, and they will hardly have a staff department at their disposal.

Another reason why strategic skills are more important than ever is that there are fewer "dumb" competitors today. All businesses work on their strategies; strategic knowledge is basically accessible to anybody.

Strategic know-how is *simple* enough for anybody to learn. It is also *important* enough to be an absolute must for any manager, something essential to fulfilling the management task responsibly.

The profound transformation that economy and society are going through is making extraordinary demands on strategic management. It needs to comprise and accomplish much more, and very different things, than is discussed in most papers on the subject. Strategic management has to solve new issues of direction and control, while external conditions are changing and getting increasingly difficult.

Above all, strategic navigation must not rely on forecasts. This is one of the most important principles of the architecture of a strategy – and the reason is that the future cannot be predicted. It could never be and will never be. Every strategic planning and/or management concept building on that possibility, or on the assumption that reliable forecasts are possible, is useless from the outset.

The Pioneers

Countless papers have been written about strategy. Fortunately, however, there are only few that every manager should be familiar with. The first publication ever on corporate strategy is Peter F. Drucker's book *Managing for Results*, written in 1964 (!). In many respects it is still the best. In this book we find the portfolio analysis that later helped the strategy consulting practices of Boston Consulting Group and McKinsey to become famous. Another book by Drucker, *Innovation and Entrepreneurship* (1985), is important with regard to the specific questions of innovation strategy.

By far the best systematics, and the only one which I feel can be deemed universally valid, was developed by Aloys Gälweiler. In the 1970s he created the basis for one of the greatest breakthroughs in strategic management. In another recommendable book which was written by Hans Ulrich, *Unternehmenspolitik* ["Corporate Policy"], the author pursues a tried and tested wholistic approach in depicting all the essential components. Ulrich places major emphasis on the formal aspects while Drucker focuses on content.

Finally, professional strategic competence requires profound knowledge of the PIMS program. Relative to their value for strategic planning, the findings from PIMS are not very widely known. Many critics content themselves with attacking marginal aspects of these research findings, instead of taking advantage of them. The standard reference on PIMS is Buzzell/Gale: *The PIMS Principles: Linking Strategy to Performance*, NY 1987. A detailed overview of the latest findings is provided by Piercarlo Ceccarelli and Keith Roberts in *I nuovi principi PIMS*, 2002.

Anyone familiar with these writings will surely have been spared from all the strategic mistakes of the 1990s: the shareholder and stakeholder nonsense, the expensive baubleries of the New Economy, the classic mistakes of bad mergers and acquisitions, the hubris of integrated technology groups, the misguided growth strategies, and the wrong judgment of risks.

I am basing my views on corporate strategy on Gälweiler's approach, which also permits the integration of all other approaches mentioned. Thus, there is no need for any other concepts besides Gälweiler's.

I have worked closely with Gälweiler myself, starting in the early 1980s. For many years he regularly contributed to strategy seminars and numerous other events at the St. Gallen Management Centre. After his untimely death I arranged for his scientific work to be published in 1990, as I consider it to be one of the greatest advances in the theory of business administration and management.[73] Unfortunately it has not received adequate

---

73 Gälweiler, Aloys, *Strategische Unternehmensführung*, new edition, Frankfurt am Main/New York, 2005. Prof. Dr. Markus Schwaninger, then head of research and development at Malik Management, was the scientific editor of this book and supervised the edition of the literary estate of Aloys Gälweiler. See also my essay "Strategische Unternehmensführung als Steuerung eines komplexen Systems", in: *Management Forum*, Vol. 5, Physica Verlag, Vienna, 1985, p. 135–154, as well as in: Malik, F., *Management-Perspektiven*, Bern/Stuttgart/Vienna, 1993, 2nd edition, 1999, p. 135–162.

recognition to this date. In his unique way, Gälweiler was able to unite practical experience with theoretical expertise.

A Cybernetic Concept

A main characteristic of Gälweiler's concept is that he explicitly approaches the problem from the perspective of control and regulation. He presents a cybernetic system of mechanisms for orientation and control. In essence it comprises the interrelations between the control and the *anticipatory* control of factors crucial for a company's subsistence and success.

From the outset, Gälweiler has explicitly focused on the idea of a healthy business and a company's viability. He was acutely aware – for theoretical reasons, but also due to his practical experience gained in a large industrial group – that achieving profit and growth is not enough. And he realized very clearly that in particular very large profits and rapid growth can be (and very often are) the root cause of later failure, or even the decline of companies.

Gälweiler was ahead of his time, just like the other great pioneers of a system-oriented, cybernetic management approach – such as Stafford Beer, Hans Ulrich, and Frederic Vester –, whose time has only just come.

What Kinds of Problems Can Be Solved Through Strategy?

According to Gälweiler, strategy means, *before you begin, to systematically think through how you need to act from the outset in order to achieve sustainable business success.* In his view, and also Drucker's, as we will see shortly, strategy operates with open time horizons as a matter of principle. According to Drucker, strategy is not about decisions in the future, but about *the futurity (the future impact) of present decisions*, including those you fail to take. As such, strategies must have an open time horizon. Someone designing a strategy, for instance, for the next ten years to come, has not understood what strategy is all about. Strategy means building the future, shaping it, not reacting to the future, as we cannot know it. Also, strategy is not about profit and profit maximization, or other financial ratios. Although they are taken account of in the context of a strategy, these terms are not part of the definition. Obviously, the purpose of strategy is a different one.

In order to correctly assess the difference between the strategic management and control system developed by Gälweiler and other concepts of strategic management, and to recognize the progress it presents, it is important to clearly understand the basic problem that needs to be solved by strategic planning and management. In the absence of a clear understanding of the problem to be solved, it is hardly possible to separate the wheat from the chaff.

The core problem is that, from a strategy perspective, a management approach based on accounting data and balance sheet figures is bound to be systematically deceptive. This observation has far-reaching implications: it implies that the common conceptual basis of business administration is being fundamentally challenged – and along with it, the entire practice built on it.[74] In practical terms this means that a company making profit does not necessarily have to be a healthy company. On the contrary, it can be facing an irreversible collapse without even realizing it. The tools of business administration are only suited for judging and controlling the operative dimension of management, not the strategic one.

This is the main reason why a profit-oriented management approach is inadequate, and will not be able to anticipate negative developments in due time. As a result, possible corrective measures cannot be taken in due time either. Thus, this type of management will inevitably steer the company into self-induced crises requiring crisis management. There are enough real-life examples of that – from Daimler Benz under Edzard Reuter's leadership, to the telecom disasters in many countries, to the demise of Swissair.

Hence, the main purpose of strategic management cannot be – as is often purported – to recognize discrepancies by comparing target and actual results and to take corrective measures; rather, it is to bring about a desired state of things and avoid undesirable, dangerous, and ultimately disastrous developments.

This cannot be achieved with target/actual comparisons in the context of financial statements. The reason is as simple as it is compelling: almost invariably, the signals triggering countermeasures will materialize too late.

---

74 See *m.o.m.® Malik on Management Letters* No. 1/98.

It is therefore necessary to identify points of reference which, owing to their information content – not by extrapolation! – permit a longer time horizon to be covered. The main effect is that extra time is gained for identifying and initiating steps to safeguard the company's existence and success.

The whole process is comparable that to the development of ever more effective sensory organs in higher organisms, permitting increasingly better orientation. Along these lines, Aloys Gälweiler's work can be considered an evolutionary leap for corporate management. Strategy is never a plan in the stricter sense. You cannot plan an expedition into uncharted territory in the same way you plan a trip to the countryside. It does, however, have its rules and landmarks. The rules follow from Gälweiler's logic; the landmarks, which are also contained in it, are further detailed and quantified by the research findings of PIMS, which will be discussed below. Strategy is trial and error with a direction, or evolution. In biology we speak of the strategy of evolution. The same applies to management.

Integral Business Navigation With Compelling Logic

Gälweiler's strategic management concept resembles a navigation system.[75] As such, it cannot relieve the corporate management of decisions on what direction to pursue; it tells it, however, what to observe in direction setting, and what indicators to use for determining the right course.

Note that I am saying "what to observe" and "what to use". It is of utmost importance to understand that Gälweiler's system – as opposed to large parts of business administration and management – has an inner logic. It cannot be modified, as some people think, in "just any" way, entirely to one's liking, without destroying its power of orientation. It is equally impossible to amend Gälweiler's model, add a few things, or "expand" it, as some people have done on the erroneous assumption that something had been forgotten. The basic logic of the control system is shown in figure 21. It is the same logic which makes Gälweiler's work a fundamental advance in corporate management. All other approaches or

---

75 At Malik Management we used this term at least ten years before it came into fashion in the context of the internet.

"theories" on corporate strategy are largely arbitrary. One can see things the way different authors (such as Porter or Mintzberg) depict them, but there are no compelling reasons whatsoever to do so.

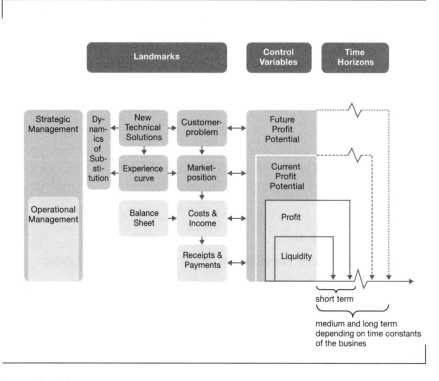

Figure 21: The corporate navigation system
(Source: Gälweiler, A., Strategische Unternehmensführung, 1990 and 2005, p. 34)

This diagram, developed by Gälweiler, comprises in ingenious simplicity all factors essential to the overall control of a company, both operative and strategic. Together with the diagram in figure 22, which was also developed by Gälweiler and will be discussed later, it forms a solid foundation for the alignment and control of all activities of a company. If you add a few aspects of structural organization, as well as some methodical guidelines for how to proceed in developing strategies, what you get is a comprehensive concept for integrated corporate development.

What Matters Most?

The following remarks refer to the above diagram. I will restrict myself to the most important points here. Figure 21 must be read from the bottom to the top, which also corresponds to the chronological order in which the navigation and control systems required for corporate management were developed.

Liquidity

The first and shorttest-term control variable for a company is liquidity. Even the most potent organization is bound to fail if it does not manage to maintain its liquidity. In a market economy it is the economically and legally defined criterion for survival. What matters, then, is not so much the factors usually listed, such as profit, growth, profitability, and so on – the important thing is to ensure liquidity.

Managing liquidity is one of the core tasks of finance, although not the only one. The parameters required for it are, at the end of the day, receipts and expenditures – as complex as modern financial management may be these days.

Obviously, liquidity control can only capture very short periods of time, while planning, and in particular strategy, must aim to cover long periods and make them accessible for entrepreneurial decisions. Solvency is a variable which focuses on the moment. Decisions to ensure liquidity always cover the shortest time horizon. The time that can typically be included in liquidity considerations is measured in months or even weeks. Even the most sophisticated analyses of the factors directly influencing liquidity – receipts and expenditures – will not reveal additional information on the longer-term development of liquidity. If you wish to look further into the future and capture longer periods in your planning, you will need to include other factors in your planning and control.

There is an additional point which even business administration professionals do not fully realize: a positive liquidity situation can be misleading. It can conceal the fact that the very basis of its future continuance – the company's financial result – has started to erode or even become negative, for a *goog* liquidity situation can also be associated with a *bad* earnings situation. Not permanently, but long enough to be misleading. It also means that a sole focus on liquidity will carry the risk of missing out on decisions that could enable one to make provisions for future liquidity. Conversely, a *bad* liquidity situation can be associated with a *good* earnings situation, simply because the liquid resources flowing from it are used for the wrong things. To summarize, one should never extrapolate from liquidity to business success, while doing it the other way round is always and reliably possible.

Profit

In order to cover longer periods of time, and thus provide an effective anticipatory control of liquidity, we need to control the financial *success* of a business – that is, its profit. It precedes liquidity in terms of logic, causality, and time. Only through financial success can the risk of systematic misguidance, which is always inherent in liquidity, be eliminated.

Profit control, or profit and loss measurement, cannot replace liquidity control; it provides the basis for it. Profit control expands the time horizon for liquidity control by focusing on another factor which also follows other principles, and not just by extrapolating liquidity as such.

Liquidity control and anticipatory liquidity control, thus, have different frames of reference and different variables. While liquidity control operates with receipts and expenses, anticipatory liquidity control includes a new layer of components situated at a higher level in terms of logic, time, and causality: the revenues and costs which determine a business's financial result. The very differentness of the factors driving success explains why they are so effective in the anticipatory control of liquidity. It is only correct, then, that success control and everything required for it – profit and loss accounting, performance analysis, and so on – are assigned to another function than liquidity control: they belong to the core tasks of accounting.

Current Profit Potential

For the exact same logical reasons, the variables immediately driving profit cannot be used for effective anticipatory profit control. Rather, control must focus on other variables which, earlier than immediate profit drivers will permit, assessing how this particular profit will evolve in the future. At this point Gälweiler leaves both the field of business administration in the stricter sense and the plans based on accounting figures. This next step takes us away from operational management and to strategic management, as shown in figure 21.

Gälweiler called the next layer, above the profit field, *profit potential* – or, to be more precise: current or existing profit potential. Note that this does not refer to just any kind of advantages, strengths, etcetera which may appear favorable – as used by most other authors – but to the "entire fabric of product and market-specific, success-relevant prerequisites that must be present, at the latest, at the point of profit realization."[76]

"Profit" here does not refer to any general kind of qualitative profit – it is profit in the quantitive sense as used in business administration, or the difference between revenues and expenses. The potential for profit in Gälweiler's meaning is not identical with the core competencies that have become so popular. There are core competencies which can never turn into a potential for profit, whereas in an ideal case both will obviously coincide, that is, potential for profit will be built on core competencies.

Thus, profit control must be based on the current profit potential, its scope and its sustainability. If lapses and wrong decisions can only be recognized based on their repercussions on financial performance, it will usually be too late to create the basic prerequisites, as there will usually be too little time left between the recognition of the crisis and its impact on liquidity. Thus, we find the same – logically explainable – reversity which can systematically lead astray: profits can still be excellent even when the potential for profit is already eroding. It is therefore impossible to identify the "underlying" potential by working back from profit (as in the tragic case of the Swiss watch industry). Conversely, financial results can be poor, even negative, while the profit potential is still excellent. Obviously the company in question did not know how to exploit this potential (that was the case with the Austrian steel industry).

Steps to protect profit and liquidity, as are often introduced when the impact of missing and/or eroding profit potential starts to show in the accounting figures, usually have a temporary effect and will often decrease

---

76 Cf. Gälweiler, Aloys, "Unternehmenssicherung und strategische Planung", in: *ZfbF Schmalenbachs Zeitschrift für betriebswirtschaftliche Forschung*, Vol. 6, 1976.

the potential for profit even further. There are countless examples in practice: for instance, it is typical of most cost-reduction programs to reduce not only costs in the sense of "extravagance", but also costs that are linked to future potential. Every potential not captured will obviously incur more costs than it will yield revenues, which does not necessarily mean that these costs should be "eliminated". They often are, though, because it is the fastest way to improve bottom-line results. The stock market rewards these moves – the profit potential, however, has been destroyed, which goes unnoticed for some time because it does not show in the accounting figures.

The two landmarks which are crucial for current profit potential – and thus, the anticipatory profit control – are the company's market position (expressed as market share) and the resulting cost implications. Or, to be more precise, the relative market shares of direct competitors, due to their effect on the lowest cost level achievable.[77]

The basis for that is the experience curve and the learning effect from which it follows: as market share ratios determine the accumulation of corporate performance (output and so on) they will generally influence the lowest cost level achievable in a market and by the individual businesses in it. The experience curve effect says that with every doubling of the volumes accumulated there will be cost-reduction potential in a certain order of magnitude, usually 20 to 30 percent of the value-added in real prices. Whether this potential is exploited or not depends on top management's skill and rigor in pursuing a comprehensive cost management approach. Delivering market performance at even below those costs defined by experience will usually be impossible – unless there are favorable external factors (such as government subsidies or costs incorrectly charged between the companies of a group).

It ought to be stressed here that the experience effect is among the least understood and thus wrongly applied parameters. I will discuss this in greater detail in the volume on strategy. At this point let me just say this much: whoever has more market share will always have a chance of achieving lower cost as well. This implies a greater ability to survive price wars – and thus to prevail in the market longer than others. That is the basic idea behind the term "defendable market share", which I created in the late 1970s for my strategy seminars. In business you do not need to be big, you need to be strong – strong enough to ward off all kinds of price

---

77 I have elaborated on this subjeect in *m.o.m.*® *Malik on Management Letters* Nos. 2/94 and 3/94.

maneuvers by your competition, which is only possible with a competitive cost base.

Future Profit Potential

Anticipatory profit control based on current profit potential also has its limits: market shares and resulting experience curve effects reach their limits where markets undergo fundamental restructuring processes.

The word "restructuring" is mostly used in a general and unspecific way; in the context of Gälweiler's system, however, it refers to a very specific kind of restructuring – namely, to changes in how the needs of the market are satisfied. They result in a much more dangerous type of competition than is common between direct competitors: it is substitution based on new technologies or on new solutions for the market. This is where key innovations take place.[78]

Again, an anticipatory control of current profit potential can never be based on the same variables used for assessment: market share and cost effects. Advance direction-setting and timely control is possible only by applying yet other parameters.

Control of future profit potential focuses on two factors: firstly, the customer or application problems to be solved by certain products and market services; secondly, the knowledge of substitution dynamics.

The key to that lies in perceiving a product as a solution to a customer problem. This understanding must be built on a certain concept: the *solution-independent formulation of a customer problem*. This term, created by Gälweiler, must be in every manager's vocabulary. As there are usually several ways to solve a problem, it is crucial to know and define a problem irrespective of the solutions already available in the market.

Only with a solution-independent understanding of the customer problem will it be possible to assess the substitution dynamics in a market, that is to say, whether and to what extent new solutions might replace the current ones.[79] There are numerous examples of substitution processes. A cur-

---

78 See *m.o.m.® Malik on Management Letters* Nos. 2/96, 4/96, and 5/96, as well as Nos. 3/01 and 4/01.

79 This idea is old, but has probably never been as important as it is today. It was first put in words by Peter Drucker in his 1954 book *The Practice of Manage-*

rent one is the substitution of chemicals-based photography by electronic and digital imaging.

The study of previous research on the emergence and penetration of basic technologies will permit conclusions with regard to the speed of substitution processes, and thus to the time available for management to take advantage of the restructuring processes, or at least adequately respond to them. These decisions, again oriented by factually different landmarks, will open up the longest timeframe of control.[80]

The better a company's current profit potential in terms of market share in a given market, and as a result, the greater the positive effects on profit and liquidity, the lesser the pressure to challenge the foundation of current profit potential – and the greater the risk that the landmarks of future potential for success will be overlooked. This is the reason why people often speak of surprising developments although they could have anticipated them long before they took effect in the markets – if only they had taken their bearings from the present control system, its factors and its inner logic.

A typical example is the internet, which was not invented in the 1990s, as many believe, but as far back as in the 60s. Anyone seriously interested in computers was aware of that. It just went unnoticed by the public and the media – until the early 1990s, when Netscape introduced the first browser for use by non-experts.

In the context of current profit potential substituted by new potential due to technological change, it is crucial to expand one's scope of attention as far as possible: original customer problems hardly change; they form a kind of "Archimedean point" within a constantly changing network of effects. To find out whether a given company provides its products and services within the scope of an original or a derivative customer problem, the entire system of services and effects that has grown around the customer's need has to be analyzed. And since customer problems and their solutions

---

ment, and with particular precision in his 1964 book *Managing for Results*, in the chapter "The Customer is the Business". Drucker's intention was to make very clear that "the customer – and not the product – is the business …". The customer or application problem, put in solution-invariant words and understood accordingly, is the Archimedean point of any corporate strategy. It is imperative for managers and companies to be aware of this.

80 At Malik Management, special approaches have been developed over the past years to analyze substitution processes and use their factual and chronological sequence as a basis for strategic decisions.

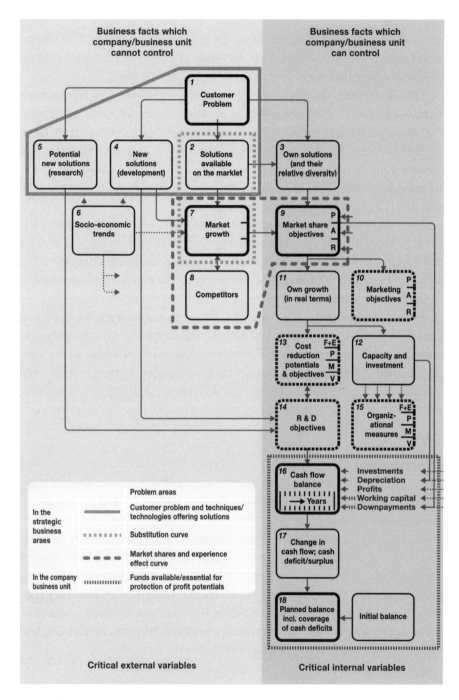

Figure 22: *Basic scheme of strategic planning*
(Source: Gälweiler, Aloys, *Strategische Unternehmensführung*, 1990 and 2005, p. 31)

are not only exposed to economic or technological influences, it is recommendable to use further-reaching methods of ecosystem analysis. This is precisely where this set of tools can unfold its full power.[81]

This is also the place where customer value analysis, one of the most valuable results of PIMS research, is applied. Customer value is the relative price-performance ratio of a company's products compared to those of the competition. It is the methodical tool not only for talking about customer value instead of shareholder value within the corporate governance context, but also for determining it empirically, quantifying it, and using it as a cornerstone of corporate strategy.

These interrelations are illustrated in figure 22, which complements figure 21. The different factors are categorized in factors inside and outside the company. Several of them together form a cause-effect relationship that can be clearly and logically attributed to the control and orientation variables of figure 21.

As mentioned before, the logic of Gälweiler's corporate navigation and control system cannot be tweaked without diluting its original purpose and effectiveness or even ruining it. Everything that has been added so far were improvements for the worse. In part they were added by people with good intentions, but who failed to understand Gälweiler in this point. I was able to clarify these aspects with him in person, in many hours of discussion.

Summary and Overview

The systematics and basic logic contained in figures 21 and 22 are essentially complete, that is, they do not need any additional factors; however, the individual factors and the relationships between them are yet to be researched extensively. In a synopsis of these interrelations and based on the current state of findings, it is fair to say, though, that they help avoid the worst of the errors initially mentioned: the limitations of anticipatory control by extrapolating relevant variables have become evident; a management approach focused on economic variables, in particular profit and growth of financial ratios, is bound to fail in the long run.

In addition, the following points should be observed.

---

81 Cf. Vester, Frederic/Hesler, Alexander von, *Sensitivitätsmodell*, Frankfurt, 1980, and Vester, Frederic, *The Art of Interconnected Thinking*, Munich, 2007.

Strategic Principles

The quality and appropriateness of a strategy do not depend on formal depictions or terminology. What matters is content, the material knowledge of the logic and rules of the market and of the prospects of certain strategies. Some of the most important elements will be discussed in the following paragraphs.

Growth is Not a Corporate Goal in Its Own Right

Growth cannot be an overriding corporate goal, in particular sales growth. Growth objectives, therefore, must never be used as *input variables* of a strategy – they must be the *output*.

Whether a company *must, can* or *must not* grow (yes, that is possible, too) can only be judged from a market perspective. There are cases where a strong growth phase will be essential for a company to build a defendable market position; there are also cases in which a company would maneuver itself into a completely unsustainable position if it grew any further. In many highly saturated markets there is no more room for growth.

It is *not* that important to keep growing; what *is* important is that an organization keeps getting better from year to year. Even companies which have no more room to grow, due to the conditions in their markets, can still keep improving their *quality* and above all their *productivity*. A very important question, if a company does need to grow, is how to accomplish that growth: by increasing volume in a growing market or by gaining market share in a saturated market? Through *acquisition or innovation?* Or through *diversification?* The latter is a very dangerous path, as countless examples have shown. Or is growth being pursued through diversification by innovation? That is even more dangerous.

Or does the company attempt to grow in that seemingly harmless but very consequential manner, by *expanding the product range?* In most companies which have grown over the past ten years, sales figures are not the only thing that has increased – what has grown even more is the range of items carried. Inevitable consequences are an exponential *increase* in complexity (which is only partly manageable with more and larger computers) and an exponential *decrease* in transparency of the business, leading to an *erosion* of profit contributions, profitability, and liquidity.

Growth – the Wrong and the Right Kind

Most corporate strategies during the boom of the 1990s were dramatically wrong, as is evident today and could have been evident back then. Stock prices have crumpled, many of the empires of old are facing their breakdown. Many impressive strategies presented by consultants and managers have turned out to be avenues leading straight into disaster. Consequences include a retreat on all fronts, capacity cuts, layoffs, imminent illiquidity in some cases.

Although the debacle is taking place in front of everyone's eyes, many managers refuse to change their thinking – among them many successors to former failures who are faced with the ruins every day. Yet they continue to operate with the same wrong categories. When asked about the most important strategic goal, they reflexively – unthinkingly – reply: growth.

Growth is undoubtedly an important factor for organizations, but as explained above, it is unsuitable and even dangerous if used as a strategic goal. It will lead a company into failure. Growth cannot be an input variable for strategy, it is an output. It cannot be a target, it is the result of thoroughly thinking through one's business and its inner regularities. As long as this is not firmly entrenched in the minds of senior executives, there will only be temporary improvements and the same mistakes will keep repeating themselves.

The high art of strategy planning can only take effect when a distinction is made between healthy and unhealthy growth. When a 12-year-old grows an inch every year he is healthy; when a 50-year-old does the same he is seriously ill. Size as such can never be a strategic goal. A company does not need to be big, it needs to be strong. There is no conceivable constellation where the size of a company has strategic importance. Those focusing on size are deceived by an optical illusion and, to use a metaphor, unable to tell muscles from fat. The deception results from the fact that good strategies nearly always lead to growth, and ultimately size, but the opposite does not hold true.

Size is measured in sales figures, and sometimes – not that often nowadays – in headcount. The recent past has shown that sales can be increased relatively quickly and easily if a business is permitted to grow the wrong way: through frivolous geographic expansion, product range expansion, misguided acquisitions and mergers. Invariably the results are an increase in complexity and a decrease in profitability. The absolute numbers go up, however, and since they are visible they are regarded as indicators of success. At the same time relative figures deteriorate, but since they are not visible or are actively concealed they go unnoticed.

There are only two variables for reliably distinguishing healthy from unhealthy growth. The first is market position: size and growth are only healthy if they result from an improvement in market position. Conversely, size and growth will not, per se, lead to a stronger market position. The second, perhaps even more important variable is productivity. Only the best companies have a sophisticated set of tools to measure it. Even today, productivity is still being neglected, wrongly defined, and wrongly measured. In its definition as total factor productivity, however, it is the only reliable basis for judging growth.

Only if sales growth is accompanied by a growth in productivity can it be healthy growth which – to use the medical metaphor again – helps build muscle and strengh. If, however, the total productivity of a growing company is stagnating, then that company is headed toward obesity. It is possible to live that way for a certain amount of time. If, however, total productivity decreases in times of growth, the company is ill.

Size Is Increasingly Unimportant

The size of a company is generally measured based on sales volume and number of employees. Without a doubt there are markets where it is important to be big in that sense. But the advantages of size are rapidly decreasing almost everywhere, due to the change in technological possibilities. More and more technologies which only large companies could afford in the past are now accessible to small and medium-sized businesses as well. The sluggishness of large organizations, the bureaucracy, the lack of orientation at middle-management levels, their slowness, and so on, have a paralyzing effect and thus offset the advantages of size.

What matters is *not size but strength, not quantity but speed and quality*. There are companies which are large by common standards, but weak in each of their business fields. That is true for most conglomerates. And on the other hand there are companies which, by these standards, are small or medium-sized at best, but extraordinarily strong in their field.

Diversification Rarely Works

A hundred years of economic history can and should teach us that diversification hardly ever really works. I am *not* saying that it never does, but successful approaches have been too rare to be recommendable. Small and medium-sized companies should stay away from diversifying on principle because they lack two inportant prerequisites: capital and management.

Larger businesses are more likely to have the financial resources required (they do not always, as numerous examples have shown) although it is often not enough to cover the *follow-up costs* of diversification. Yet in most cases they, too, lack the quantitative and qualitative level of management required for successful diversification.

Even the world's largest organizations do not have many "best people". And that is what is needed the most for successful diversification: *a large number of excellently qualified managers* – by which I mean experienced, "battle-tested" people who have weathered the ups and downs of management. You need people you can rely on for better or worse, and about whom you know how they think and act. People of that kind are few and far between, even in the largest of corporations.

This is not to say that diversification cannot work. But it is the most difficult and risky task one could possibly take on, the least likely to be successful, and the most likely to lead to mediocre or even poor results. Taking on this sort of management task without good cause is imprudent. Foundering on a difficult task will not make you look successful – mastering an easy task as a manager will often afford you wealth and recognition.

The fact that there are precious few examples of successful and, above all, skillful diversification strategies proves my point. As a matter of fact, only General Electric under Jack Welch's leadership makes for a really good role model – and even that is not really convincing, for Jack Welch's success was by no means owed to diversification only.

Eliminating Weaknesses Is Rarely a Strategic Goal

An organization which has eliminated all its weaknesses is *mediocre*, not *good*. Therefore, existing weaknesses must be considered in any strategy; there may even be cases where their elimination is crucial for success. True corporate success, however, always results from *using* and *exploiting* a specific *strength*, and this is usually an *existing* strength, not one that the company aims to build over five years. Nobody in business has that much time.

This is why corporate strategy development must *first* and *primarily* focus on *identifying strengths*. Determining weaknesses is easy – identifying strengths is difficult. Discovering an organization's strengths is worth almost any consulting fee. Weaknesses that are not eliminated may limit the potential for success; that said, their elimination will never suffice to bring about success, or provide a basis for it.

The High Art of Strategy: PIMS – Profit Impact of Market Strategy

> "When the history of business strategy is written, PIMS will remain as a milestone."
> *Philip Kotler, marketing professor*

Breakthrough in Strategy Research

One of the greatest advances in management, and in economics overall, was achieved by a program called PIMS – "Profit Impact of Market Strategy". When it started, its focal point of research were market strategies. Meanwhile, PIMS has provided empirically based answers to virtually all relevant questions of strategy; answers that could not be obtained any other way.

The PIMS program is the largest strategy research program to date, and the one stretching across the longest period of time – from 1972 to the present. Its beginnings reach back to the 1960s. No other projects are comparable.

Metaphorically speaking, the PIMS findings signal no less than the end of 'the era of blind flight' in strategy development. What used to be a mixture of guessing games, individual experiences, intuition, copying the competition, and extrapolation of the past, has now become an almost perfectly executed flight with state-of-the-art satellite navigation technology.

The PIMS research has added enormous substance to business administration knowledge in the narrower sense. Pioneer work has been done and new territory charted in the definition and operationalization of terms. Some of the cateogries and terms were created from scratch. Data collection, data structuring, and data evaluation were raised to a new level of professionalism. The results are largely original; hardly anything had previously been known. Only a fraction of it is used in university education to date.

For economics, too, PIMS has brought a unique increase in knowledge. Business organizations' microeconomics were largely neglected before, which in my view is one of the reasons why virtually all economic theories are based on unsustainable premises of entrepreneurial behavior, in particular an oversimplified profit maximization premise.

The basic idea behind the PIMS research program, and the resulting approaches to designing and developing corporate strategies, are both simple and fascinating. Should it not be possible to distil from the data of numerous business divisions of numerous companies the precise factors responsible for lasting business success? Should one not expect approaches that have long been customary in other sciences, in particular comparative structural analyses, to render better results than intuition and individual experience?

What factors are decisive for the strategic profit potential of a business enterprise, in terms of sustainable profitability as measured by the return on investment? How can these factors be quantified? And what does the management of a company really have to do to build justifiable and quantifiable potential for success?

Results of the Program

In the following I will outline the most important aspects of PIMS. A comprehensive discussion of its results, and of the opportunities arising from PIMS for strategic practice, will follow in the strategy volume of this series which is currently in progress. It will also include an adequate appraisal of, and response to the criticism so far put forward.

The PIMS research program uses a database comprising financial figures of over 3,500 business units to derive the strategic factors of success. This broad empirical basis, the evaluation of which is computer-assisted, provides an excellent foundation for strategic decisions. Tom Peters expressed his opinion as follows: *"PIMS has the world's most extensive strategic information database ... provides compelling quantitative evidence as to which business strategies work and don't work ... an unparalleled database."*

Today, the PIMS data material comprises more than 20,000 years of business experience. It can be structured in different ways, depending on the issue to be solved. In addition, there are several databases for special topics, such as start-up stategies, business overhead and customer value. Thus, PIMS is the only database enabling a scientifically founded benchmarking. One result of PIMS research, for instance, is a database on over 250 European marketing and distribution organizations of international consumer goods companies, permitting any kind of benchmarking for marketing and distribution. A similar benchmarking database exists for the pharmaceutical industry. For the first time, substantiated and quantitative answers are possible for questions including the following:

1. What are the truly decisive strategic success factors of sustainable profitability?
2. How are these factors related to each other, and how can they be influenced by the company?
3. Where do "winning" and "losing" strategies differ, specifically and quantifiably?
4. With a given set of strategic factors, what is the minimum level of profits required for a company in each of its business units, and what is the maximum level of losses?
5. How must diversification and innovation projects (start-ups) be designed to have a chance at success? What quantifiable strategic prerequisites must be created for that, and how long will it take for such endeavors to yield returns?
6. What are the quantifiable effects of business acquisitions, and where are quantifiable synergy effects?
7. From a strategic point of view, what is the maximum level of expenses to be tolerated for marketing and distribution, research and development, and other factors, relative to sales?
8. What are the levels to be reached at minimum/maximum for value-added, vertical integration, productivity per employee, and capital intensity, in order for the company to remain healthy in the long term?
9. What can/should the rate of innovation be from a strategic perspective?

These questions, and a series of similar, equally important questions, can be answered with unprecedented precision and speed by using PIMS findings. Precision is not always crucial for a strategy; speed, however, is invaluable for strategy development.

One of the most important findings of PIMS is that 60 to 70 percent of the success of a business, measured by the return on investment, can be traced back to around a dozen success factors. Eight of these are particularly important (see box below) and it is imperative to have them under control. A favorable set of these factors will make a business strategically robust enough to offset weaknesses in other fields. Conversely, weaknesses in one or several of these key factors cannot be offset by other strengths, even if there are many of them, or by even the best operational management.

Whoever needs a higher degree of precision can include additional factors in the analysis. Together, the available factors explain a major share of the statistical variance in business success.

Factor	Definition	Effect
1. Relative market share	Own market share divided by the sum of market shares of 3 largest competitors	High relative market share is always favorable. It is particularly important in case of: high marketing intensity, high R&D intensity, bad economic climate.
2. Productivity	Value-added per employee	High productivity is always good; it is indispensable in case of high investment intensity.
3. Investment intensity	Investment/ value-added	High investment intensity negatively affects profitability.
4. Relative customer value	Product, service, and image quality offered relative to the competition, in conjunction with the relative price position.	Positive for all financial data, and indispensable in case of a small market share.
5. Innovation rate	Share in sales of products not older than 3 years	Above a certain share in sales, innovation has a negative impact on the ROI.
6. Growth rate of served market		A high growth rate is positive for absolute returns, neutral for relative returns, and negative for cash-flow.

7. Customer profile	Number of direct customers accounting for 50 percent of sales	An extremely small number of customers may be good, depending on industry specifics; otherwise a broader customer base will be better.
8. Vertical integration	Value-added / turnover	Particularly positive in mature, stable markets.

Basis and Key Factors of PIMS

The following diagram provides an overview of PIMS and its data basis, along with the most important findings.

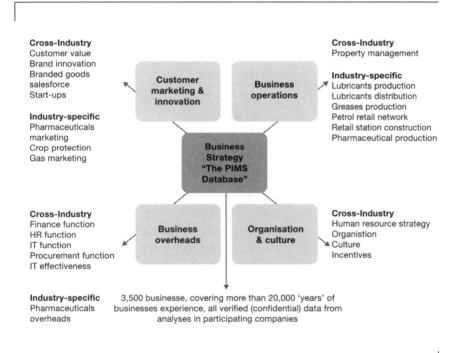

Figure 23: PIMS: The data basis and most important findings

The key factors can be grouped in three categories, as shown in figure 24.

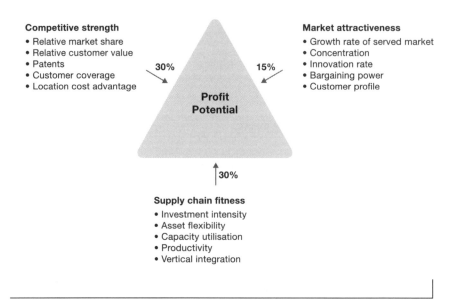

Competitive strength
- Relative market share
- Relative customer value
- Patents
- Customer coverage
- Location cost advantage

30%

15%

Market attractiveness
- Growth rate of served market
- Concentration
- Innovation rate
- Bargaining power
- Customer profile

Profit Potential

30%

Supply chain fitness
- Investment intensity
- Asset flexibility
- Capacity utilisation
- Productivity
- Vertical integration

Figure 24: Key factors determining the ROI
(Source: PIMS Strategy Database)

Among other things, PIMS is a confirmation of the fact that right management is identical everywhere, and the same factors are crucial for all institutions. The widespread opinion that there are major differences between conditions in the U.S. and in Europe has also been studied in detail, and has been largely refuted. The same is true for the opinion that investment goods and consumer goods are different. The essential structures of strategic parameters are identical for consumer and industrial goods.

Navigating With Network Structures

Using the PIMS findings is particularly interesting when different factors are linked to each other.

Figure 25, for instance, shows the relation between relative customer value (quality of market performance) and relative market share, as well

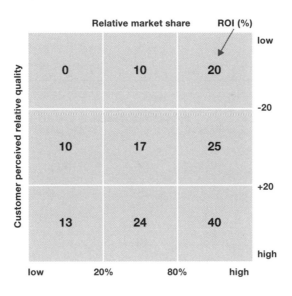

Figure 25: Relation between relative market share and relative customer satisfaction (Source: PIMS Strategy Database)

as the resulting figures for Return on Investment (ROI). It is hardly surprising that the highest ROI (average of 40 percent) results when top quality coincides with high market share. However, businesses with high market shares still achieve relatively good ROI values (20 percent on average) if the quality offered is inferior to that of the competition. On the other hand, businesses with relatively small market shares can offset this advantage only by offering superior quality. This is one of the most important and not immediately obvious findings from PIMS. It means hope and a strategic option for many small and medium-sized companies: with a well-designed quality strategy they can reach a 13-percent ROI on average despite their smaller market shares. By contrast, businesses with small market shares and inferior product quality are in a hopeless situation – generating 0 percent ROI (before interest and taxes are taken into account).

Figure 26 can be interpreted similarly: it shows the relation between relative market share and the extraordinarily important factor of investment intensity (= investment over value-added), again with its effects on the ROI.

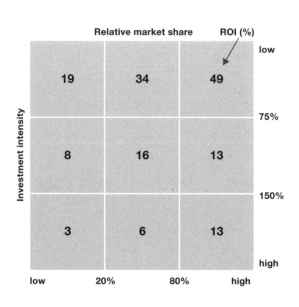

Figure 26: Relation between relative market share and investment intensity (Source: PIMS Strategy Database)

As a last example, figure 27 shows how customer value is captured in PIMS. The very conceptualization of customer value was a research breakthrough. Analyzing the data material then enabled findings of immense significance for strategy development. As mentioned before, relative customer value is one of the central strategic factors for sustainable success.

These few examples should suffice for the purpose of this book. Many other relations could also be shown, such as the interdependencies between market shares and marketing expenditure, customer value and R & D expenditure, value-added and productivity, productivity and current assets, and so forth.

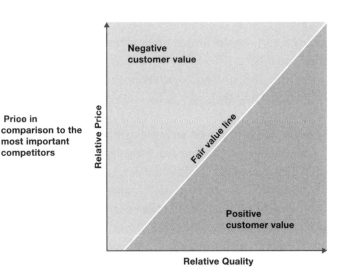

- Prioo in comparison to the most important competitors

Relative Price

Negative customer value

Fair value line

Positive customer value

Relative Quality

- Quality from the perspective of the customer
- Measured by attributes affecting customer's choice
- Compared to main competitors

Figure 27: Customer value according to PIMS (Source: PIMS Strategy Database)

Benefits to Companies

Specifically, PIMS provides value to companies in the following points:

1. The strategically relevant factors, which before could only be vaguely estimated with regard to their impact on current and future business success (return on investment and cash-flow), can now be quantified very reliably. As a result, it becomes possible to verify them empirically and thus place one's own strategic considerations on a sound basis.
2. The knowledge of what is feasible has been enhanced; the definition of realistic strategic and operative goals now rests on a much sounder basis than it did in the past.

3. Companies can systematically benefit from the experiences and mistakes of others with similar structural characteristics and in similar competitive situations.
4. Strategies developed and steps planned can be simulated, thus achieving optimal strategic variants.
5. Not only a company's own strategic options but also those of its competitors can be analyzed and their effects on one's own business quantified.
6. Potential targets for acquisitions or mergers can be analyzed with regard to their current strategic position and future prospects.
8. Executive and skilled personnel at different levels can be deliberately and selectively involved in the strategy development process. As a result, strategic thinking firmly takes hold in the corporate culture.
9. Through efficient control of these problem solution processes, any resistance to change is constructively managed, and consensus, understanding, and commitment are built as crucial prerequisites for the effective implementation of strategies.

Criticism of the PIMS-Program

Over the years, the PIMS results and research approach has aroused some criticism by proponents and opponents – not all of them thorough, competent and reputable. PIMS is one of the few cases where, at least by intention, a serious scientific discussion was conducted. The PIMS results refuted so many positions held in business administration to date, challenged so many ideas and provided new, consequential and partly provocative results, that serious criticism was highly welcome. Consequently, PIMS was open as regards access to its data material, and generous whenever scientific interest was credibly demonstrated.

The key findings of PIMS have not been disproved to this date. There are stories going round but so far no evidence has been presented. Most standard points of criticism frequently repeated in literature are mere conjectures which could be invalidated upon closer examination. A large part of negative criticism results from a lack of knowledge about PIMS as such, and in particular of the statistical methods applied; hence this criticism carries little weight, even if it continues to be copied uncritically.

Chapter 11

Structure

After the environment, governance, and strategy, the next element of general management is the structure of an institution. It is in vogue today to put processes and structure in contrast to each other and give priority to processes, as if that was something new. For three decades at least it has been acknowledged that processes are fast-changing structures, and structures slow-going processes. They represent two sides of the same coin. Nothing remains unchanged, so there is no generally valid distinction between structure and process.

"Structure follows strategy" – not vice versa. It is an insight which goes back to the 1960s, formulated by one of the most productive management thinkers, Alfred Chandler. Nothing has changed since then. If you do not know where you are going (strategy) you cannot possibly know how to organize yourself to get there.

The changes going on in business and society are forcing most companies to rethink their structure in ever shorter cycles. Corporate organization has long been a central issue, and will continue to be – with the exception of the very few firms engaged in a rather simple business, and of very small firms. Practically all institutions have to rely on experiments, as the suggestions offered by business administration experts are largely stagnating and becoming sterile. New impulses emerge from very different directions, as mentioned in the chapter on complexity, including life sciences.

---

82 Alfred P. Sloan – CEO and Chairman of General Motors from 1920 to 1956 – in the chapter entitled "Concept of the Organization" of his book *My Years with General Motors*, New York, 1964, p. 53.

By far the most fruitful structural model is the so-called "Viable System Model" by Stafford Beer, the management cybernetician I have quoted before.[83] Elaborating on it would exceed the scope of this book. It will be discussed in the volume on structure.

At this point I wish to remind readers of my initial remarks on the language to be used, where I explained two meanings of "organization". An institution *is* an organization, and an institution *has* an organization. The first is the term's institutional meaning, and both terms are used synonymously. The second is the functional meaning of the word: an institution needs an organization – or needs to be organized – to be able to function. It will be clear from the context what is meant in each individual case. In this chapter it will mostly be the functional aspect.

Organizing

I am not in favor of permanent organizing, which is actually reorganizing. It can easily develop into a neurotic disorder, into "organizitis", and I have little sympathy for managers (there are quite a few of them) who think an institution should constantly be reorganized, in order to "keep thinks moving" or to "keep going".

It is true, people can cope with changes – in my experience, better than many experts think – but they also need phases of calm and stability to be productive. Managers who keep changing and reorganizing for the sake of change risk a dramatic deterioration of business results and produce attentism, lethargy, and fear. So what has to be kept in mind?

Reorganizing Is Always "Surgery"

Metaphorically speaking, organization changes are comparable to surgical interventions in an organism – a living organism. Surgeons, however, are in a more comfortable situation than managers: they can anaesthetize the patient during the operation; managers cannot. Their "patients"

---

83 Beer, Stafford, *The Heart of Enterprise*, London, 1979, and *Brain of the Firm – The Managerial Cybernetics of Organization*, London, 1972.

are wide awake, clearly aware of what is facing them, and they respond accordingly.

Good surgeons have learned to use the scalpel as a last resort. Only if all other means fail will they go ahead and cut. Good managers act the same way. They never reorganize without good cause – and if they need to, it will always be after thorough preparation, after carefully thinking about how to proceed and after taking all accompanying measures required.

Good surgeons do not simply cut and then think about what to do next. They are prepared for all conceivable occurrences, always ready to take the necessary steps in case of emergency. This way they can cope with possible surprises by improvising.

On the other hand, if a surgeon, after careful consideration of the problem, finds that an operation is indispensable, he will perform it quickly and resolutely. This is how reorganizations must be handled.

There Is No "Good" Organization

Most people, in particular if they have little experience, think that there are organizations without frictions. There are not. At least, they have not been discovered so far. All organizations are bad, all of them produce conflict, coordination effort, information problems, interpersonal frictions, ambiguities, and interfaces.

It is therefore better to assume that the choice is not between a good and a bad organization, but between a bad and a worse one. All organizations require compromises.

Thus, an organization should not be judged by the problems it creates but by those is does *not* create. It may be a somewhat unusual thought, which one may have to think about more than once, but it helps avoid organizitis. It does not make sense to demand organizational changes as soon as conflicts and lapses occur. Experienced people do not respond that way. They do see the problems and are confident that a reorganization will solve them. But they do not deceive themselves into thinking there will be no problems left afterwards. They know that a new organization will create new problems – and they will be of a kind they do not know yet and cannot judge. Today's problems may be a nuisance but at least they are known. That is their attitude.

Moreover, it is seldom possible to inplement a "pure" form of organization, as is taught in economic organization theory. Those only exist in textbooks. Real organizations are mixtures of several "pure" forms; they are hybrids. That is nothing negative, it is just something not dealt with in textbooks.

Never Start With Organization Charts

As soon as a discussion turns to the subject of organization, most people immediately start sketching org charts. That is a strong indicator of a lack of experience with organizational issues. It is the least appropriate thing one could do. Organization charts are an outcome of organizing, not its beginning. It begins with the basic purpose, basic issues, and basic prerequisites for functionality. Organizing begins with a business mission and strategy.

The reason is simple. Even the best org charts do not say much; they do not contain what is most important to the functioning of an institution.

Firstly, the usual organization charts do not show the institution's environment and its main elements, customers and competitors. Customers, however, are what a company works for, where it fulfills its purpose. Competitors are whom the organization measures up against in its attempts to do better. Customers and competitors, thus, are the main points of reference for both, organizing and management as a whole. Yet they do not appear in the institution's "most important" chart.

Secondly, org charts do not contain secretarial services, except for maybe those assigned to top management. I do not know many institutions, certainly none of the large ones, which could function without secretarial services. If there was a secretarial strike – and I am not talking about typists but about secretaries managing their bosses, or assistants – every major company would come to a standstill in a matter of hours.

Thirdly, organization charts do not contain the different committees, work groups, task-forces and teams that are increasingly becoming the actual work units in a company.

Fourthly, organization charts do not contain the meeting structures and cycles. The function of an institution and its speed depend on decisions, and decisions are largely taken in meetings. Consequently, the question as to who will attend what meeting is essential for any organization. None of it appears in an organization chart.

Fifthly, organization charts consist of boxes. They do not show what happens between those boxes. And that is what really matters. That is where the potential lies – for conflict, cooperation, and synergies. Even "in the olden days" people used to know that, as the motto at the beginning of this chapter shows: "Interaction is the thing ... "

Basic Functional Prerequisites

The Basic Purpose of Any Organization

It is the purpose of an organization to enhance the strengths of the people in it and to offset their weaknesses. Attempts to eliminate weaknesses are seldom successful, but it is possible to ensure that they lose significance. This is one of the basic prerequisites for the functioning of an organization.

An organization should make it easy for people to perform and be successful. Most organizations, in particular modern ones, do the opposite. This is particularly true for the matrix structure.

The key consideration must always be: what can people accomplish, and how can we make it easier for them to accomplish it?

The Three Basic Questions of Organizing

There is always a risk in not seeing the forest for the trees. This is particularly true for organizing, where one can get hopelessly caught in a maze of targets and criteria which the organization is supposed to meet. The worst thing one can do is to overburden an organization with demands. The greater the number of requirements, the less the organization will be capable of.

In essence, there are exactly three questions to be answered; they are the basic questions of organizing:

1. How do we have to organize ourselves to ensure that what the customer pays us to do can take the center of attention and will not slip from there?

2. How do we have to organize ourselves to ensure that what our staff is paid to do will actually get done?
3. How do we have to organize ourselves to ensure that what our top management is paid to do can actually be done?

The organization forms the bridge between these questions.

These questions may seem simple, even trivial. No company will explicitly say that customers do not matter. However, in these times of shareholder dominance not too many of them have stated the opposite: that customers are what matters the most. Shareholders have been and still are considered the central object of attention; everything revolves around them, not around the customer. Managers do have their eyes set on the market – but on the wrong one: the stock market, not the market consisting of customers and competitors. Hardly anyone will admit it, but this is the reality of the shareholder approach. This is why it is so dangerous.

Apart from that, it is not so easy to implement customer focus. Firstly, it is difficult to find out what customers actually pay a company for. Secondly, even if it is known, it is always much easier to miss the mark than to hit it, as there are so many ways to fail in building a truly customer-focused organization. This is a consequence of the immense complexity of the market and environment. Thirdly, remember my remarks on business mission: even if you know what customers pay for, you still do not know what non-customers pay for – and where …

With employees it is similar. It is worth the effort to regularly ask one's employees: why are you on this company's payroll? In many cases you will find that people have no answer, or a rather fuzzy one at best. They will quote from their work contracts, or from the titles of their job descriptions. But that usually does not say a lot. What their contribution really is about, what it should be about, is not at the center of their thoughts.

Further, you will often find that organizations constrain their people rather than really support their work. Quite often, the boss himself is the bottleneck.

One case in point – which also helps to clarify questions 1 and 2 – refers to those insurance companies where field staff need to do administrative work on top of their sales calls. Analyses still show that sales representatives at many insurance companies spend no more than 40 percent of their time with their customers; the rest is needed for different administrative tasks. In cases like these, customers are not the main focus and employees cannot do what they are really paid to do.

The third basic question of organizing refers to the issue of what top management actually spends its valuable time on. Is it really the true top-management tasks? Or does top management get drowned in the details of day-to-day business? Are top managers truly released of everyday duties, to solve the problems that require an overriding perspective and comprehensive knowledge of the organization as a whole? Or does it cost so much time and effort to keep the organization going that there is hardly any time left for those tasks?

Related questions will be discussed in the paragraphs on top management structure.

In addition, two more basic questions may be important:

4. How do we have to organize ourselves in order to grow?
5. How do we have to organize ourselves in order to cope with increasing complexity?

Basic Rules of Functioning

Instead of working with organization charts, the first step should be to apply the basic rules of functioning of an organization. It will not always be possible to observe them 100 percent, but compromises should only be considered after every effort has been made to comply. If compromises are made, they must be closely monitored at the beginning, in order to be able to react quickly when things go wrong.

1. **Develop an organization suitable for strategy development: pull together the elements suitable for a joint strategy; separate them from the rest.**

    The size of an organization unit is not as important as its strategic homogeneity. This follows from my earlier remarks on complexity. Variety, not quantity, is what creates problems. When managers basically deal with one product only, as is the case with Coca Cola, it is relatively easy for them to be successful. If they have a multitude of different things to do, they will need managerial "good weather" to be successful. Note that not every kind of variety creates the same problems. Product variety can be managed well, if the same strategy basically applies to all products.

2. **Separate current business from innovation – make room for new things.**

This principle will be mentioned again in the chapter on innovation. It is one of the most important principles of effective innovation. Mixing old and new, known and unknown is one of the root causes of innovation failure. Wherever possible, this should be taken account of in the organization. The same is true for substitution. It results in coordination problems. These, however, are easier to solve than the problems that result from mixing things.

3. **Form small units but make them big enough so they can afford their own infrastructure.**

"Small is beautiful" has its justification but should not become a dogma. Well-trained people, equipped with the right technology, can also manage larger units since, as I said before, it is variety and not size that creates problems. Organization units can be too big, but they can also be too small – which is the case when they cannot survive on their own. Units should be granted organizational independence only if they can afford the functions needed to operate successfully.

4. **Separate result-producing units and supporting units.**

In a business unit structure, this is usually the case. Structuring by business units is not always possible, through. Moreover, within the business units there will usually be functional entities. It is important to ensure here that supporting functions can never become dominant but will always remain aware of their supporting nature. In an industrial company there are basically only three functions which directly produce results: developing, producing, and selling. All other functions are there to support them. HR, IT, procurement, accounting, and so on, are only required in order to develop, produce, and sell.

5. **Do Not Tolerate Internal Monopolies.**

Monopolies have a tendency to develop into feudal structures, to become arrogant, sated, and parasitic. Everything in an organization must be compared to the competition again and again. That is the only way to prevent organizational "obesity" and parasitism.

6. **Decentralize as far as possible, but maintain a strong center. The more decentralized structures are, the stronger the top management must be.**

There is hardly an argument against decentralization. But in and by itself, decentralization would lead to the decline of an organization. There must be a coordinating and optimizing force, a center. The art is in having not a large center but a strong one. That is the secret of holding structures that work.

7. Minimize interfaces.

Networking is in vogue these days. Hardly anyone talks about disentangling, though. If everything is linked to everything, nothing will work because the system will block itself. Networking tends to keep increasing the number of interfaces. Every interface creates additional problems, potential conflicts, communicative distortion, and delays. It is therefore important to aim at minimizing the number of interfaces. Even if this is successful, there will still be a sufficient number of them left.

8. An organization must be clear – not necessarily simple.

I have talked about the one-sided – and sometimes naive – demand for simplicity in the chapter on complexity. Simple systems, as desirable as they may be, are not capable of higher performance. Simplicity is often mistaken for clarity. Not every organization can be simple, but it must always be clear. As a building, a gothic cathedral is anything but simple. But it is clear in every respect – which cannot be said of every modern administrative building.

Top Management Structure

It goes without saying that the elements constituting top management are among the most important ones of any structure. Two organizational elements take center stage: the supervisory and the executive body.[84] I am using these general terms in order not to have to deal with the differences between individual legal systems and the terms they use for these organizational bodies. For the organizational aspects discussed here, legal terms are of secondary importance.

Organizing top management is not a purely structural task. More than at any other point, structural issues coincide with questions of person and function, as well as with questions of working methods. Top management organization is one of the most difficult tasks. It must be solved specifically for the individual case. Schematisms are misleading; most of what we find

---

84 Regarding the following, see my book *Effective Top Management*, Weinheim, 2006.

in the textbooks is of little use. The organization of an institution's top management must support the fulfillment of clearly defined tasks, yet it is extremely dependent on the individuals concerned, other commitments, subject-specific expertise, management skill, personal working style.

The organization of top management depends on the current situation of the company and the level of sophistication of its management systems. There is always a danger of creating "impossible jobs".

It is all the more important, then, to work out clearly the fixed points and principles that have proved useful, and to abide by them rigorously.

The Supervisory Body

Every institution needs effective supervision. It is structured differently under the different legal systems. The main difference is in the one- or two-tier structure of top management, and I am not counting the General Meeting among the core elements of top management. In Germany and Austria, a two-tier structure is mandatory for public companies; also, the dividing line between the supervisory and the executive body is precisely defined and binding. Most other countries have the one-tier model, which does not mean that a two-tier structure would not be possible.

In professionally managed companies, a two-tier structure – a separation between executive and supervisory body – will emerge even when a one-tier structure is admissible. There are compelling logical arguments and experiences clearly showing that nobody can effectively supervise themselves. The dividing line, however, can be drawn in very different ways, which has certain advantages. Under German law it is not possible for one and the same person to have a seat on the supervisory board *and* on the executive committee. In Switzerland and in Anglo-Saxon countries, by contrast, the double function of Chairman-cum-CEO is quite frequent (albeit with a decreasing tendency).

Purpose

The purpose of a supervisory body is quite easy to explain: it ensures that the company is managed rightly and well.

The supervisory body does three things to ensure this. *Firstly*, it ensures effective self-organization. In essence, this depends on the composition and efficiency of the group. De jure, its personal composition is not for the supervisory body but for the company owner to decide. In most cases, however, individual members of the supervisory body have decisive influence, at least with regard to removing incompetent members. In family-owned companies this can be a rather difficult issue.

Secondly, the supervisory body provides for the organization and effective work of the executive body. This is done via the executive body's personal composition (which is usually at the supervisory body's discretion), the rules of procedure, and the assignment of businesses.

Thirdly, the supervisory body ensures clarity on corporate governance, including both the essential guidelines and their content. It is the center of discussion, evaluation, and decision of the issues discussed in the corporate governance chapter. Explicitness and clarity, which also implies the written form, are among the key factors to the supervisory body's effective work. If part of its members think in shareholder categories, others lean towards a stakeholder principle, and a third group wants the company to have highest priority, the result will be endless discussions on questions that are insolvable as long as basic principles have not been clarified.

The correctness and significance of a logic that will give the institution itself top priority will dramatically reveal itself when, in companies with employee representation, the supervisory body includes representatives of the work council. Neither the shareholder nor the stakeholder approach will then provide a basis for constructive cooperation. However, if the well-being of the company is the ultimate goal there will be no use in taking sides. Of course there will always be incapable work council representatives, but they will usually unmask themselves, and likely lose influence. The good ones, however, with their usually excellent knowledge of corporate facts and goings-on, will make a substantial contribution to the right management of the company.

Tasks

The tasks of a supervisory body are described quite incompletely in the different legal systems, solely focusing on the legal perspective, and have little to do with the right management of a company. Complying with legal requirements is by far not enough to conduct effective supervision. Therefore, the rights and obligations of the supervisory body and its members must be defined in other regulatory works, such as the articles of association and the bylaws, as well as in individual contracts.

Genuine supervision requires professional executing of the following five tasks.

1. **Retrospective function.** This is the traditional task of the supervisory body. It is the most pronounced and takes up a major share of the group's time. In practically every meeting this task will be on the agenda. In the absence of strong resistance, many meetings will restrict themselves to this task. It will not be done well, however, as the group will concentrate almost exclusively on financial figures. The retrospective function needs to refer to all six CPCs discussed in the corporate governance chapter. This is a first indicator of whether the supervisory body has an understanding of proper corporate governance.

2. **Preview function.** As important as the retrospective function may be, it can only deal with the past which cannot be changed. The only thing to be done is to learn the right lessons from it. It is therefore much more important to look ahead. Instead of determining what has worked out and what has not, it should be ensured that the right things will be done in the future. Therefore, the supervisory body must deal with strategy, structure, and culture, and place a strong emphasis on the monitoring and evaluation of environmental changes. The members of the supervisory body do not need to be experts in those fields, but they need to know enough to be competent discussion partners to the executive body.

3. **Selection, management, evaluation, compensation, and removal of top executives.** In all legal systems, the supervisory body is responsible for HR matters relating to the executive body. Together with task No. 4, this is the strongest lever for supervisory effectiveness. It is the most difficult task, and it requires the most time. In an alarming number of cases its execution is mediocre or poor. The quick staffing changes and in particular the excesses[85] at the top of many companies impressively prove that point. Irrespective of how legal HR responsibilities are defined in the individual case, the supervisory body should be a role model

---

85 See, for instance, Linda Pelzmann on the vanity of managers in: *m.o.m.® Malik on Management Letter* No. 9/02.

to the entire organization in terms of conscientiousness and carefulness in staffing decisions.

4. **Organization of the executive body, business assignment, and rules of procedure.** By performing this task, the supervisory body determines the division of tasks among, and the working procedure for, the executive body. Together with task No. 5, it can exert practically any influence required to ensure right and good management.

5. **Shaping relations with stakeholder groups.** This task should be performed jointly with the executive body, depending on the company's current situation. Experienced members of the supervisory body can make an invaluable contribution here, be it in the basic design and maintenance of relationships or by working to improve burdened or broken relationships.

How the supervisory body complies with its tasks is a matter of internal organization and dependent on the number and skills of its members. If committees must be formed it is important to ensure that they work effectively and efficiently, which is a challenging management task for the chairman. It is advisable here to assign specific tasks to the individual members of the supervisory body, as this can clearly improve its effectiveness and commitment. If people do not have active assignments, if they only attend meetings to hear reports and ask questions, truly professional work cannot be accomplished.

It is crucial that the supervisory body not perceive its tasks as consisting predominantly (let alone exclusively) in ex-post monitoring and identifying mistakes of the executive body, which, however, is often the case. When ostracism is a regular feature at the meetings of the supervisory body, with the members of the executive body finding themselves on trial by the inquisition, it will neither be possible to fulfill the supervisory task nor to build a trust-based corporate culture. The supervisory body will destroy the very foundation of its work, as the executive body will reduce its cooperation to the minimum required by law. Before long, the whole organization will be characterized by distrust, hostility, and intrigue.

A good supervisory body acts as a competent discussion partner to the executive body, an advisor and helper in difficult situations. And it does not necessarily reduce its "bite", as is occasionally said. On the contrary: if and when controlling and corrective measures become necessary, it gives them weight, respect, and impact.

The Executive Body

Every company needs an executive body. What I said about the supervisory body and its different appearances in different legal systems also applies here.

One point should be made very clear, though, as the adoption of English terms in other languages and the translations of business papers and websites create some confusion. Under the German and Austrian stock corporation law, the executive board of a company has collective responsibility. This cannot be changed. In other countries, responsibilities can be defined at liberty. According to the CEO principle, power and responsibility are mainly with the Chief Executive Officer – he is the boss, and the other members of the executive board are helpers who more or less depend on him.

Under German and Austrian law this is not possible. There, the head of an executive board, the *Vorstandsvorsitzender*, cannot be the remaining members' superior – which does not mean that, depending on the individual's personality, he or she will not act that way if permitted. Struggles for power and rank are not fought through legal and corporate regulations, but through staffing and resignations.

The position of *Vorstandsvorsitzender* under German and Austrian law has no equivalent in English-speaking countries. They have CEOs – which is not the same and must not be perceived that way, even though many *Vorstandsvorsitzende* today carry that title in their papers and on their business cards. A CEO has plenty, almost unlimited power; a *Vorstandsvorsitzender* has very little. He presides over the meeting of the *Vorstand* and coordinates the members' areas of responsibility, but he is not their superior nor authorized to give them instructions. The members of the *Vorstand* are appointed and recalled by the supervisory board, which also deals with disciplinary issues (usually via a dedicated committee).

Purpose

As for the supervisory body, the executive body's purpose can also be described succinctly: it is to manage the company rightly and well. This is the second place where corporate government manifests itself – right or wrong governance, good or bad, depending what is jointly discussed and agreed on in the supervisory and executive bodies.

A detail worth mentioning is that Section 76 of the German Stock Corporation Act stipulates that the *Vorstand* has to manage the company "on its own responsibility". As Michael Hoffmann-Becking points out in his book on company law, "the power of control is granted to the *Vorstand* not only in the shareholders' interest; rather, its purpose is to enable the *Vorstand* to manage the company in sole consideration of the company's interest."[86] Against this background, the shareholder value discussion in Germany appears amusing if not morbid, as legislature has clearly expressed its intentions. What these words describe is identical with right governance from a management perspective, which is why I have always been of the opinion that German corporate governance – despite all its flaws – is by far ahead of the American one, and has been ahead since the 1936 reform of German stock corporation law.

Strictly speaking, German companies managed by the shareholder or stakeholder approach are breaking the law. It would be interesting to see the outcome of a test case on this issue.

Tasks

I will make the following very brief, as the tasks have been discussed at length in the chapters of Part III.

1. **Thinking through and determining the business's purpose and mission, and developing a strategy.** In coordination with the supervisory body, the essential decisions regarding corporate governance, business mission, and strategy must be taken, all in consideration of the company's environment. These are tasks which, while the executive body may get help from consultants, must be completed on its own responsibility. Mind you, I am not talking about granting approvals here but about active work.
2. **Defining standards and criteria.** Institutions are not only managed via objectives, strategies and such, but also by establishing values, rules,

---

86 Hoffmann-Becking, Michael, *Münchener Handbuch des Gesellschaftsrechts*, Vol. 4: "Aktiengesellschaft", Munich, 1988, p. 123 [translation of quote provided by another].

standards, and criteria for the behavior of the overall organization and its groups and individuals. They define what the organization stands for, and reveal the gap between actual and target performance. This is where basic decisions are made as to how excessive privileges, ostentatious extravagance, incompetence, and arrogance will be handled, and whether everything will be valued in monetary terms only. The most visible and weighty standard is the example set by the individuals in senior management positions.

3. **Developing and maintaining human resources.** Organizations can never be better than what people and their abilities permit. It is therefore a joint top management task (not one of the HR function, for instance) to ensure that the institution is equipped with the right technical and management staff, that tomorrow's managers are being prepared for the task today, that they have the best possible knowledge, are continually trained, and ready on call.

4. **Thinking through and defining the institution's overall structure.** Just as top management must contribute to strategy development, structuring is another one of its responsibilities. Many top managers do not know enough about organizational issues. This is why companies almost invariably hire consultants to help them – which, by the way, is no guarantee for quality. At the very least, top management must make sure that the points discussed here are adequately observed.

5. **Maintaining the company's key relationships to outside parties.** This is obvious and will hardly require any further discussion. The members of the executive body have to ensure that relationships are maintained in a professional manner. It is no solution to delegate this to external experts, as is done in most cases. The institution must be visible to the public via its own representatives.

6. **Representing the institution.** This task is closely linked to point 5. Representative functions must clearly and visibly be performed on behalf of the company, and must not serve the egos and personality cult of managers. Some are talented in that area and fulfill the task with skill and pleasure. Others abhor representative duties and would prefer to stay away from such events. Usually they are not very good at representing, either. In those cases it is important to ensure that the task is not neglected, be it by smartly dividing responsibilities or exerting appropriate pressure.

7. **Being prepared for crises and opportunities.** Executive members' tasks are complex, difficult, and time-consuming. Yet there must be consider-

able degrees of liberty, without fixed obligations. The executive body must be able to respond to changed conditions at any time. That is not possible if schedules are too busy. The two most important special missions are crisis and opportunity. In both cases, it is usually only the top representatives of an institution who can make the right decisions within the time available.

There are many more tasks to be performed in an institution, from research and development to marketing, from production to finance. It goes without saying that the members of the executive body will be involved in those tasks as well. Usually they head the respective divisions or departments. Yet, heading a division is not really a top management task, although it is often perceived that way. Heading a division is essentially an *operational* management task. True top management tasks, as evident from the list, are of a different nature.

It is due to the fact that top executives usually carry responsibility for a division, be it a functional, business, or regional one, that the true top management tasks are often poorly executed. They are done en passant, or delegated to others, such as consultants, or – even worse – not done at all. Thus, the third basic question of organizing, as mentioned above, is not answered at all or only partially. For all these reasons, it is one of the crucial responsibilities of the supervisory body to ensure that top management tasks are given appropriate attention, and that they are perceived and handled as priorities rather than minor matters.

Top Management Teams: How do They Work?

Contrary to zeitgeist opinion, executive top management teams are not characterized by specific emotional states or the much-cited "culture" or "chemistry". The secret of effective top teams is their abidance by guidelines and rules they have agreed on. Whenever the failure of a top management team is investigated more closely, it turns out that one of the main causes is their ignorance of this fact – which is remarkable, as one should assume familiarity with these issues to be one of the core elements of training in organization, management, and above all, leadership.

1. Three Principles

The first principle is that the *tasks* of the executive team must be clear. A team is not a place of individual or collective self-realization, nor of a democratic consensus discourse. Teams are needed wherever tasks need to be done which would exceed the strength and abilities of individuals. Otherwise we would not need them, and could spare ourselves all the fuss typically associated with working in teams. It may seem superfluous or trite to demand clarity of tasks. The fact of the matter is that this demand is seldom complied with.

The second principle is that effective teams need a precise *division* of *responsibilities*, for tasks are executed *in a coordinated fashion*, not *jointly* in a stricter sense. Everyone contributes his or her part; the rest need to know what it is and must be able to rely on it. Therefore, good teams have well-thought-out, succinct rules of procedure, or something of the sort, which clearly define who does what.

The third principle of functional teams is easy to put in words: it is strict *discipline*. This point cannot be emphasized enough. A lack of discipline is the kiss of death for any team, not only in management or at the top of an organization. There, however, a lack of discipline will have the most serious consequences. Among other things, discipline means renouncing any kind of personality cult or vanity, and it includes subordinating one's personal goals to those of the company. As long as the two kinds of goals are not in conflict that is not a problem, but anyone misusing a company – or any other organization – as a vehicle for his or her personal goals constitutes a risk.

2. Six Rules

In addition to these basic principles, highly functional teams follow six rules:

1. Every member of a top management team has the last say in his or her sphere of responsibility. He speaks on behalf of and commits the whole team.
2. Nobody takes a decision in any of the other areas of responsibility.

    These two rules condition and complement each other. They create clarity and speed, and guarantee the capability to act. Violations of these two rules will not only create enormous confusion in an organization, paralyzing its effectiveness, they will also lead to power struggles.

3. Certain decisions must be left to the team as a whole. These cases have to be specified.

This rule is a safety net against the misuse of the first two rules, which, in the absence of a corrective mechanism, could give rise to "feudal lordships" within an organization, and thus to the quick breakup of the team. Speed and an ability to act are important, but they need to serve the whole. Therefore, certain decisions must not be taken by individuals but require the whole group's assent. Typical cases include acquisitions or alliances, large-scale innovations, or critical staffing decisions.

4. Outside the team there may be no judgement comments of any one team member about another. The members of a team do not have to like each other, but agitation is not permissible. This rule applies to the outward behavior. Within the team there may be fierce debates. That can hardly be avoided when it comes to making crucial and risky decisions. In outward communications, however, there must be no uttering of personal opinions about team colleagues, no judging of others – no matter whether it is criticism or praise.

5. Each team member is obliged to keep the other members informed about what is going on in his or her area of responsibility. That, too, is a corrective to rule No. 1. If there is autonomous decision authority in each area of responsibility, there must be comprehensive information for the others.

6. Contrary to widespread opinion, a well-functioning team is not a group of equals with equal rights, even if – formally – the legal system requires it. Teams have nothing to do with democracy. What matters is effectiveness. Everyone is a member of the team because he or she has to make a distinct contribution. That is why functioning teams have an inner structure and a management.

The leader of a team must ensure that the team performs its tasks and obeys the rules for the team's functionality. In addition, he is the key person in situations where the team is paralyzing itself. For such cases the team leader needs to have the authority to overcome a stalemate situation. In an ideal case he will never have to use his right to a playoff decision; yet it must be possible in crisis situations. It is a serious warning signal if the team leader has to use that right frequently. Usually, it means that either something is fundamentally wrong with the team, or that the leader is incapable.

3. Decisions at the Top

When decisions must be taken, several formulas are possible and customary: decisions with ordinary majority, qualified majority, or unanimity. For the top executive body unanimity seems preferable, although it has its disadvantages. In a case of crisis, however, the decision-making ability is most important.

Although polling must be possible on principle, it should remain an exception. The head of the executive body must make every effort to establish consensus – not, however, the superficial kind so often found, and which only serves to conceal problems instead of solving them. It is important, therefore, that the head of the group is skilled in dealing with disagreement. Sustainable consensus – the kind that will hold even during difficult phases of implementation – only arises from open disagreement.

Wherever polling becomes necessary because consensus cannot be reached, it is indispensable that the minority back the majority decision and act loyally. They need to do everything possible to contribute to the timely implementation of the decision. Neither active nor passive opposition is admissible. Misbehavior of that kind, even if subtle and only insinuated, undermines the executive body's authority and effectiveness. If someone is definitely unable to back a decision, there is no other option for that person than to leave the company.

As long as these principles and rules are followed, the much-cited "chemistry" in the group is largely meaningless. If it is good, so much the better. If it is not, there will still be a functional team – not because of "chemistry" but thanks to the established rules. No rational person will leave an organization to the contingencies of "chemistry".

What Makes Teamwork So Difficult?

The team is one of the most important elements of action in every institution. Its significance is increasing, and in many institutions all the work is done in teams, such as in consulting, in engineering, in the fashion industry, in advertisement and communication. In these industries, the team is the chief organizational element.

This is the reason why it is so important to have a clear understanding of the pros and cons of working in teams. Team and teamwork are both fashionable words, and whoever wishes to be particularly up-to-date on zeitgeist puts them in diametric contrast to performance of individuals: the latter incorporates anything bad and outdated while team work is good and "en vogue". For quite some time now, teamwork has been one of the most frequently used terms in management. Almost without exception it is used in a positive sense: teams and teamwork are not only considered a necessary form of working under certain circumstances, not one form of many, but the *only desirable* one. In very categorical and general terms, teams are perceived as *superior* to the individual. Teams as such are considered to be good, efficient, creative, and successful. Unfortunately there is no evidence for the correctness of this hypothesis.

Not that teamwork is not necessary. It always has been. What is so new about this? Why does it warrant so much emphasis? And how can the related, almost medieval dogmatism be justified, according to which team work is the only sensible form of work?

Ever since man first walked this earth, working together has been one of the realities of everyday life. What is referred to as teams today is the basic unit of any social structure. It is even the constitutive element of everything social: the cooperation between human beings in various forms in order to cope with life, from the various different forms of families to prehistoric hunting communities, tribes, and agricultural farm communities, to craftsmen's workshops, village communities, and so on. Without cooperation no-one could have survived. Robinson Crusoe is fiction.

For all these reasons it was never a problem for anybody to work in and as teams with others. Life as such occurred in teams; living was teamwork. What, then, are the changes that apparently require something so natural throughout the millenniums to become such a priority all of a sudden? What makes it so important that it must be specifically taught, and is considered a key criterion for people's professional development, even their very suitability for employment? Perhaps today, due to certain training efforts, we have in our organizations a slightly greater share of people who have never learnt to finish something on their own because they were allowed too often to hide in learning or experience groups of some kind. Perhaps we have a slightly greater share of those who have not clearly felt the difference between success and failure in school, because they were never rated correctly and now believe it is an exceptional achievement to make it through school. Certain misguided developments in pedagogy have left their traces, and people that were harmed by them are now struggling to learn. However, they are in the minority.

What has definitely increased are nonsensical forms of organization and division of labor which almost prevent any kind of productive work, or at least make it inhumanly difficult. For instance, someone having to work in a matrix organization – which in most cases has been introduced much too hurriedly and has never really been thought through – needs teamwork capabilities to an extent that is seldom found in reality and is usually impossible to develop, no matter how much training a person receives. It is therefore much better, more effective, and more economic to change the organization structure. The purpose of organization is not to make it difficult for people to work. On the contrary, it should facilitate things. If people are not burdened with organizations hindering performance, it quickly shows that most can work together without major problems – precisely because that is one of the normal abilities of ordinary people.

What About Really Excellent Performance?

In a nutshell, people may, under reasonable conditions, be assumed to already possess the abilities generally needed to work together. But how about truly excellent performance? Is it not true that real top performance – the creative break-through – arises in teams, and would the ordinary teamwork ability of ordinary people suffice for this? Or should specific training not begin right there? This thought is fascinating enough to investigate it further. Whether or not you will consider the result surprising depends on how much you have studied the work and achievements of "great" people. Practically all great achievements, in particular those commonly referred to as breakthroughs, were achievements by individuals, sometimes with helpers and supporters, but hardly ever by teams. This is true for all forms of art: there are neither musical compositions by teams nor works of world literature created by teams; neither team painting nor team sculpturing are known art forms. Contrary to a widespread view, this is also true for science – true enough to take it seriously. Apart from very few exceptions, the great works of philosophy, mathematics, natural sciences and the humanities were created by individuals.

Teams are tools, as is individual work. Neither of these forms of work should be categorically excluded or praised to the sky. How to work, and what form of work will be optimal, depends on the task as such and not on dogmas. In the world of organizations, tasks must be designed in such a way that they can be performed by ordinary people (because there is no other kind) with ordinary skills (because no other kind can be acquired). Whoever wants results needs to be capable of both: team work and individual work – each wherever it is appropriate. Anyone who wants to climb the career ladder – or, better perhaps: deliver sustainable performance – and who, as an executive, depends on the trust and respect of others, must abstain from using buzzwords and falling for fads.

To summarize, I am not against teams but against the tendency to consider them the only sensible form of work. In other words, I am against idealizing teams and underestimating individual work.

Chapter 12

Culture

"Don't change culture; use it ..."
Peter F. Drucker

"Culture is not an excuse."
Friedrich Dürrenmatt

Many of the essential factors of right corporate culture have been included in the foregoing considerations on right and good management. Right management is right culture, as I have mentioned before.

What organizations need is a culture of effectiveness, of performance, of professionalism and responsibility. It is also a culture of trust and noticeable human companionship.

I do not think much of the line, "we are all one big family". Like all other organizations in society, companies are communities of purpose. Regarding and treating them as families would overburden organizations and the people in them, as family is associated with other emotions than institutions.

It is, however, important for people to feel a sense of community, which obviously is not the same as family. In this point, neoliberalism is right to the extent that the state and modern society cannot be communities, nor can they replace them. That was a socialist illusion. It seems, however, that neoliberalism is incapable of accepting man as a social being with a deeply rooted, evolution-based need to experience community. In particular large organizations face a paradox: on the one hand they perceive themselves as vehicles of market-economic rationality, on the other hand they are the place where their employees experience both community and the emotionality that comes with it.

The Standard Model of Effectiveness covers most of what is needed. Its guidelines, tasks and tools comprise most of those values which make a company function, and which make living and working in an organization humanly bearable. I will get back to the notion of responsibility later.

There are some additional issues which are crucial for an organization's culture. One is the erosion of values caused by neoliberalism and the shareholder approach. Another is shared management knowledge. A third concerns staffing decisions, the fourth some open questions of motivation, and the fifth – and perhaps most essential – the question of meaning that was already commented on in the business mission context. First, however, I would like to bring up for discussion some thoughts on changing cultures.

Cultural Change

Corporate culture became a major topic in the early 1980s, essentially due to Peters and Waterman's global bestseller *In Search of Excellence*[87] as well as Deal and Kennedy's book on *Corporate Cultures*[88]. For years, corporate culture was *the* hot topic. Great hopes were placed in the possibility of changing a culture. However, results have been sobering.

In retrospect, I believe – and I was not aware of this back then – that we were dealing with an import of U.S. American notions which were really out of place in Europe, or at least in the German-speaking part of it. What the Americans meant when they talked about culture, and what they probably needed in their organizations, was a non-issue in Europe because we already had it. As happens so often, we were led to believe that American companies were better than ours, due to their culture. The same myths, by the way, were spread about Japanese businesses.

There are two ways to achieve a true, profound, sustained and quick change of cultures. The first is through crisis; the second is through the staffing of key positions. They provide an opportunity to get people into positions where they can be a visible example to others.

---

87 Peters, Thomas J./Waterman, Robert H. Jr., *In Search of Excellence*, New York, 1982.
88 Deal, Terrence E./Kennedy, Allan A., *Corporate Cultures*, Reading, Mass. 1982.

All other ways are highly questionable. The impact of most programs has been superficial and there has been no real change. Everything takes much too long, momentum and credibility are lost. I am not saying that all of the countless cultural change programs, which today are almost standard in every company, are useless – although many are. They belong in the category of entertainment rather than serious management development.

It goes without saying that a crisis which cannot be ignored, and which is clearly addressed as such, will not remain without effect. Yet most managers hesitate to acknowledge a crisis situation and to openly pronounce the word crisis. Playing it down is the most common strategy, although a crisis, if used in the right way, can be an enormous opportunity.

When, for example, Austria's state-owned enterprises – and hence the state itself – ran into a crisis at the end of the 1980s, the way to serious reform (also implying a cultural shock) was not opened until, at a turbulent general staff meeting and in the presence of television cameras, the head of the executive board openly admitted that the group was bankrupt.

A crisis permits the replacement of key people – although in a somewhat risky manner, as numerous new faces will have to be recruited from outside and there is no way of knowing how they will act in certain situations.

Once again, Peter Drucker has shown the way to a right perception of corporate culture: "Don't change culture; use it." Recognize and use your strengths; do not worry about culture but find out what you can do better than your competitors. Then leave your people alone and let them do their work. In discussing the key issues mentioned above, I let myself be guided by this attitude.

Values

When it comes to values, once again I need to come back to the disastrous effects of neoliberalism. Under its influence, society has undergone a change of value of historical dimensions over the past decade, with dangerous repercussions. As mentioned before, neoliberalism has led to the *economization* of society, albeit to a *primitive* form of economization: one in which everything is perceived, measured, and judged in monetary terms.

Indeed, not all managers and only few entrepreneurs have committed themselves to shareholder value. It has established itself in very few industries, such as banking and insurance, telecommunications, parts of media and entertainment, and in IT. The industries and some of their top managers, their mistakes, their income excesses, and their demeanor in public have met with so much attention from the media that this part of the business sector is regarded as *representative of all business enterprises* by many people.

As had long been predicted[89], these developments have caused a new anti-business attitude in the population that would hardly have been considered possible after the collapse of communism. They have – justifiably – created widespread contempt for this kind of manager which had not existed before, but unfortunately also contempt for management in general, even when it worked well.

This *purely money-driven* climate permitted people to rise to the top of large corporations who would not have stood a chance before – not entrepreneurial personalities but gamblers, showoffs, bluffers, partly even criminals. Quick money was the highest value to them. A swamp of mental corruption and deal-making developed and replaced other values. Although some corrective action has been taken, we are still far away from the values of a well-functioning economy and society.[90]

For *commercial enterprises* the shareholder value concept must be replaced by the notion of a healthy organization. The highest values must be its *viability* as well as sustainable economic operations. Customers, not shareholders must take the center of attention. Companies with satisfied customers – this cannot be repeated often enough – will also have satisfied shareholders. The opposite does not work.

Jobs must not be the highest goal. When many employees are required to achieve customer satisfaction, there will be many jobs; when only few people are needed, there will be few. Companies must not be hindered from being competitive; whether they are competitive or not is up to the customers.

The highest value for management must be to serve the institution. Anyone giving priority to his own personal interests should do this on his own

---

89 See my book *Effective Top Management*, Weinheim, 2006, p. 109.
90 See Krieg, Walter in: Krieg, Walter/Galler, Klaus/Stadelmann, Peter (eds.), *Richtiges und gutes Management: vom System zur Praxis* Bern/Stuttgart/Vienna, 2004.

account, not with other people's money. Personality cult and self-enrichment must not be allowed in business because they harm employees' motivation. Hence, new solutions will be required for the responsibility and liability of managers.

As we know from Viktor Frankl's work, what matters most to people is not money but a meaning in life. This also includes human values like brotherliness and communal solidarity. When people lose the Why, there will be neither motivation nor performance – and ultimately, no society.

The Unity of Management Knowledge

Some consider shared values to be the most important element of corporate culture. As important as it may be, I would like to place another element above it – not to create a ranking issue but because it is neglected or even violated in most organizations, based on the conviction that this will particularly contribute to culture and demonstrate a modern and professional attitude. As a matter of fact, it is the worst obstacle to the development of a culture that will serve the organization's function.

It is the neglection or active destruction of the unity of management, of Unité de Pensée and Unité de Doctrine, by splitting up management training. It is done with best intentions, in the interest of diversity and openness. It is utterly wrong. It is diversity in the wrong place, and openness to the wrong things.

There should not be blind dogmatism, though. Every institution should verify over and over again whether its management kow-how is still right, whether there is anything new and better, what others are doing, what competitors are focusing on, and what is happening in science. It must be verified what alternative approaches might accomplish and where they could possibly be adopted. That is an obvious task for the experts of HR management, executive development, and employee training. Regardless, the solution certainly cannot be for every manager to pick his "favorite dishes" from the menu of international training offers.

No organization can function well if everyone has different perceptions of management. One would think that is obvious. In fact, this is what the reality in most companies looks like. So far I have never read anything about the indispensable unity of management thinking in any book on corporate culture or knowledge management. There is much talk about "shared knowledge", but what knowledge that refers to is not revealed.

Many people have never had any management training because those in charge do not think they need that kind of knowledge. That per se is a mistake. Many had poor, too little, and/or the wrong training. Only few organizations have understood that all employees, no matter what their function or level, need to have the same perception of management in order for the organization to work, to be error-resilient and able to cope with heavy workloads, to be productive, possibly even to function perfectly, as well as – even more importantly – to be able to do the right thing quickly and without debate in the event of an extraordinary crisis or opportunity.

Management training must include anyone who is a boss and anyone who has a boss – that is to say, everybody – and they all must be taught the same things. That does not mean that everybody needs to study the same subject matter with the same intensity. The basic elements, the inner logic and the main principles need to be the same for all, and everyone must know that they are binding for all.

Scope and intensity must differ depending on the organizational level, the content must not. This shared management knowledge is at least as important for corporate culture as shared values. However, to repeat what I have said before: it is not a question of culture and thus – as some apostles of shareholder value disparagingly put it – of the organization's "soft" elements. It is an indispensable prerequisite for the functionality of an organization.

The Strongest Signals: Staffing Decisions

Staffing decisions are the most important of all decisions. In the final analysis, any large organization can only be managed from the top via finance and staffing.

Filling a post – in particular at the top – requires great care. Organizations are ultimately managed through staffing decisions. Everything depends on them. Does that warrant special emphasis? In view of the overall outcome of European and American top management staffing decisions since the early 1990, the answer must clearly be Yes.

Senior, competent managers therefore dedicate a major share of their time to staffing questions – and they do not only do that when they are in charge of the HR division. In well-managed organizations, weighty decisions on the staffing of management positions are not a responsibility of the HR division. They are taken by the executive board, and its chairman is well advised to personally ensure their quality. Alfred P. Sloan from 1920 to 1956, at the helm of the General Motors Corporation, dedicated up to half his time to staffing decisions, including those at lower hierarchical levels. Staffing decisions and everything that they include – selection, promotion, transfer, demotion, and dismissal – determine almost everything important in and of an organization. It is all the more remarkable that management trainings, corporate culture and change programs, and business literature contain very little about the subject.

1. Staffing decisions determine an organization's performance capability. All other resources have their significance – equipment, funds, computers, and so on – but the true factor driving performance is people.
2. Staffing decisions are the linchpin of corporate culture. No matter what programs the organization conducts in order to foster and change its culture – if there are discrepancies between these programs and the staffing decisions taken, people will pay attention to the signals sent by the staffing decisions. If these two elements contradict each other, even the best and greatest programs will evaporate into thin air, and may even be perceived as a higher form of cynicism. Staffing decisions are the main source of frustration, of inward and formal resignation, of agony, bitterness, and cynicism.
3. Staffing decisions involve the greatest risk – firstly, because they are hardly corrigible and therefore have long-term impact. That is particularly true for decisions regarding the company's top, as well as key position in divisions and subsidiaries. Secondly, because they are visible to anyone. Staffing decisions cannot be kept confidential. Many other wrong decisions can be hidden from the majority of the workforce. Failed investment decisions, innovation projects, and so on, are rarely interesting to all employees. For a while they may be newsworthy and take the center of attention; over time they are forgotten. They lose topicality and appeal. With staffing decisions things are different. They are interesting to workers, media, and the public, and when they are wrong, everyone will be reminded of them on a day-to-day basis.

4. Anyone failing here will not only create problems for himself but also run the risk of losing his organization's respect. How often can a supervisory board make mistakes in staffing top executive positions before everyone starts questioning its competence? How often can the executive board afford to make the wrong choices when filling management positions in divisions and subsidiaries?

Yet I do not know of any usable studies dealing with the quality and success of staffing decisions. It seems we are largely dealing with uncharted territory here. Based on many years' experience and discussions with executives of all levels I dare say, however, that no more than a third of all staffing decisions are good all around – that is to say, of the kind of quality that makes everyone say, even after years: "This is the right person in the right place". Another third of decisions is good enough to live with; the last third is downright wrong. There is no other field in which such success rates, or rather: failure rates, would be tolerated.

Critical Incidents[91]

The best way to prepare decisions about people is to test them over years. Confronting people with new, bigger and more difficult tasks over and over again is a great way to get to know them, judge their results, and learn to assess their behavior in critical situations. This is why it takes some time until you have truly reliable information on your staff.

The most difficult and most critical staffing decisions concern the top management bodies. People coming from within the organization are not really prepared for a top position. Every preceding position they held as they were being tested for the "real thing" was not a top position but another step on the way. It is ultimately impossible to know how a person will act when getting into the top position with all its possibilities – and its temptations.

Things are even more difficult with people coming from outside. If someone previously had a top position in another organization you will know how that person acted there, but since he or she does not know your

---

91 See Linda Pelzmann in: *m.o.m.*® *Malik on Management Letter* No. 1/02.

organization, there is no way of knowing how employees will respond to the new boss. Whichever way you look at it, the risks are considerable.

In situations like these, the so-called Critical Incidents method can be useful, which is not very widely known. Looking at the misguided staffing decisions taken over the last years at major corporations in almost every country, some of which resulted in widely publicized resignations, I seriously doubt that this method was used, otherwise decisions could not have gone so wrong.

Linda Pelzmann writes: "An old rule among Hungarian magnates stipulates what to do before you can trust a business partner. You have to have experienced him in three critical situations, situations in which it will not remain unnoticed if he is lacking in terms of personal integrity: first, you need to see him drunk. He will not hold back the truth then. Second, you need to share an inheritance with him. He will not hold back his greed then. Third, you need to be in captivity with him to see whether he will lose his head and abandon his peers."

Of course it is impossible to arbitrarily create these three situations, but they illustrate what this is about. Analogous everyday situations can be observed often enough to gather information.

In every single case of a spectacular resignation or dismissal of a top manager, there were enough critical incidents in his vita to justify *not* staffing him. For instance, if someone, once arrived at the top, demands privileges for himself and fosters a personality cult, it is highly probable that this person had that inclination before and also displayed it, but nobody paid attention.

There are negative and positive critical incidents. "Critical" here does not imply a judgment; it refers to an unusual, untypical behavior that could not have been expected in that situation. This includes occurrences and behaviors which, in and by themselves, may not really be that relevant but which, over time and in combination, provide a basic pattern for what can probably be understood to be the person's character.

If you examine more closely what people did who had to make numerous staffing decisions in the past and were quite successful with them, you will often find that they kept a "little black book" in which they noted all their observations. In most cases, they got their most valuable information not from official files but from what they had had collected over the years. Again and again they took the time to watch people and test them with ever more demanding tasks. They also noted seemingly irrelevant occurrences, in case they would need them at some point, and paid particular attention to three things: to the results a person delivered in the course of his or her life, to the way that person dealt with his or her mistakes, and to the so-called critical incidents.

Questions of Motivation

An institution's culture must be based on more than the usual motivational dogmas. One way to achieve this is by role models displaying more than the usual degree of motivation.

The thesaurus defines "motivation" as follows: *the psychological feature that arouses an organism to action toward the desired goal; the reason for the action; that which gives purpose and direction to behavior.* And Charles Lattmann, who was extremely thorough in these matters, writes: "the term 'motive' stems from the Latin verb 'movere', which means 'put into motion'. Literally translated, it therefore means 'the reason that moves': a motive is the cause for what an acting person does or does not do. Its meaning includes everything contained in a number of everyday terms, such as 'drive', 'urge', 'desire' and the like. They all have in common the notion of striving for a state of satisfaction."[92]

It seems to me that, firstly, there are more reasons for people's actions than those caused by the "strive for a state of satisfaction"; reasons that have nothing to do with drive, urge, or desire. Secondly, the general interpretation of motivation is usually about very specific motives which are associated with emotions and emotional states. In recent years, the motivating emotional state has been interpreted almost exclusively in terms of pleasure – that is, in a hedonistic sense.

Motivation is perceived to be something that gives you pleasure, is fun, "turns you on", gives you a "kick", and so forth. "I am not motivated", thus, usually means "I don't feel like it." Likewise for frustration; "I am frustrated" means "it does not give me pleasure" or "I don't feel like it". Hence, it is all about emotions, about feelings of pleasure and displeasure.

This may be acceptable for private matters. It does not suffice, however, when it comes to managing people. For these reasons I have always, and

---

92 Lattmann, Charles, *Die verhaltenswissenschaftlichen Grundlagen der Führung des Mitarbeiters*, Bern/Stuttgart, 1982, p. 105 [translation provided by author].

to all the fashion trends, recommended holding on to terms such as "obligation" and "will", which are hardly ever used.

In good times, and when it comes to doing pleasant things, it may suffice to be motivated as usual. In bad times, and when true and serious requirements are at stake, that is not enough. Even the careless use of these terms in everyday language cannot change that.

I would like to counter the superficial use of the term motivation, and above all, the view that someone needs to be motivated in that way in order to do something, with an alternative point of view. People do most of what they do because it is their *obligation* and, even more, because they have *committed* themselves. Whether this is associated with emotions, and to what extent, is meaningless in this context.

It would be a romantic illusion to believe that the majority of people go to work on Monday morning because they are motivated in an emotional sense. They have contractually committed themselves to doing certain things, and they must comply with that contractual obligation – among other reasons, because they have entered into other contractual obligations besides that, such as rental contracts, credit agreements, and many more. Some of these obligations have been taken on voluntarily, and some motivating emotions may have played a role in that. The resulting obligations themselves, stretching across many years, are entirely independent of such feelings.

Then there are commitments which we do not have for contractual reasons but because we are humans. Someone taking care of his or her elderly parents will usually not do that because he or she is motivated in the usual sense of the word. The same is true for helping co-workers in difficult situations.

Another element is volition: people do much of what they do because *they* want to do it, no matter whether they are motivated or not, whether they feel a drive, urge, or desire, or not. It seems not to make too much sense to me – expect perhaps for the childhood years – to speak of motivation when referring to matters of personal hygiene, such as brushing your teeth. You do it because you know it is important and, as a result, you have the will to do it, regardless of motivation, irrespective of whether it gives you feelings of pleasure or even satisfaction.

The same is true for sports. A person waiting to be motivated for exercise will never get anywhere. I will not deny that exercising can sometimes give you feelings of pleasure or even happiness, but anyone with higher ambitions as an athlete cannot afford to wait for such feelings. She will exercise because she wishes to deliver a good athletic performance and she knows how important it is to exercise regularly.

There are two more reasons for people's actions which are not sufficiently dealt with in literature and to which the psychologist Linda Pelzmann directed my attention: it is our *habits*, which play a crucial role for how we act, and the *orientation by other people's actions*. Many things are not done for reasons of motivation but because other people do them as well.

Becoming Motivation-Independent

I would also suggest adopting the notion of motivation-independence into corporate culture. People need to abandon the notion that there will always be someone, a superior or some other person, to motivate them.

Even if this notion can be considered to make sense for ordinary people, it is surely not feasible for *executives*. Anyone wanting to be an executive will need to take another step: he will need to progress from motivation to self-motivation. If he waits to be motivated by others he will never get anywhere. He will be dependent on others; he will remain someone led by others all his life, essentially a servant, even if by accident, by happenstance or through wrong staffing decisions he may be able to rise to higher positions.

Anyone waiting to be motivated by third parties will keep getting disappointed, for there will not always be someone to motivate him. Hence my suggestion which strongly contradicts the usual notions of motivation: *Make yourself inwardly independent of motivation by others! Learn to motivate yourself!*

True humaneness in management and true performance orientation require people to not only motivate themselves, but also to make as many co-workers as possible aware of this approach – in particular those who also have to lead other people – and enable them to motivate themselves.

Trust: More Important than Motivation

The fifth of my key principles initially listed is that trust is more important than motivation. In *Managing Performing Living* I have elaborated on this subject, which has largely been neglected by the usual motivation theories. When in the 1980s I talked about trust in the context of corporate culture and motivation, this was new but also plausible to managers. Now there are some publications on the subject[93] which deal with it in greater detail. There can be no such thing as corporate culture if it is not based on trust. Effectiveness and performance directly depend on trust.

Trust does not replace motivation and it is not the same as motivation. Trust is the key prerequisite that enables motivation. When there is trust there is no need to motivate people. If it is done anyway, so much the better. Effects will surely show.

The true significance of trust becomes evident when it is lacking: when there is not even a minimum of trust, it is useless to try to motivate people; all attempts will remain without effect. Even worse, in the absence of trust all attempts at motivation will usually have the opposite effect – they will be perceived as manipulation, even as a particularly shrewd form of cynicism.

It is precisely for this reason that many well-intended and competently designed motivation and culture programs remain ineffective or even turn out to be detrimental, much to the experts' surprise. Such programs are usually started when management thinks they are necessary due to deteriorating performance, or to motivate people to deliver even better performance. In most cases the trust base is not examined or even considered. Once a reasonably stable trust base can be established, motivational programs usually become superfluous.

Trust is the basis of any reasonable, humane, and, in particular, any well-functioning form of management. It does not require any special skill or talent, let alone sophisticated theories of the sort that are currently being cited for all sorts of things. Contrary to popular opinion, trust and distrust are not emotional phenomena, although certain emotional states may be linked to both. Also, it is entirely unnecessary to speak of a "culture of trust" right away as often happens reflexively. What is really necessary is consistent behavior, reliability, and perhaps what is commonly referred to as personal integrity. Meaning what you say, and acting accordingly. Keeping your promises.

---

93 Such as Sprenger, Reinhard, *Vertrauen führt: Worauf es im Unternehmen wirklich ankommt*, Frankfurt am Main/New York, 2002.

Culture and Meaning

The Best Has Been Overlooked

Amazingly enough, a theory directly dealing with the motivation of people has largely been overlooked or neglected so far: it is the theory of the Austrian psychologist and psychiatrist *Viktor Frankl*.[94] I have been using his basic findings in my seminars since the early 1980s, and have also written a management letter about them in early 1997.[95] In my seminars I regularly find that less than 5 percent of the managers attending have ever heard of the name Frankl, and less than 2 percent are more or less familiar with his teachings.

Frankl's theory is the best that has ever been expressed about motivation. In my view, anyone claiming to have an understanding of motivation should at least know Frankl's work. To what extent one will accept his views is another question entirely, but in any case it takes strong arguments to refute what he said.

To put it very briefly, Viktor Frank's hypothesis is that man is motivated by meaning. He refers to his theory and the therapy based on it as "logotherapy". Occasionally this school of thought is also referred to as the third Austrian school of psychotherapy.[96] According to Frankl, man is motivated by meaning and the search for it. Once man has found meaning, when (and as long as) he manages to see meaning in something, he will be willing and able to deliver outstanding performance, and also willing and able to make sacrifices and abstain. Evidence of that can often be found in the cases of people who have mastered the most difficult situations in life. And if man no longer sees a meaning in life, he will no longer be willing and able to perform, and will even be inclined to end his life.

Viktor Frankl goes to the very roots of human existence and he views the human being as a whole, which cannot be said of all psychological schools of thought. Therefore, not every aspect of his theory will be relevant specifically to managers and their profession. For this context, two or

---

94 I regret not being able to mention Gertrud Höhler's book *Die Sinn-Macher* as an exception. Ms. Höhler has also overlooked or ignored Frankl's work.
95 *m.o.m.® Malik on Management Letter* No. 3/02.
96 The first and second are those of Sigmund Freud, and Alfred Adler.

three of Frankl's thoughts are relevant and even essential. For managers as human beings, however, and in particular for those in one's sphere of responsibility, his entire teaching is highly relevant.

The Essence

Frankl's key hypotheses can be summarized as follows:

Man is a being in search of meaning. This search is his main motivating force. Meaning, however, cannot be provided or made by anyone. Everybody must search for it for himself.

It is possible, however, to take away meaning from people; their search for meaning can be frustrated, and as a result their main source of strength and the foundation of their lives can be destroyed. Avoiding this, instead creating the opportunities for everyone to find their meaning, is one of the noblest tasks of managers. In my opinion, this is probably the only thing one needs to do – and has to do – to motivate people. All other motivational approaches are irrelevant by comparison, for without meaning they are ineffective, or worse, cynical.

Frankl goes further, however: he does not only say that everyone is motivated by his search for meaning but needs to find it for himself; he also says that everyone can find it, that there is a meaning in life for every individual. Hence he does not content himself with raising a major issue, he also provides answers which are down-to-earth, simple, and comprehensible. Based on his findings from numerous, partly international research projects, Frankl shows how people can find a meaning in life.

They mainly do it in three ways, of which the first is significant for management, the second for private life, and the third relates to borderline situations.

This is how people find meaning:

1. Service to a cause: by fulfilling a task, delivering a performance, creating something, or undergoing an important experience. It goes without saying that here is the key to motivation in the management context.
2. Service to a person (or several persons): for instance, in dedicating oneself to one's family, to friends, but also to people in need of help. This way of finding meaning may occur in professional life when particular collegiality and helpfulness are called for, but apart from that it is mainly

a matter of private life, of life partnership and other interpersonal relationships.

3. The third way in which, according to Frankl, man finds meaning is by transforming pain into achievement, by bearing testimony of the most human of all accomplishments: mastering one's fate and enduring a hopeless situation, such as an incurable disease, with dignity.

Self-Realization – by Doing What?

One of the main aspects of Frankl's theory is that, as he persuasively points out, the search and the finding of meaning are connected with self-transcendence, with man's reaching beyond himself, putting aside his own interests and throwing himself into service to something different and more important. Thus, the theory is in diametric contrast to all the self-realization approaches finding such broad acceptance, and which probably originated from the motivational theory of Abraham Maslow – or perhaps in its misinterpretation. Not that Frankl is against self-realization. On the contrary: finding meaning is the highest form of self-realization. Yet the way there, according to Frankl, is different from what Abraham Maslow and neoliberalism teach.

While self-realization theories – at least as they are commonly understood – lead to egocentrism, to man placing himself at the center of things, Frankl teaches the opposite. Man forgets himself over his search for meaning and selflessly dedicates himself to his task or work. At one point Frankl uses a vivid comparison with the human eye. A healthy eye cannot see itself. As soon as it senses something related to itself, it is ill and notices its own functional disorder.

It is this same kind of selflessness that we find in managers whom we would consider candidates for true leadership. One example: one week after the allied troops successfully landed in Normandy, Chief of Staff General Marshall inspected the front. Over lunch, sitting on ammunition boxes, Marshall turned to Eisenhower and said something along the lines of: "Eisenhower, you have chosen all these wonderful commanders who have accomplished this great mission – or you have accepted those I had suggested to you. What is the main virtue you look for when choosing people?" Almost unthinkingly, Eisenhower replied: "selflessness."

Chapter 13

Executives

> "Make them brave, upright and honorable men!"
> *Empress Maria Theresia, speaking to the*
> *first commander of her military academy in 1745*

Concepts and models are doubtless important. Without them, coordinated action is not possible. It is people, however, who do the actual work, and in organizations it is above all the managers who have to shape, lead, and develop things. Every executive is a center of effectiveness, or the lack of it, in his or her organization. Managers are centers of self-regulation and self-organization in the strictest sense of the word in that they have to control, guide, and organize themselves. In a broader sense they are also centers of the capability of self-regulation and self-organization, and of the evolution of the institution as a whole. In cybernetic terms they are also amplifiers and attenuators of complexity. As a group – or rather, as a system – they personify Ashby's law of requisite variety, which I have mentioned in the chapter on complexity.

More nonsense has been published about executives than about any other management topic. More than for any other management topic, it is evident that most publications have been written by people who have no or very little first-hand experience with managers. Still, I would find it more persuasive if such research was based on personal experience in strategy development. It cannot be replaced with questionnaires.

For the topic of executives I consider personal experience to be indispensable, and it has to be substantial and comprehensive, developed in years of working with them hands-on. More on this later.

Does Management Need a Concept of Man?

Almost every important subject in management – motivation, performance, satisfaction, values, corporate culture – seems to depend on a certain idea of man. Inevitably, the same two concepts have repeatedly been introduced into the debate, which Douglas McGregor has presented decades ago in *The Human Side of Enterprise*[97] and referred to as "Theory X" and "Theory Y". Even then, these two concepts of man were ages old. They have permeated the entire intellectual history, and have probably originated in the two state models of Sparta and Athens.

One of the two concepts (Theory X) views man as a weak being in need of help, depending on the solidarity of his community and unable to shape and take responsibility for his life, a being that perceives work as something distressing and troublesome, therefore tends to shun it, and is in need of "redemption". The second (Theory Y) is the concept of a strong and capable being who works and performs of his own volition and with pleasure, decides over himself and his life, and finds meaning and self-fulfillment in that fact.

Whichever concept one may lean towards emotionally, I suggest working *without* a concept of man in the field of management. I recommend resisting the idea of having a concept of man, as it involves a risk of falling into the trap of cliché and bias.

What are my reasons for this somewhat unusual suggestion? We simply do not know what man *as such* is like. Presently the world is populated by close to 7 billion people, but no two of them are identical. And even if there will be some 11 or 12 billion in a few decades, there still will not be two that are identical. So what are human beings like? We will probably never know.

And we do not need to know. Management does not involve the task of managing *humankind*. The task is to manage one's dozen or so people who, by choice or coincidence, have become one's direct reports. It is therefore only necessary to know what these few people are like, only these concrete persons, no academic abstractions of any kind. And that can be found out even if science will never detect anything universally valid for all humans.

The refusal to accept a generalized concept of man is very consequential: it leads to the task of *finding out* what the individual co-worker is like instead of letting oneself be guided by clichés.

---

97 McGregor, Douglas, *The Human Side of Enterprise*, New York, 1960.

It will soon turn out that hardly anyone conforms to a general concept. There are people who seem to be a Theory X type at the workplace, apparently thinking of nothing else but the end of their workday. Then, all of a sudden, the picture changes: with great passion and commitment they dedicate themselves to an honorary function in a club, or work in a nonprofit organization or a political party, or pursue a hobby or sport. So what kind of person are they?

Then there are people delivering excellent performance at work, obviously Theory Y types, but who never get anything going in their private life and spend their evenings watching TV. There are people going through periods of high performance, only to take it easy for days or weeks after. What types are they?

Every sports coach has learnt not to pay attention to types but to the individual performance profile of every individual athlete. Anyone focusing on concepts of people will not only run the risk of doing them injustice – he will also neglect what is most important in management: finding out what the individual person is capable of, what his or her strengths and capabilities are, and then placing that person wherever he or she can make a difference.

New Qualifications and Requirements

There is constant talk about the new requirements that managers supposedly have to meet. Hardly a week passes without something of the kind being published in one of the numerous magazines, trade journals or books. Discussions around managers' qualifications and the competencies they should have do not seem to end. Every real or perceived change, be it in technologies or the market, in the economy, the environment, or inside the companies, fuels the same old discussion leading to the same old result: *managers need to change dramatically.*

Usually no one talks about how realistic this demand really is. Fortunately we must not take it all that seriously, as it is the result of a series of misunderstandings. Anyone with the usual qualifications obtained through normal upbringing and good education, and who has been trained in the craft of management, has a fair chance of getting quite far.

Who Is Making the Demands?

Those making all these outrageous demands are not always familiar with management practice, but that does not keep them from writing and demanding. Many of them are young journalists with limited professional practice and hardly any first-hand experience with managers, apart from their own bosses. Others are book authors for whom the same is true in a surprising number of cases. Many come from the training and consulting scene, some from academia. According to my research findings, *more than half* have no management experience whatsoever. A surprisingly large number have never borne managerial responsibility, never had to deliver and account for economic results, and have not worked with nearly enough executives to know their situation or be able to assess their situation. Quite a few never graduated, others failed in their professional careers.

It comes as no surprise, then, that tangible and crucial questions are never asked: for instance, how much time managers should take at maximum to learn something new – in particular if it will be radically new; how much spare time they have left for that; where they can get the new qualifications. None of the people making the demands seem to actually go to the effort of verifying the skills that truly competent managers – not necessarily those mentioned in the papers – already have, perhaps always had.

These questions would have a welcome, sobering effect and draw attention to the one and only key question: how can we use the managers we have today – because there are no others – in such a way that they can bring their current strengths and abilities to bear and deliver results?

The constantly changing demands are blocking the view of what is essential, and are causing false doctrines to emerge. Even more importantly, they make solid management training *impossible*, or difficult at minimum. When managers are asked to learn a new kind of management, fulfill new requirements and meet even higher standards every few months, some of them will just *give* up mentally, others will cease to take those trainings seriously. At the same time, it will be grist to the mill of those skilled in throwing around buzzwords and meaningless rhetoric, and whose goal it is to impress that way.

Many of the new demands people believe must be made have originated from the so-called New Economy. Now that the stock market frenzy of the boom years, the New Economy fantasies and the internet and E-business illusions have faded, we may have an opportunity to carry on a *critical and sensible* discussion – at least for a while, until we will be deluged by the next wave. This, however, will require some *distinctions* to be made and some *standards* to be observed.

Bad and Good Managers

Once again, the distinction between good and bad management which this book is based on proves enlightening. If this distinction is made – and only then – it will be possible to recognize misconceptions. Surely nobody has ever doubted that there are bad managers, and lots of them. The important point is that there are good ones, too. Their number may be smaller, but it is still much larger than is commonly assumed. They are just not that visible. They are not always found at the top of corporations, and there is nothing about them in the newspapers because there is nothing bad to be said about them. After all, the media are primarily interested in publishing bad news on managers.

Good managers must serve as benchmarks in terms of qualifications and requirements. When that happens it quickly turns out that the so-called new qualifications are not that new after all, and that good managers may always have had them. In other words, they are nothing special – except for people who do not know that much about management.

Being or Doing

New requirements mostly refer to how managers should be, as opposed to what they should do and how they should act. Certain qualities are demanded. Managers, so we hear, should be emotionally intelligent, socially competent, visionary, communicative, and dynamic. That may appear plausible; however, it has long been known that the search for qualities leads nowhere. I have elaborated on this topic in my book *Managing Performing Living*.

Demands of this kind miss one of the perhaps most important facts: managers are as different as human beings can be. In their qualities, their personality, their character and temperament there are hardly any commonalities. What matters is not how managers are, but what they *do*.

That is obvious in particular when looking at executives who have made great achievements in the course of their lives, the real performers: those who have not only established businesses but made them successful; those who have not only managed well but also successfully passed on their responsibilities to their successors. The greater a person's achievements, the less he or she conforms to the usual standards, as can easily be seen from their biographies.

This applies to managers not only of commercial enterprises but of any kind of organization. Let me just mention a few names here which are widely known; similar things could be said about people who are less famous or not known at all. Politicians such as Roosevelt, Churchill, Ghandi, Adenauer, and de Gaulle could not have been more different with regard to their personalities and qualities. The same is true for military leaders such as Eisenhower and Patton in the U.S., Montgomery and Alexander in the U.K., or Rommel, Guderian and von Manstein in Germany. Similar can be said of leaders in the sciences, health care, and administration. Of course it also applies to female leaders. For all we know, Maria Theresia and Elisabeth I., Grete Schickedanz and Marion Gräfin Dönhoff had very different personalities. By contrast, there are remarkable similarities in what they did. As an aside it is worth noting that many of these persons would have come out badly in the usual HR and headhunter selection processes, which only serves to reinforce existing doubts in such procedures.

Requirement Profiles – A Trap

It is a short way leading from the "new requirements" frequently stated to a requirement profile. It is one of the tools most frequently used in HR management, and as weird as it may sound, it leads to the exact opposite of what is really needed. Like almost the entire field of HR, it is dominated by the concept of the ideal manager.

We should not ask whether someone conforms to some ideal profile; instead we should ask whether he or she has learnt to be effective. Effective people do not match requirement catalogs. They have learnt a few things:

- They have learnt to recognize their strength(s) and to focus on using them. They do not pay much attention to their weaknesses.

- They have maneuvered themselves into a position – according to their possibilities, but very deliberately – where these strengths are particularly helpful and can be translated into results.
- They follow a set of guidelines and use them to establish discipline in their work.

It is impossible to learn how to be a universal genius. You may work on yourself as hard as you can, it won't get you there. It is possible, however, to observe and implement the three points listed above.

All of the aforesaid does not mean, as some people may conclude, that I am against requirements as such.

My remarks are only directed at those that – intentionally or not – form an ideal type or universal genius when pieced together.

This is why I am not very much in favor of the demand for social competencies, which has been put forward with great verve over the past years, or all the calls for emotional intelligence. Not because they are unnecessary but because we have enough of both. Once again, these are fads uncritically imported from the U.S.

As a matter of fact, it is quite easy to avoid the trap of requirement profiles: All it takes is going from the abstract to the concrete. Instead of asking: "What requirements must managers generally meet?" the question should be "What do we need here and now?" Or, in more detailed terms: "What do we need in this specific position, in this specific organization, and in this specific situation?"

Perhaps some elements can be generalized, as they may be important in more than one situation. Take, for instance, sports: Fitness and strength will always be important here. But this is as far as generalizations go. What fitness and what strength? Athletes competing in 100-meter sprint will need a different kind of fitness than those doing a marathon, and the practice they need for the two disciplines will be so different that they almost exclude one another. The strength you need for lifting weights is very different from the strength required for high-jumping.

For each of the disciplines, specific requirements can be stated quite precisely, as can the performance that athletes need to aim for with their work-out. As soon as it is summarized, aggregated and generalized, however, all that information becomes useless.

Of course a ski racer needs to be able to ski. However, in and by itself that does not mean much. Only when we talk of the individual disciplines – downhill, slalom, Super G – will we reach a reasonable degree of concreteness. The point where it gets truly useful, however, is when we talk about the individual case. For instance, a downhill racer weighing less than her competitors may be able to make up for that difference by practicing a particular technique. Some racers are better on long tracks, others on short ones. At this level, everything becomes more tangible and useful.

We can define requirements to the 100-meter runner, the high-jumper and the discus thrower in relatively reasonable terms. We cannot do the same for athletes in general. Nor can we do that for managers – or only in such general and vague terms that it is not useful. At this point, one or the other reader may think of decathletes. Well, there are very few really good ones – just as there are very few ingenious managers.

To avoid a possible misunderstanding: I am not against the management tools mentioned above. Although opinions may vary with regard to the details, I think that performance evaluations, for instance, are necessary, as are procedures for recruiting, methods to determine compensation levels, and so on. I have always been sceptic about the potential analysis, though. Indeed, I believe that to this date we do not have a reliable method to determine the potential of a person. Still, I am against using criteria in all these tools that will define the ideal, universal manager.

Major Tasks Ahead for HR Management

Setting an End to Mind Pollution

> Don't read anything stupid;
> brains can be poisoned, too."
> *Ernst Jünger, quoted according to Helmut A. Gansterer*

There is environmental pollution, which is dangerous enough, and there is mind pollution.[98]

---

98 I used to think I had discovered that myself. By reading an essay by Helmut Gansterer, one of the sharpest observers of management and other interesting things, I learned that Ernst Jünger had realized the same thing long before me.

In retrospect – provided that case historians will ever be seriously interested in management – the past 15 years will probably be considered an era of fashion trends, superficiality, deception, and seduction in what concerns management. Over the past years I have often been amazed at the extent to which executive and supervisory bodies permit people's thinking and actions to be influenced by entirely meaningless buzzwords and illusory concepts, and at the amounts of money paid for those things.

I consider a major share of the content of current management training programs to be scientifically unsustainable, useless in practice, and even detrimental. This applies to most of what is said about leadership style, motivation, communication and corporate culture, but also – as I have pointed out several times before – for large parts of the common views on visions and synergy, to name just a few examples. Just as useless, even misleading, are the requirement profiles, criteria catalogues in performance evaluation systems, and the assessment of people's potential.

In my opinion, mind pollution is one of the main reasons for nearly all management mistakes made over the past two decades. Therefore I think it is absolutely necessary for executive and supervisory bodies to discuss staff development and training programs not only in terms of budgets, but also in terms of content.

In discussions about executive training, I have very rarely observed top management members to be genuinely interested in the content. The top management, however, is where the responsibility lies – not only for how much but also for *what* employees are taught. There may be some discussion on the topics of the training, that is to say, on the headings of the different sections and chapters, as well as on the duration and costs, obviously, and occasionally on the didactic methods used. Content in the stricter sense is hardly ever discussed, although that is what matters the most and what the discussion should focus on. It is the content, not the titles of the training program, where expectations and attitudes, skills and knowledge are conveyed.

Improvement in Effectiveness

The second major area is *managers' effectiveness*, and in particular that of an organization's *brainworkers*. Even the best knowledge, the greatest talent, all of the intelligence and capabilities available are worthless if they are not used. In this respect, almost all organizations are machineries that hinder rather than foster their people's effectiveness.

While I am unable to present any quantitative statistics as evidence, with the benefit of twenty years of experience I dare say that the coefficient of performance hardly exceeds 50 percent for most managers and brainworkers, and perhaps less than 30 percent for many. There are exceptions, but they are few and far between. On the other hand they may be helpful as a basis to determine what kind of reserves should be mobilized. The performance differences between people working effectively and those working ineffectively are such that no one – neither organizations nor individuals – can afford to ignore them. Effectiveness will be a prerequisite for every company to remain competitive, and for every individual to stay in employment.

The effectiveness of brainworkers, both in expert and management functions, their quality and productiveness are almost exclusively a matter of HR management. No one else plays a part in this. And it is more of an understatement than it is an exaggeration to say that half of the value-added in an economy will result from brainwork in the future. In an increasing number of companies this rate will be close to 80 percent, in some it will comprise the total value-added. Thus, HR management is turning into the most important management function besides finance management.

Brainwork focused on finding better solutions for known problems is productivity. Brainwork focused on finding solutions for unknown problems is innovation. As such, brainworkers are a species of their own, just like the "matter" they work with – knowledge – is something entirely different from classic economic resources. As a consequence, traditional management categories are not only useless here, they are wrong and detrimental.

Humane Organization

A third major field of HR management will be the *design of organizations*. As I said before, most organizations are machineries that hinder rather than foster the effectiveness of their people. If the intention had been to create something to hinder people, the outcome would have been the organization forms we have today, most especially the matrix organization.

Organizational responsibility must be moved from where it gradually shifted over the past two decades – to information technology – back to the responsibility of HR management. We must realize that, despite all the difficulties, it is much easier to change computer systems and organizational structures than it is to change humans. Trying to adapt people to systems is a communist concept at heart. We know it cannot work.

As trivial as it may sound, people must be treated *humanely*. The widespread lip service regarding this principle conceals the facts rather than being truly helpful. No two persons are the same, so they cannot be managed the same way.

The following analogy may be quite fitting: no one would think of treating cats and dogs the same way just because they are both animals. Dog lovers know that every dog, even compared to those of the same race and litter, is a distinct individual, even an individualist. They will never treat two dogs the same way. Only people are continually exposed to the dogma of equalization which is expressed in different forms – in service contracts, job profiles, evaluation systems, and organization structures. This way we deprive them of the only thing that makes them valuable, or, to express it in cynical and economic terms, useful: It is their individuality, their specific strengths and capabilities. At best we leave them untapped.

When we need things that are equal, it is better to work with computers and robots. When we need *differentiated* things, when dealing with complexity, adaptiveness and flexibility matter, we need *people* – and they must not be fictions created by some management theory but humans with all their individuality.

In the classic industrial enterprise, individuality was something rather annoying, in particular at the assembly line. It was all about standardization and normatization. In a knowledge society things are different. What matters here is that the owner of a value-adding resource deploys it of his own accord and in his own responsibility, because he alone will be able to realize what is required, what needs to be done in the specific case and how it must be done. And since individuality cannot be managed in the traditional way we will not primarily need the information-based or network organization. These terms conceal the key point. What we need to create is the *responsibility-based* organization. At every single workplace, in every job, individual responsibility for performance, quality, and results must be established. That is the true purpose of Total Quality Management – and only where this has been implemented can quality standards be considered to have been reached. The establishment of individual responsibility in the job is, incidentally, also the main purpose of Management by Objectives – something that is often disregarded or forgotten. Peter Drucker, its "inventor", has explicitly used the words "Management by Objectives, Self-Control and Responsibility". That can only be achieved by humans, not robots. Therefore, the task of designing an organization must be given back to those who know the most about people: to HR management.

Career Planning

The *fourth* major contribution by HR management refers to *professional development*. The questions to be asked here are what a "career" will mean in the future, what it will look like, where it will lead, and how it should be shaped. One thing seems certain to me: it must be very different from what we have seen so far. If that is true it also means that the entire spectrum of staffing decisions – selection, development, promotion, transfer, demotion, and dismissal – will follow very different criteria.

It begins with basic training and related hopes and expectations. For my generation a university degree was almost a guarantee for what is generally referred to as a career. For the young people of today it will be an essential prerequisite for getting a good job.

We would be well advised to tell our young ones who, as a result of their upbringing and education, still harbor the same now obsolete career expectations, that these expectations *cannot be fulfilled*. It will be a shock to many and may initially lead to a phase of disorientation. Most still bear in their minds of the old model. *"If you are not promoted every three years you are a failure."* But where can people be promoted to when hierarchies are dismantled and organizations become flatter? A "career" will no longer lead "upward"; it will consist in getting a *bigger* – not higher – job, perhaps also *a more interesting* and *more important* one, but not one that is superior in rank. We will have to point out to young people that it is a great privilege and implies career and success when you have a great and interesting task to do.

Career planning will also have to be linked to life planning. It will have to deal with questions about the meaning of a professional occupation, the meaning of a career, and ultimately the meaning of life.

Creating an Elite

The fifth major task of HR management – in particular in large corporations – is to create an elite. I am very aware of the potential dangers of this proposition. After the experiences of the 20th century we need to operate with maximum caution.

Yet, the major transformations that the business sector and society at large are going through will call for *more* and *better* leadership than we ever had in previous epochs. Note that I am not saying we need leaders – we need leadership. We will not get by without a management elite, but it must be an elite which is *not elitist* – and which *cannot become* elitist because constitutional provisions have been taken to prevent it.

It is a difficult task, and it would be (almost) the first time in world history that it would succeed. It is not impossible, however. If we invested only a fraction of the intelligence that went into the creation of the welfare state to solve the elite issue, we should be able to expect perhaps not ideal solutions, but much better ones than we have so far.

Senior managers, especially in large companies, have high visibility. In the public's perception they represent the entire business sector, even if that is not really the case. Whether they want it or not, they personify general standards of leadership and elite. Thus, their behavior must conform to the strictest standards of exemplariness. They must be raised and trained to be role models. Whoever is unable or unwilling to meet these standards does not belong in a senior management position and should not stay there. Even minor lapses can have disastrous effects on the public perception, in particular in a media society.

Unfortunately, in the German language we are unable to express the difference between management and leadership, as both means "Führung". The leadership discussion that has recently been going on is at a lamentable level.

This is all the more worrisome as we do have a considerable pool of leadership knowledge and experience. At one point – if only temporarily and in a historically unique context – the issue of leadership was almost solved: it was during the Allied Forces' military leadership training during World War II.

To successfully cope with the ongoing transformation in a peaceful, humane way, every society needs a large number of competent, effective, and responsible leaders/managers. Not only engineers are needed but engineers who can manage; not only scientists but scientists who can manage themselves and others, not only business economists but economists who can translate their own knowledge and that of others into value by means of management. This is true not only for business but for all organizations, not only for senior levels but for everyone with management tasks.

While investments in management and management skills cannot be calculated at present, they will determine the performance and competitiveness of organizations, industries, countries, and economic blocks more than they ever did. They will be decisive for wealth, for the elimination of poverty and misery and the correction of ecological damages; and they will be decisive for whether our young generation has a future and what it will look like. The task and the responsibility for it are largely in the hands of HR management.

Money: Managers' Compensation

Managerial Salaries and Leadership Quality

„If we don't pay the highest salaries we won't get the best managers. The market calls for the highest pay." These are the arguments used to justify extraordinary managerial income.

Compensation excesses among U.S. top managers dominate the headlines. In Europe and Asia we may not have such record numbers as yet, but – to put it in polite terms – we have made great "advances" in this respect in Europe.

Are the most expensive managers really the best? Is there a correlation between income levels and leadership qualities? Does the market really bring the best people into the best positions?

As long as the stock market boomed and before scandals became visible, it may have been justifiable to argue like that, although there has long been reasonable doubt and criticism even before the recent occurrences. After the scandals came to light, the argument no longer holds.

No doubt good people must be paid well, or rather: very well. The opposite is not true, however – well-paid people do not necessarily deliver good performance. Why should not cheaper people do a better job than expensive ones? If some corporations with extraordinarily well-paid top managers, such as Enron or Worldcom, had been spared these people, not only would they have saved a lot of money but they would probably still exist. No-one could have managed these companies more poorly than these big earners did. A ruined company or a bankruptcy can be had for less.

It is an unproved supposition that a top income will ensure great performance, let alone top performance. There are numerous examples of the opposite – top performance for little money –, enough to take them seriously. No great politician has ever gone into politics because of the money. German chancellors, American presidents, and Swiss government representatives are relatively poorly paid, although there have been people with top qualifications among them. The same is true for scientists and top government or military officers. Or take the medical profession, which is often criticized for its high income levels: there are quite a few doctors who do not measure their services in money.

When senior positions are automatically measured in extra pay, there will inevitably be more and more among those pushing to the top who are only out for the money. The more of them actually reach the top, the more the organization itself will be money-driven. Money focus, however, is not the same as profit focus. Enron and Worldcom made no profit, as everybody knows, but they were money-driven.

Years ago, Peter F. Drucker reported on a remarkable case. At the beginning of the 20th century, the U.S. tycoon John P. Morgan, one of America's great founder figures and a die-hard capitalist, initiated a study in his widely ramified business empire. He wanted to know what the main differences were between his successful businesses and the less successful ones. It turned out that there was only one point where performers differed from non-peformers: it was the difference between the salary levels within each organization. In successful businesses it was no more than 30 percent from one level to the next; in less successful ones it had gotten out of control. J.P. Morgan then introduced that 30-percent ratio everywhere.

Today, more than 100 years later, we can be a bit more generous about these proportions, especially in case of success. Absolute top performance should be rewarded with top bonuses. But I have not found even one financial analyst so far – nor an executive searcher – who would have paid attention to this factor in distinguishing performers from non-performers.

Perhaps it is some food for thought to supervisory and executive bodies that one of the grandmasters of capitalism had a clear concept of how compensation should be determined.

Fresh Start for Managerial Income

After the numerous scandals it is about time to stop justifying systems that have never worked and never will. Decades ago Drucker said: *"There are no good executive compensation plans. There are only bad and worse."* It is time for a new beginning, and a good opportunity at that – in the very interest of the top managers taking so much criticism, in the interest of all those who have not taken things too far, and in the interest of reinstating managerial credibility.

Even the most sophisticated reforms now undertaken to save the remainders of stock option programs, for instance, will not solve the problem. There is no effective arithmetic-mechanical system to determine the right compensation for the complex job at the top level. No such system will do justice to the rapid change of conditions under which it is supposed to function. Most of these conditions have not been taken into account by the inventors of those systems, as they could not even begin to imagine that they would ever come about.

No arithmetic system will work for both rising and falling stock prices, in boom phases as well as recessions, for business as usual and for turnaround cases, for acquisitions as well as divestitures. There is no system that, by using mechanical calculation, could take proper account of the essential dimensions of corporate management – operational and strategic, short and long-term, today and tomorrow.

What are the alternatives? There is only one: *an autonomous decision by the supervisory body, impartially appraising all relevant circumstances.* This solution is far from an ideal one, but it is the least unsatisfactory one, once it has been realized that the ideal is an illusion and cannot be implemented.

This way the supervisory body wins back its most important function which it had to cede to rigid mechanics: to evaluate the company's overall performance and determine and assess executive's contributions. This is undoubtedly one of the most difficult tasks in the context of management and control, but it is also the most important and noble one. This is how the supervisory body fulfills its core function; this is where its true significance lies. Without the competent and responsible fulfillment of this task there will be no corporate governance.

The implications are unpleasant, but beneficial to the function of the company and indispensable for its health. With this kind of compensation design, management can no longer simply derive its performance from the relations of some monetary factors – which can be manipulated to no small degree – but must present, prove and substantiate that performance. The supervisory body must look at the overall situation of the company and its managers closely enough to fulfill its task competently. That requires some work, but the supervisory body is appointed and paid for it. In companies with a sophisticated management system it has always been that way.

The most frequent objections can easily be invalidated. One argument is that the supervisory body is not in a position to fulfill this task because it is too detached from day-to-day reality. Wherever that is the case, it will have to move closer to it. Another argument is that the supervisory body does not have the competencies. In that case it is time to bring some competent people in. A third argument is that managers would make less money under this concept. That depends on the supervisory body – it could also be more. Some say the decision is of a subjective nature. That is right but irrelevant. Every court decision is subjective because it is taken by a thinking, considering, judging person or group of people. It is important that the decision not be arbitrary. This can be ensured, as we know from 200 years' practice with the rule of law. Yet another objection is that managers would not know in advance what they earn by year-end. Correct. This was and is the situation of an entrepreneur: his income is never known in advance.

Two further considerations will have to influence the compensation decision for managers in the future, due to the income excesses of the past. Why should a manager automatically make more money as he gets older? Probably this idea will be expanded to include everyone in the workforce. The need for a high income is not automatically linked to increasing age or tenure. Young families need more income than older people, whose financial obligations are much lower at times.

In particular for top managers we will have to ask why they should get paid more with each move up the hierarchy. It is imaginable and desirable for compensations to begin decreasing again when certain positions are reached. That would have the very positive effect of people no longer aiming for senior positions with one eye on the extra pay. On the contrary, these positions would be filled with people willing to accept a loss of income to have more possibilities to shape and influence things from a more senior position. Money focus, or even greed, should not be drivers of the strive for top positions.

The circle of candidates for top positions would drastically shrink. Quality and motivation would improve noticeably.

Chapter 14

Innovation and Change

> "Only few people are creative
> but any institution can be innovative."

According to the logic of my standard model, the management of new activities – unknown activities – is not much different in nature from those of existing, familiar activities. Thus there is no need for a specific innovation or change management.

Management of new activities is the same as for everything else. However, it requires a maximum of professionalism and virtuosity in mastering the craft.

As we have seen in the chapters on strategy, structure, and culture, questions of innovation and change are natural elements of these areas. It is not possible to talk about them without considering both the existing and the new. Renewal and change are not something that is added to the company. They are capabilities which must be established in the company; they are part of a well-functioning organization just as cell division is part of an organism. The organism arises from cell division; once it stops, what remains is a carcass. The enterprise arises from innovation and change; once they stop, what remains is a ruin.

In other words, we do not have strategy here and innovation there, structure and culture here and change there. That perception would only create confusion and conceal what is important – namely, that strategy, structure, and culture are the entry gates to innovation and change. If the latter do not occur here they will not occur at all. Innovation and change, just like culture, belong to the so-called emergent properties which were discussed earlier. As I had pointed out in the culture context, that does not mean they cannot be treated as subjects of their own; only they cannot be directly "made". Today and tomorrow, the existing and the new, the operative and the innovative, the known and the unknown, the familiar and the unfamiliar, they all belong together. They do not require different kinds of management.

In addition to what I have said so far, there are some more aspects that warrant special attention. In particular for market- and product-based innovation – that is to say, for start-up businesses – there are excellent findings from PIMS research which are invaluable for the innovation process. At least half of the dot.com flops could have been avoided had these findings been applied. Among other things, they will be the subject of a special volume of this series.[99] For the purposes of this book I will restrict myself to dealing with the main misunderstandings and the guidelines to avoid them.

False Doctrines and Misconceptions

There is no doubt that innovation is important; the future of almost every company depends on it. Most attempts at innovation fail, however – a fact that cannot be stressed enough. Eight out of ten innovations have always failed, incurring enormous costs. The New Economy nonsense has raised the quota dramatically.

The main reason is that in most companies there is a lot of innovation *romanticism* but little innovation *professionalism*. Most managers do not master the craft. Every innovation is an "expedition into uncharted territory", a "first ascent to the mountain top" – but most are treated like a walk in the park.

What needs to be done above all is to eliminate widespread false doctrines and misunderstandings. Next, the experiences and insights we have been having for many years must be rigorously evaluated.

The *first* false doctrine says that innovation is created in labs or R&D departments. It is not. What is created there are ideas, or maybe prototypes and experimental results. Innovation must be defined from a market perspective. Only when market success begins to materialize can we speak of innovation. Only this perspective allows choosing the right strategies

---

99 Part of them has been published in the *PIMS Letters* as well as in my *m.o.m.*® *Malik on Management Letters.*

and making halfway reasonable assessments on the time and money required. The key question is not: *What new things have we developed, invented, or discovered?* The key question is: *What would we need to do and what would be required to successfully launch this development, discovery, or invention into the market?*

The *second* false doctrine says creativity is key. As a consequence, creativity is demanded as a quality in managers, creativity trainings are conducted in companies, and supposedly creative methods are used. Obviously there is a feeling – and it is expressed often enough – that there is a lack of ideas.

There is no lack of ideas. There is a lack of ideas that are *implemented*. Even the most uncreative companies have many more ideas than they could ever realize. *Generating* ideas is something entirely different from implementing ideas. That, and that alone, is innovation. The idea as such is not unimportant but it is the least important, least costly, and least difficult of all by comparison. Following an idea, a functioning prototype must be developed or clinical tests carried out. That incurs much more effort and expense, and it takes much longer. After that, the new development must be taken to maturity for full-scale production, which takes even greater an effort. And finally the marketing phase must at least be initiated. It can safely be assumed that each successive step incurs ten times the expenditure of the previous one.

The *third* erroneous belief is that only small companies are innovative. It is one of the stupidities often repeated during the New Economy euphoria. It is always easy (and a popular practice) to criticize large corporations for their sluggishness and praise the advantages of small units. Indeed, small companies are capable of many things that large companies are not. Innovation is not one of them. Small entities are often more creative, they develop new ideas more easily and make it to the prototype rather quickly. But this is the point where they often run out of steam. Small companies always have two problems: they are *underfinanced* – or if they do have money they cannot handle it – and they are undermanaged. As a result, small and supposedly innovative companies are often doomed, or taken over by the big ones. Small entities are good sprinters but poor finalizers. Effective innovation, however, is a long-distance run, an endurance discipline where it is crucial to have enough strength left for the second half of the track.

A *fourth* popular superstition says that innovation is mainly or exclusively about high-tech. That, too, was one of the basic beliefs of New

Economy propagandists. The fascination by and fixation on high-tech result in deception. No doubt we will have some more high-tech in the future, and there are businesses that will have to deal with it to a particular extent. But that is not relevant for all. As a result of this fascination, there is a tendency to overlook many opportunities existing in low- and no-tech areas which involve less risk and offer better opportunities at lower cost.

The *fifth* error – the most harebrained and also most dangerous of all – is that innovation requires a special type of personality: the proactive, creative, entrepreneurial, risk-taking pioneer character. That is a major source of arrogance and personality cult. People of that kind exist, but they are few and far between. Taking a closer look at supposed pioneers, you often find that they were talked up in hindsight by over-enthusiastic biographies and media reports. Most pioneers were very ordinary people. Before their successes became evident they were often regarded as cranks or freaks by other people. They had nothing in common with the radiant "innovator type". But they did have one thing: a systematic work approach. They mastered the craft of innovating. Although their biographies hardly ever mention it, this is what we can learn from them.

The Guidelines

There are some lessons to be learnt from innovative companies, and using them as guidelines will not only help avoid errors and mistakes, it will help to succeed in managing innovation.

1. Aim at Market Leadership and Notable Change

When it comes to product-market innovation, the aim must be *market leadership*. For all other types of innovation (organization, processes, information technology, behavior, and so forth) the goal must be clear, *notable* and *consequential* change.

I am saying: it must be the goal. This does not necessarily mean one will always achieve it. Even with goals of this kind, results may sometimes be of minor significance or entirely useless. Yet only if you really want to *win*, you will mobilize the resources and strengths that will give you at least a chance at reaching the goal. If you content yourself with *some* kind of goal from the start, you will achieve *some* kind of result. That is true for sports, and it is true for innovation. You will only muster the necessary thoroughness and care, and seriously deal with the methods and procedures required, if you aim for the top, whether in sports training or in innovation management.

Another point is that small changes often trigger the same kind of resistance as *major* change does. You will have to be prepared for people fiercely fighting for each and every one of their vested rights. Thus, you will face the same struggle in any case – all the more reason to go for something that really makes a difference.

2. Make Room for the New

Innovation must begin with *systematically disposing* of what was there before; otherwise the new will not have enough room. It will be choked off in the "waste" of the previous. Hence there must be *systematic "waste removal"*.[100] The fastest, most radical and simplest way to implement the new is: *Stop doing the wrong things!*

3. Separate the New from the Old

This guideline complements rule No. 2. Wherever the old and the previous cannot be disposed of, at least we need to *separate* the old from the new wherever possible.

The new requires a factually different logic; there must be different rules, measures, strategies, and so on. Almost everything will be different from how it used to be – with regard to the matter as such, not its management – and must therefore be handled differently as well. Cars are different from horse carriages, even though both have four wheels. Handling things differently, however, will only be possible to the extent needed – or the maximum extent possible – when things are cleanly separated. Some points warrant special emphasis here:

---

100 See my book *Managing Performing Living: Effective Management for a New Era*, new edition, Frankfurt am Main/New York, 2006.

a) Other Benchmarks

A growth rate of less than 5 percent is usually excellent for *mature* products in *mature* markets. Nowadays you can consider yourself lucky if such businesses grow at all. New businesses, however, should have the potential to achieve *two-digit* growth rates. Similar is true for productivity increases: 2 to 3 percent are very good for most of the older operations, but new processes and systems should achieve *markedly* more (also in the two-digit region) in order for the effort to be worthwhile.

b) Other Budgets

Actually you need *two* budgets, one for current business and one for the new operation. The former can be based on experience values; for the new budget there can be no experiences to draw on. Familiar activities can be budgeted quite precisely and in detail; new activities can only be roughly delineated, calculating with larger margins of error and planning correspondingly large reserves in terms of cost, human resources, and so on. While ongoing activities are based on *experience*, new activities can only be based on *assumptions*.

When these crucial differences are leveled down by mixing everything together in the same budget or plan, each of these tools loses part of its significance. Neither the old nor the new can then be reasonably judged and controlled.

c) Other Schedules

The time a manager needs to dedicate to familiar activities can be predicted and assessed quite well; usually it is also clear *when* that time will be needed. Not so for new businesses. The only sure thing is that managing an innovation *always* takes much more time, and it is impossible to tell when exactly that time will be needed.

d) Other Reporting Approaches

Familiar activities can be controlled relatively well – if not exclusively – based on key variables and their variations. Good managers never rely on numbers alone; they also try to keep themselves informed on qualitative aspects, moods, and so forth. Still, figures are quite expressive here, not least because they permit comparisons, for instance to earlier periods.

Figures relating to new activities, however, are always unreliable; it is always necessary to monitor things closely. You need to listen to people and watch them do their jobs; you need to let them think aloud and accept the fact that they may utter vague presumptions, hopes, and fears.

All these "weak" signals are necessary to squeeze at least some information from the maze of presumptions, to get a whiff of the scent, as it were. Managers who are after "hard facts" only, who always want everything "in black and white", should not be given any innovation responsibility.

Again, this is yet another factor speaking in favor of clear and clean separation between new and familiar activities wherever possible.

4. Seek Opportunities in Problems

A major share of managerial work consists of solving problems. However, if you only see problems everywhere, you will *overlook opportunities and possibilities* – and this is where all the innovation potential lies. To put it bluntly, when all problems have been solved not one opportunity has been exploited. A company may then be mediocre but not good. To be successful, companies need to identify and exploit *opportunities*.

Very good and effective managers apply a very special way of thinking, in that they keep asking themselves: *"What are the opportunities even in this problem?"* Even when a situation is particularly dreadful they still look for the positive sides, for possibilities and opportunities. This is what makes them potential innovators.

They are so insistent in this that their attitude may sometimes appear somewhat compulsive and naive. But these people are not calculated optimists, nor are they naive. They call things by their names, euphemize nothing, and judge the situation soberly and realistically. They know that managers are ultimately not paid for solving problems but for exploiting opportunities.

5. Demand a Second "First" Page from Controllers

The fifth rule reinforces the fourth and leads further, beyond the general attitude and to a practical method.

What does a *good* controller do? Writing a report and presenting the numbers is not all he does. For management's particular attention he will also carefully seek out all *negative* deviations and list them (marked in red) on the first page of his report, so they *cannot be overlooked.*

What does an excellent controller do? He will additionally single out all positive deviations and list them (marked in green and just as impossible to overlook) on the second "first" page of his report, so that *they cannot escape management's attention.*

This is far more than playing around. It calls top managers' attention to the indicators that typically point to hidden opportunities. Where are we doing better than we had expected and budgeted? Where are we making progress faster than we had planned? Positive deviations must have their *reasons*, just as the negative ones do. These reasons must be figured out and outlined, and they should be examined further. In most cases there will be a particular strength that has not been recognized so far, or a special *opportunity*. Even small but concerted additional *efforts* will often lead to considerable extra *results* in these areas, and it is worthwhile directing one's resources there.

If you don't have that kind of information you will inevitably focus on problems and negative deviations in your meetings. It is important, however, that opportunities and strengths be exploited, too, and that requires preparing and providing the relevant information in an appropriate manner.

6. Write Down Your Expectations

The written form is a basic principle of innovating. I have met people who, in their function as innovation managers, kept special diaries and made painstaking notes about everything.

The human memory is fragmentary and very elastic. Our brain does *not* work like a computer. It does not store information but keeps processing and reshaping it.

Good innovation managers write down their expectations regarding the future course of a renewal process. Even if they cannot draw up precise budgets, they have clear concepts of how things should go if they stay on course. They take notes of discussions with employees and their observations. They do not permit their memory to play tricks on them because they are aware of its shortcomings.

7. Clarify the Limiting Conditions

One point is particularly crucial for effective managers dealing with innovation: they know when to stop. The way to do that is to outline the limiting conditions precisely by asking themselves: *"What are the conditions which, if and when they do occur, will make me accept that I have been wrong, that something fundamental cannot be right?"*

They write down these things very precisely and keep checking the reality against these criteria again and again. "If we have not achieved such and such in three months' time, something fundamental must be wrong." They define in advance where the *cut-off point* will be, in order to prevent having to throw good money after what has already turned bad.

8. Make Sure You Have the Best People

Whenever an oganization deals with something new, there will inevitably come a point when the question is raised as to who will be in charge. Reflexively, the next question is: who has got the time? That is a sure-fire way to making the wrong choice. For innovation you need your best people, and they never have time because they are constantly swamped with work. Note that I am not saying everyone drowned in work and having no time is automatically one of the best. However, those who do have time are definitely not among the best. The basic principle must be: get the *best* people, wherever possible, *and get 100 percent of their capacity.*

Not only should they be the best people but also those with *credibility* in the organization. Why do people have credibility? Not because of rank or status, position or title. There is only one reason for credibility and only one way to get there: *visible, demonstrable, convincing results.* Whoever has no results to show is not credible. He may be a *hope* but he will not have people's trust.

The implications of this principle are significant: it means that three groups of people are *not* suitable to be innovation managers, although they are put in charge of innovations *most often*:

a) The young ones, as they will not have any results to show. Young people hopefully have potential, but they do not have results. They can and should contribute to innovation projects so that they can learn, but they can usually not be given overall responsibility.

b) People in staff functions, as with very few exceptions they will not have any results to show, either. The worst case, obviously, is a combination of (a) and (b), young central staff members.

Things are different if you have people in your staff functions who bring operative or line-management experience from former stations of their careers, or who have been given opportunities to show what they are really capable of. There are organizations, by the way – although precious few of them – where staff functions are exclusively staffed with people with this kind of background. A very recommendable approach.

c) Organization developers, HR developers, and the like, for the very same reasons.

9. Run Tests

Effective innovation managers particularly dread a specific kind of innovation – the kind that must immediately be rolled out over the *whole* organization or market. There are such cases, but they should remain absolute exceptions.

New activities should always be *tested* as far as possible. Everything may look nice and perfect on paper; still it is safe to assume that even the best plan contains mistakes, that things have been overlooked, the significance of some things has been underrated, and so on. It is therefore highly recommendable to run two or three tests.

Capable people use tests to detect and eliminate mistakes, and for something *even more important: to remove the basis for possible later excuses.* The time spent on the tests will be won back later through speedier implementation – once there is evidence that the new really works out.

10. Absolutely Concentrate on Few Things

Since every major innovation requires *full attention* and the best people, and is fraught with risk even then, experienced innovators concentrate on *a small number* of innovation projects. They never let themselves be fooled into dissipating their energies and fragmenting their strength.

Rather, they create a situation in which the plan succeeds and has break-through success, or else, in case of failure, they can say with *deep conviction*: *"We have done everything this organization is capable of. We have not made mistakes nor bad trade-offs. If the effort has not been successful nevertheless, it is definitely beyond our capabilities. We will give it up with dignity, keeping our losses low, and find another solution."*

11. Innovation Teams: Don`t Overlook the Individual

Attentive readers will have noticed that I have not spoken of work groups or teams to this point. Obviously, teams are important in most innovation projects today. The rules I have listed apply to them just as they do for *individuals*. Almost always, however, it is *individuals* who ensure that the right rules are observed, owing to their discipline, their expertise and *experience*, and above all, their *role model behavior*.

12. Don`t Worry about Criteria for the New

Some managers are constantly, almost desperately, in search of *criteria for distinguishing* the new from the old. In most cases such criteria are not necessary; the answer is usually clear. The key question is not whether something is new "to the world" but whether it is new *to us*. If we, the people in *this* organization, have no experience with something, it is new, no matter how often the same thing has been implemented at other places before. Perhaps it is possible to get help from there. Regardless, it is new to us.

If there are still doubts or if it is a borderline case, I recommend treating an effort as if it was new. Perhaps then you will make easier and faster progress than expected, because you realize that you do have considerable relevant experience. You may have paid too much attention to the project then, but that will not seriously hurt anybody. It is much more dangerous to manage a borderline case "hands down", only to find out later that it is much more difficult after all.

Part IV

Management is Getting Things Done

Chapter 15

Implementation

"We have no shortage of concepts. Our problem is implementation!"

This, or similar, is one of the things you hear from managers all the time – irrespective of the hierarchical level or industry, and largely independent of the size of their organization. Every organization seems to have this problem to some degree; the reasons are manifold.

One of the causes of implementation deficits is humans. Man is a creature of habit, as we all know. Each of us in his own way is *dependent on habits*. This is also true for creative people, by the way, as any study of their lives will reveal.

Habits are not laws though. We can change them, even if it is usually not that easy. There are people who are good implementers *although* they have their habits, even strong ones. We can learn some helpful practices from them.

Concentrate on a Few Things

Anyone determined to get somewhere will have to learn to focus on few things. Focus is the alpha and omega of implementing, it is the basis of every implementation success.

Especially in management, the danger of *dissipating* one's energies is enormous. Organizations tempt executives to do just that, and too many of them succumb to the temptation. Many even think it is a sign of management competence to juggle lots of things at any given time. That view could not be *more false*.

Do just a few things at a time – but do them properly! That is the motto of all good implementers, be it individuals or organizations. Nothing is more typical of success, implementation, and realization, than strictly focusing on *one* thing at a time.

Making Agenda Entries

Managers control things. They are also controlled – by their diaries. Whatever has been entered in the little book will usually get done; whatever is not written there is very unlikely to be carried through. The agenda – or, generally speaking, the structuring of one's time – is one of the most important tools for *changing one's habits.*

One simple example: someone making a resolution to work out at the gym two or three times a week, and who has many other obligations, will probably need to enter this in his agenda, at least initially. Otherwise he will probably not get around to it. He will not work out at all, or only irregularly and at random. There will be no training effect, no new routine, and after some time he will give up again, just like most people do – he will not have implemented his plan.

Almost anything crucial to managerial effectiveness can be implemented by entering it in the diary. It is also the only way to make it succeed. Nothing ever happens just like that, or because good resolutions have been made. For instance, someone planning to adopt what is assumed to be the most effective way to build a constructive relationship with his co-workers will probably enter this in his diary. The same is true for those planning to do a regular and systematic "waste removal" in their divisions.

Monitoring Outstanding Tasks

Capable implementers are usually very disciplined workers. They do not forget anything – not because they are memory geniuses but because they *write down* their ideas, intentions, and the like. For this purpose they usually have a little notebook lying on the bedside table. They note all their to-dos – because they *want* to get them done.

I suggest not trusting people who believe they can memorize everything. Either they are very inexperienced or they have relatively little to do or they are incompetent and never really get anything done. More than anything, successful implementation is a question of *persistence* and *endur-*

ance. It requires checking over and over again, which only works if ongoing activities are recorded and monitored.

Thinking Things Through to the End

Many plans and decisions are not implemented because they *cannot* be. *Why?* Because they have not really been thought through to the end.

The ability to think something through, thoroughly and carefully – really *to the end* – is not very common. In my view, thinking through a problem, a process, a decision, and the like systematically, carefully and rigorously is still the *most important* and best problem-solving approach. Unfortunately it is seldom taught and hardly ever mentioned in management books.

Actually, in this context we should speak of *discipline* rather than a *capability*. By and large it is not that difficult to think things through to the end. In most cases it is just a bit tedious; it takes some time and effort.

Some people feel particularly great in saying they never care about the details. This attitude may be justified in certain cases and sometimes even unavoidable, especially for high-ranking executives. It is not permissible, however, if the aim is to implement something. In that case it is indispensable to make reasonably sure that everything has been planned realistically, that crucial contingencies have been considered and alternatives devised for cases of emergency.

Testing

Experienced managers go one step further. They know that even the best and most careful consideration is not always enough to discover mistakes of a *certain kind* – those that will become apparent during *application*. Therefore they test things prior to their actual implementation wherever possible. They are aware – often from painful experience – that even the most elaborate concept, the best plan, the most careful decision will often have its flaws, and that they will be of the kind that you cannot find by reflection *alone*.

There are enough real-life examples to prove that point: even if the greatest diligence is applied in development, construction, and manufacturing, new car models still need to be tested. And so far there has not been a single computer program that was absolutely bug-free in application. Everything needs to undergo one test after the other.

The great implementers in management do not, as is often clichéd, charge at things like raging bulls. Quite to the contrary: they study, try out, experiment, probe and – metaphorically speaking – test the ice before actually walking on it.

Experienced managers find it dreadful to imagine they should implement something *system-wide* without prior testing. Consistently and sometimes almost stubbornly, they demand that two or even *three convincing trials* be run, wherever possible, before something new is rolled out across the organization. These tests cost money and, even more importantly, they take time. Still they are the *only* way to detect the kind of mistakes that will only show in practical usage.

Only after these tests have been carried out and the flaws and deficits found have been eliminated, will experienced implementers go system-wide – and then it will be *at full force*, no trade-offs accepted, and at the highest possible speed. This way they make up for all the time they have "lost" by doing previous tests, usually even much more than that.

Even more importantly, this approach will gain them *credibility* and *respect* in the organization. People trust them because they can see they are competent. This kind of standing cannot be gained any other way. Even if mistakes do happen in the course of implementation, even if something goes wrong, it does not harm the esteem these managers enjoy from those around them. People know and understand perfectly well that there are different kinds of mistakes, and they distinguish very sharply.

Putting Someone in Charge

Managers who are successful at implementing have a deep-rooted aversion against collective and anonymous responsibilities. They delegate responsibility not to groups, not to teams, not to committees or other bodies, but *exclusively to individuals*. They stubbornly hold on to the principle of *individualized personal responsibility* – and they do not care if others consider that old-fashioned. They know that collective responsibility does not work.

At this point I want to pre-empt a potential misunderstanding: in corporate law there is collective responsibility borne by the organs of a corporation. I find this regulation to be right and important; it does not contradict my above demand for individual responsibility. These two kinds of responsibility refer to very *different* aspects. The collective responsibility under corporate law refers to cases of *liability* and has nothing to do with the topic discussed here, the *implementation deficit* of organizations. The first is a legal issue; the second is an issue of *managerial* effectiveness. These are two very different things, which require different regulations of responsibility.

Hence, the following model applies mutatis mutandis: the executive body has collectively made a decision; the responsibility for implementing it is with executive board member XY. The individual liability of each executive board member resulting from the board's collective responsibility remains unaffected.

Never Trying to Win Everyone Over

Many things are never implemented because those responsible think they need to get *everyone* in the organization on board. That is one of the after-effects of a *misunderstood* participation principle, which I believe originated in the protest movement of 1968. As praiseworthy as the attempt to involve people may be on principle, and as necessary and useful it may be in many cases, it does have its *clear limits*.

As a manager you can never expect to win people over for all your plans and intentions, except for those that will not hurt anybody. You should not expect it and you should not even try it. The stronger an interference with the organization and the more profound a change, the more people will be negatively affected. As regrettable as it may be, it is a fact. Consequently these people will oppose the effort no matter what. Perhaps they will not openly resist or actually undermine it, but it would be downright inhuman to demand their approval to changes that will harm them and run counter to their interests.

This is one of the typical situations so common in management which require power of judgment and experience. Trying to enforce something against unanimous resistance is usually not very smart nor will it work, apart from some borderline situations. Trying to convince *everybody* and to get everyone's approval is usually not possible either, and fortunately it is not really necessary.

Experienced and successful implementers try to mobilize what physicists call *"critical mass"*. How many people it includes in the specific case depends on the circumstances. As a general rule, however, 30 percent are usually enough, in many cases a smaller percentage will do.

What is much more important than numbers and percentages is *who* must be won over. There is only one criterion for the correct answer to this question: it must be the people who have *credibility* in the organization. When and why is someone credible? Again, there is only one answer to that: people are credible because of the *results* they have achieved. Academic titles, ranks in hierarchy, status symbols, image, and so on – all of that will not convince anyone nowadays, and if so, it will be somewhat naïve persons as will hardly be needed for the implementation. People are convinced of a person when that person has achieved visible, presentable, consequential results that are important to the company.

Experienced implementers will therefore try to get a critical number of such people on board. It does not need to be a large group in terms of absolute numbers or percentages; what matters is that it is a *weighty* group.

Thinking Through Who Needs What to Take Action

Although strong implementers do not try to win everybody over, they do something else: they think very carefully about what those involved in the implementation will need in order to be effective. They think about what *information*, what *tools* and what *training* these people will require.

Above all, there is one mistake they do not make: they never take for granted that everyone else probably knows what the change is about, just because they themselves know it. Too many executives commit this – truly fundamental – error again and again, although they should really know better. They themselves may have discussed the issue for weeks and months with their management colleagues before a decision was finally made. They are probably familiar with all the facets and dimensions of the problem; they have gone to sleep with it and woken up to it. The people now supposed to implement the decision, however, *were not part of all that*. So how can they effectively implement it?

Note that this is not about motivational issues. They may have to be considered in addition. First of all, however, a much more important question must be clarified which has nothing to do with motivation: *Who needs to know, understand, and be able to do what, in order to make a correct and effective contribution to the overall result?* For this reason – and not primarily for reasons of motivation – good implementers think very carefully about how to explain and make a case for their decisions, so that those involved will *understand* what is at stake.

Not Relying on Reports

It should be obvious that progress in the implementation phase needs to be monitored and controlled. Indeed, among the so-called modern management coaches there are those unwilling to accept that fact and who propagate that controls are dispensable. I cannot get anything out of that, and my suggestion here is not to listen to these pied pipers.

However, even if control is accepted *as a task* and taken seriously, it still remains to be clarified how it should be done. The – otherwise very welcome – advances in information technology involve a considerable *risk* when it comes to implementing things: it has become too easy to produce reports... *The essential point*, however, is that one should *not rely* on reports – least of all when the implementation of major projects is at stake.

What is the alternative? You need to *go there and see for yourself*. This is the only way to form a view on the situation and the progress made that is sufficiently comprehensive and adequately reflects the real state of things. All through history this type of behavior has been common to *all implementers*: even if they had the most sophisticated reporting systems available, as, for instance, in military organizations, they would never allow them to replace their personal observation. Conversely, there is enough evidence to show that a lack of personal, direct observation has often been a major cause of incomplete or faulty implementation, sometimes even utter failure.

As we have seen, implementing is not that difficult really. Observing a few rules and applying some relatively simple practices may not help to solve all implementation problems in this world, but it will surely help to make considerable progress in one's own sphere of responsibility.

Epilog – Management Responsibility and Management Ethics

> "Questions that are not decidable
> must be decided by us."
> *Heinz von Foerster, cybernet(h)ician*

Management is the transformation of resources into value – by shaping, regulating, guiding, and developing complex societal systems.

Based on this book, I believe I can define quite clearly, for top management issues of corporate governance, what management responsibility and management ethics should be. As long as the significance and function of management are unclear, there is no way one can determine its responsibility and ethics. Once it is clear, however, what management is and what it is not, and in particular what right and good management is, there seem to be no problems that cannot be solved, provided one has the courage to make decisions. The guiding line is there; decisions are up to the individual.

I am using the word ethics in this context only because I am asked about it so often. As a matter of fact, responsibility is enough. I think that ethics should be reserved to the more serious problems of humanity, such as genetic engineering, and should rather not be strained for the relatively simple questions of management. We need no ethics to resolve the question as to how much money top managers should make or how they should act in public. To behave correctly as a manager and fulfill one's responsibility, some common sense, fundamental decency, and empathy for people's circumstances should suffice.

Managers are, firstly, responsible for themselves, their own capabilities and performance. Secondly, they are responsible for those working for them, their capabilities and performance. Thirdly, managers are responsible for their institution, its capabilities and performance according to the standards described in this book. They are responsible for ensuring that everyone can deliver adequate performance by utilizing his or her strengths.

These three responsibilities have to be judged against the purpose of the institution. That is one of the reasons why this purpose must be clear and unambiguous, as otherwise neither performance nor responsibility will be possible. The purpose must be a contribution to society, not in a vague metaphysical sense but in the sense of the customer value outlined earlier, and in line with the business mission and strategy, as explained above.

A manager is responsible for fulfilling his or her function, as described here, with a maximum of professionalism. This requires striving for right and good management, continuing to perfect it in accordance with one's own strengths, and preparing oneself for bigger and more difficult tasks.

There can be no responsibility for things you cannot influence directly or indirectly. Managers cannot be responsible for changing people, in particular their personalities. Changing oneself is up to each individual. Right management does not require universal geniuses or saints. Demands along these lines will lead to the opposite of good management. It is not necessary to demand of people – including the managers themselves – more than the decency and morality that can be expected of a person with ordinary upbringing and education. Solutions are not inherent in individuals and their personalities, as important as they may be. It is practices rather than virtues that matter, actions rather than motives, results rather than intentions.

Managers are responsible for having the factual and managerial knowledge required for their tasks, as otherwise their ability to perform will be impaired. They must be expected to distinguish reality from appearances, content from packaging, right from wrong, tried and true practices from fads. A manager who is incapable of those things lacks professionalism and will turn into a risk for his or her institution.

Managers are responsible for not promoting anyone to a position he or she is not ready for, in the sense described here. Usually it is possible to find out whether or not someone is capable. If it is not, that person should not be given the task until his or her qualification can be assessed. If it turns out that the decision was wrong although due diligence was exercised, it is the manager's responsibility to remove that person from the job and give him or her another task. For every failure in business there is someone who has got him there, and someone who has failed to remove him in time. Not only failure itself is a question of responsibility, but, much more than that, the wrong staffing decisions that have permitted it to happen.

The top of an institution must be designed in such a way that wrong staffing decisions, even if they do happen, will not cause permanent damage, and that they can be detected and corrected quickly. This responsibility is honored by means of providing constitutional regulations and ensuring that the institution will never entirely depend on individuals, as they are bound to make mistakes. In staffing decisions, existing rules of independence must be carefully observed in order to prevent conflicts of interest and ensure, above all, that the supervisory body can take its decisions in the sole interest of the institution in question. The members of the supervisory body must be committed accordingly. This is the authority to ensure reasonable contractual arrangements and compensations for top executives, including liability regulations, and thus ensure role model behavior and prevent privileges and mental corruption. It is also the authority which can enforce the honoring of responsibilities.

As a manager in a key position, knowing that trade-offs will always be required to some degree, you base your decisions on the following question: What would be right for this organization in this situation? You do not go by general popularity, state of the art, or zeitgeist considerations. You act on the assumption that management is the most important function in society.

You have the responsibility to represent to the public the kind of corporate management that corresponds to the standards described here, and which can be understood by people. This responsibility cannot be fulfilled by holding pastoral or militant speeches. It is honored by means of delivering results and setting an example, as these are the only things that will really convince people. You have particular responsibility if you represent a major corporation, not because it has particular power but because in our media society it is visible to everybody. People's perceptions of business and management are influenced, rightly or wrongly, by major corporations. They are regarded as representative of the business world.

As a manager you are also responsible for ensuring that your actions will not provoke anti-business attitudes, causing neither future burdens nor restrictions for a functioning economy. You are responsible for demonstrating through your actions that healthy companies need a functioning economy and that the economy needs a functioning society.

You fulfill your responsibility in such a way that people will see and understand that the business sector is too important – not to be left to managers but to be left to bad managers.

Appendix

The Malik Management System
and Its Users

The first impulses for the development of my management system go back as far as the 1970s, when both the *System-Oriented Management Theory* and the *St. Gallen Management Model* were created under the guidance of my former academic mentor and superior, Prof. Dr. Hans Ulrich, and my friend and colleague Prof. Dr. Walter Krieg. There were even earlier origins in General Cybernetics, strongly influenced by my first contacts with its main creators, above all Heinz von Foerster, Francesco Varela, Gordon Pask, Hermann Haken, Gotthardt Günther, Stafford Beer, and Frederic Vester, the strategy pioneer Aloys Gälweiler, the evolutionary theoretician and biologist Rupert Riedl, and the art historian Ernst Gombrich. Other major influences were my encounters with Karl R. Popper, Friedrich von Hayek, Hans Albert, Cesare Marchetti at the legendary Alpach University Weeks and, above all, with Peter F. Drucker .

With my habilitation thesis, the title of which translates as "Strategy for the Management of Complex Systems"[101], I developed my own theoretical concept, based on which an open, networked, dynamic system of cybernetic principles emerged through an ongoing pursuit of both theory and practice – the *Malik Management System*. As such, it refers to wholistic management in all three meanings of the word:

1. Management as a societal function
2. Management in the sense of institutional organs, and
3. Management in the sense of what managers do.

---

101 Malik, Fredmund, *Strategie des Managements komplexer Systeme*, Berne/Stuttgart/Vienna, 1984, 9th edition 2006

Designations and Identities

The official and probably most straightforward name for my overall system is the *Malik Management System*. It corresponds to *Malik Management*, the name of the organization that I founded and whose purpose is to develop, disseminate and apply my management system.

When studying and describing complex systems, one does not know at first what the outcome will be. In their early stages the systems usually carry working titles, and it often takes a while until they are given their final names or brands. This is what happened with my overall system and its subsystems. There is a host of different names for them, for the most part improvised during different development stages, projects, publications, seminars, programs and the like, often even by readers and customers. Examples include *The Integrated Management System (IMS®)*, *Right And Good Management*, *Managerial Effectiveness*, *Effective Management*, *The General Management Model*, *The Standard Model*, the *"Management Wheel"*, *The Malik Model*, *Malik on Management*, and several others.

Experienced users are aware that the actual identity of systems is never defined by their names but always by the systems themselves, their contents and versions. From the very beginning I have tried to make this transparent in my publications for reasons of accuracy and trustworthiness, in so far as straightforward descriptions were possible at all.

History of Development

It has been over 30 years since I started developing my system, and I have been dedicating all my time and resources to it ever since. The extraordinary turning point from the industrial era to the era of complexity was clearly in sight back then, but it was equally clear that the general awareness in both society and the market of the resulting, complexity-driven problems and opportunities would be a long time in coming.

Hence, securing the elaborate research and development work in my company required much persistence and it has been a difficult balancing act over all these years. From the very start we had to meet the requirements of our customers while, at the same time, striving to develop a General Management System independent of time, culture, industry, and company function. On the one hand we needed to address the tasks, questions, and issues that were entering into society's awareness at any given point; on the other hand we had to think and work ahead as far and as comprehensively as was possible.

The time is now right for the advanced development of the cybernetic foundation of the overall concept, which were the first to be developed as they constitute the basic prerequisites for my management system's ability to function. The technical conditions for their practical application were just recently created and there is now a sufficient number of practitioners who have gathered enough experience with complexity to develop an interest in it.

Thus, after several decades, my strategy and policy of dedicating all my resources to the requirements of management in the era of complexity – which was a rather daring step back then – has finally been confirmed.

Applications and Effects

The *Malik Management System* has been designed for the life situation of man in the hybrid system world of the age of complexity. Such systems for management and self-management need to become the new civilizing and cultural techniques which have become necessary in this still-young world. Without them, existing and potential resources can neither be recognized nor transformed into results. The latter requires the kind of information and knowledge which, in the *Malik Management System*, I have organized as navigation systems, models, sets of rules and tools.

While our world is complex and we face numerous highly complex issues this does not necessarily mean that the solutions have to be complicated, too. On the contrary – they can be very simple, provided they contain the potential for unfolding the necessary complexity. The fact that the *Malik Management System* meets these requirements is owed to decades of persistence and focus.

Anyone will understand that there is information which, while being brief, clear, and simple, triggers exactly the kind of action within a system that is required at the time. One example is the fire siren: it mobilizes all the forces required for safety because everyone can hear it, everyone knows what the alarm means and what to do when it sounds. Thanks to its modular structure, my management system meets this requirement of providing that kind of relatively simple but highly effective signal-effect information, which will support and maintain a system, as well as configure, activate and vitalize it as necessary.

The modules of the *Malik Management System* have been designed for maximum effectiveness, efficiency, and viability, based on the forces of the information-driven coherences that typically exist in systems. As such, they can be *combined, configured,* and *applied* without limits. Depending on the configuration and combination, it is a management system for entire organizations and their subsystems, as well as for the self-management of the individual, both including their environments.

Hence, for any conceivable purpose, for any size and kind of organization in any development phase, for any area of activity and for any order of magnitude, the *Malik Management System* provides a system-logical basis that is capable of evolving. It is suitable for both nature and mind, and is certain to help focus on the essential. It is the evolutionable "operating system" for complex institutions.

The *Malik Management System* grows with an organization or person. It interacts with them. It ensures that they both keep developing in a mutual evolutionary process. The interface between them is the human brain and mind.

Autonomy for Management and Managers

From the *Malik Management System,* every person and every organization can configure their *"Own/Our/My Management System"*, provided they observe certain rules; just like it is possible to configure one's own computer according to one's individual requirements. This is crucial because in the age of complexity managers need a degree of intellectual autonomy that they can only achieve and maintain, without major times losses, by resorting to general management systems that are organized to the last detail – systems that are generally valid but adjustable to their individual requirements.

Hence, the challenge in creating my management system was to provide a basis for management that does not conform to a certain period of time, a region, or even a fashion, but only to those principles that are generally and permanently valid. Just like technicians create systems which obey the natural laws of physics, I had to create a system that obeyed the natural laws of information, communication, systems, and complexity. The key foundation for that is the science of cybernetics, the laws of which govern the nature of complex systems.

Consequently, the systemic structure of the *Malik Management System* is based on applied cybernetics; and the system itself *is* applied cybernetics. It follows the cybernetic principle to *design a system in such a way that the greatest possible number of applications can arise from the smallest possible number of modules.* This principle renders the user autonomous. It depends on him, and him alone, to what degree he will mentally conquer such a system. He will not be dependent on the developer.

Modularity and Interfaces

The *Malik Management System* has a *modular* structure. Its modules are compatible with each other and with the user's world and can be combined in any way. Their interfaces are:

1. All the cybernetic management models that provide the necessary insight in crucial active elements and connections
2. All the tools required for generating and applying the required information
3. All the methods required for solving tasks
4. All the concepts helping to reflect on things
5. All the rules of application by which every system can be brought to maximum performance.

Users can apply the whole *Malik Management System* or its modules in different forms and across different languages. They are available in books, numerous essays and articles, training courses, entire training programs, DVDs, CDs, MP3 format files, e-management learning programs, and, as far as is sensible and system-supported, also as digital tools and software.

Above all, however, the *Malik Management System* must be a program for the brain, because a good executive must be able to identify current themes and respond to them faster than they could be fed into and processed by a computer. As far as sensible and helpful, however, modules can be randomly combined and configured by information-technological tools, due to their evolutionary structure. Moreover, when it comes to transferring knowledge and information and complex problem solutions from one brain to another, there are experts available in my organization whom I have trained myself.

A Management System for Self-Thinkers

Anyone working on organizational solutions for maximum effectiveness and efficiency is essentially working on becoming superfluous. Accordingly, one of the major goals of my management system is to render managers independent of management consultants. In the 20th century there were certainly good reasons why management consultants played a major role, as the discipline of management was only just emerging.

In the 21th century and beyond, however, the world needs executives who are aware why in management there can be no simple, fail-safe formula for success, and why no one can spare them from making their own observations and deliberations. They will have to master their profession comprehensively enough to know that, particularly under complex circumstances, it is much more important to ask the *right questions* than to have the right answers. The reason is that under complex conditions it is impossible in many respects to know for sure whether one's answers are correct. This is exactly what the *Malik Management System* has been designed for, in order to prevent any potential malfunctions or aberrations.

Potential for Success Rising With Qualification

One of the typical effects of the development history of my management system was that, for a long time, only the simplest and most plausible-seeming models would meet with broad acceptance and even become standard. The much more sophisticated cybernetic functional backgrounds preceding them have largely remained unknown to this date.

Anyone interested in making full use of my management system should know, however, that his autonomy will grow along with his command of not only the simplest functions but also the deeper grounding. Everything required for that is available to him – the management system in everyday user language, the cybernetic models, and pure cybernetics itself. The latter, above all, will help him solve individual management or subject-specific issues without making unnecessary deviations.

At the same time, users should know that the use of even one single principle from the entire management system can and will have enormous systemic effects. The manager's own effectiveness, however, is maximized by his ability to combine all the relevant contents of the system quickly and correctly; the more so as others can communicate and cooperate with him on this basis.

Self-Motivation for Self-Developers

A manager making use of the *Malik Management Systems*, and in particular developing his own solutions on this basis, also needs to know that he lives in a time when he is increasingly given more credit for what others can understand of him than for what he actually accomplishes.

For the most part, the motivation to shape and handle systems in the way they require by nature will not come from outside – he will have to find it in himself. After all, users and other parties concerned will naturally assess the performance and value of a system by what they can get out of it, irrespective of what and how much is actually in it. The developer, by contrast, most values the intricate backgrounds of this system because he knows that everything depends on them. Therefore, good developers will inevitably get much more credit for achievements they themselves do not value so much, while those that they are really proud of are often disregarded and hardly ever appreciated. That, however, should neither pain nor discourage them: proper acknowledgment will come from the system itself, because it only really functions when people allow themselves to be guided by its "needs", that is to say, its inner laws and regularities.

Care versus Kudos

It is the fate of responsible executives and experts in the age of complexity that to the majority of those around them they can do things either the *right and good* way or the *popular and desired* way. Reconciling both is getting increasingly impossible. It will continue that way as long as common thinking and knowledge have not sufficiently adjusted to the requirements of the age of complexity.

More than ever, the true professionals and pioneers will face problems created by self- or media-acclaimed gurus, dilettantes and dazzlers in pursuit of fast but short-lived successes, who attract not only plenty of attention but, lamentably, also a host of misconceptions which are difficult to dispel. In the age of complexity, such superficiality will become more than dangerous. We therefore need a solid fact basis for management enabling people to distinguish the real experts from *gurus, spin doctors,* and *pseudo-enlightened* individuals. This is what I work for. This is what my management system stands for, this is what my motto *right and good management* is meant to express.

Hence, here is one final practical advice to the self-thinkers and self-developers among my readers: The motto *easier said than done* may be true for many situations, but it does not apply for dealing with complex systems and cybernetics. Quite the opposite is true here: *easier done than said.* It is much easier and, above all, takes much less time to *show* what the matter is and to *do something about* it than to describe it.

Anyone working with the *Malik Management System* will find that it will help them solve many tasks quickly. They will, however, need a lot of time to describe their *own* developments to others in a comprehensive, correct, and comprehensible manner. For classical management practice, the latter is not really necessary anyway. It becomes relevant once people use my system to develop their own, intending to provide a reliable help to others.

In the age of complexity, more than ever before, managers and experts will be alone with their really great achievements. They will meet with less appreciation than ever, and often get no encouragement. They will also find that they are admired for trivial things while their true accomplishments are ignored. They will feel like Albert Einstein would have, had he been celebrated for his ability to explain gravitation. The recognition they deserve for their successful brain work and system work will come from the systems themselves, which they shape, direct, and regulate based on solid foundations.

Authors and Acknowledgments

To my knowledge, the *Malik Management System* is currently the only comprehensive, wholistic, integrated general management system consistently based on cybernetics as a science of regulation, explicitly geared toward the coping with complexity, and designed specifically for the management of complex systems. The majority of related concepts were developed by me. My greatest contribution, however, has been the development of the overall system itself. After all, the *Malik Management Sytem* is ultimately owed to long-standing, close cooperation and friendships with the best minds of the areas of management, cybernetics, and management cybernetics, as well as system sciences. All rights for all modules have been reserved by me. They predominantly follow from the copyright; rights for other authors' developments have been contractually acquired.[102]

In my publications I also refer to numerous leading authors of management theory, in particular Peter F. Drucker, Hans Ulrich, Walter Krieg, my former colleagues at the St. Gallen University's Institute of Business Economics, Stafford Beer, and many others in other areas. My sincere thanks go to all authors and customers, all discussion partners and friends, and the people in my organization.

---

102 The work, including all its parts, is copyright-protected. Also subject to copyright protection are all modules, terms, models, depictions, etc., referred to here. Any exploitation, application, or use, etc. outside the narrow defines of the copyright is not permissible, without the prior written approval of the publishers, and is liable for prosecution. That is true, in particular, for duplications, disseminations, reproductions , translations, micro-fiches, the storing and processing by electronic systems, as well as any form of commercial distribution.

About the Author

Hardly anyone has managed to do what Fredmund Malik has been doing for several decades: make the necessary concessions to traditional, everyday understanding and, at the same time, work for a new era. It has polarized managers into adversaries and advocates, as inevitably happens with pioneers.

After graduating from high school, with a focus on economics, and gathering several years of industry practice, Fredmund Malik studied economics, business administration and social sciences as well as the philosophy of logic and epistemology at the universities of Innsbruck and St. Gallen. In 1971 he wrote his master thesis on *Cybernetic Models and Management Concepts*. In 1975, he took his doctoral degree with his PHD-thesis on "System Methodology – Foundations of a Methodology for Exploring and Shaping Complex Sociotechnical Systems"; in 1978 he submitted his habilitation thesis and received his Venia Legendi for corporate management theory. This thesis was entitled *Strategie des Managements komplexer Systeme* ["Strategy of the Management of Complex Systems"].

In 1977, Fredmund Malik became Managing Director of Management Zentrum St. Gallen, from 1979 to 1984 he also was a member to the board of directors of the Institute for Business Administration at St. Gallen University, in charge of its management consulting department. In 1984, he took over Management Zentrum St. Gallen in a friendly buy-out and established *Malik Management*. Since that day, he has been the chairman of the Board of Directors of MZSG Holding AG and its subsidiaries, currently with offices in St. Gallen, Zürich, Vienna, Berlin, London, Shanghai, and Toronto, which employ some 250 consultants specially trained on his management systems.

Fredmund Malik owns several companies and holds seats on several Corporate Governance boards, as well as in various administrative, supervisory, and advisory (foundation) councils. As a management consultant and educator he has been working for numerous renowned companies of all sizes, sectors, and industries in Switzerland and elsewhere, as well as with executives at all levels, for over 30 years. From 1978 to 2004 he also taught at the University of St. Gallen; he was a visiting lecturer at the University of Innsbruck from 1981 – 1982 and a visiting professor at the Vienna University of Economics and Business between 1992 – 1997.

Fredmund Malik is the author and publisher of the monthly management letter Malik on Management (M.o.M.); the overall list of his publications comprises over 300 items. As a columnist, Malik writes for several newspapers and magazines including *Trend, Cash, Basler Zeitung, Handelsblatt, Die Welt, Manager Magazin online, Süddeutsche Zeitung*, and *Junior Consult* (a magazine for students at St. Gallen University).

Fredmund Malik is married with two children. His main interests are philosophy, in particular philosophy of science, as well as history with a special focus on the history of ideas and of art, spanning all epochs and cultures. He dedicates his leisure time to literature and music, sports, and his passion for mountaineering.

Malik Management
Geltenwilenstrasse 18
CH-9001 St. Gallen
Switzerland

Telephone: +41 (0) 71 274 34 00

info@malik-mzsg.ch
www.malik-mzsg.ch

Literature

Albert, Hans, *Traktat über rationale Praxis*, Tübingen, 1986

Ashby, Ross W., *An Introduction to Cybernetics*, London, 1956, 5th edition, 1970

Beer, Stafford, *Beyond Dispute*, Chichester, 1994

Beer, Stafford, *Brain of the Firm – The Managerial Cybernetics of Organization*, London, 1972

Beer, Stafford, *Decision and Control*, London, 1966, 2nd edition, 1994

Beer, Stafford, *The Heart of Enterprise*, London, 1979

Beer, Stafford, "The World, the Flesh and the Metal"; 1964 Stephenson Lecture; in: *How many Grapes went into the Wine*, Harnden, Roger/Leonard, Allena (Eds.), Chichester, 1994

Blüchel, Kurt G., *Bionik: Wie wir die geheimen Baupläne der Natur nutzen können*, Munich, 2005

Blüchel, Kurz G./Malik, Fredmund, *Faszination Bionik. Die Intelligenz der Schöpfung*, Munich, 2006

Böckli, Peter, *Corporate Governance: Swiss Code of Best Practice*. Zürich, 2002

Bresch, Karsten, *Zwischenstufe Leben – Evolution ohne Ziel?*, Munich, 1977

Burckhardt, Jacob, *Weltgeschichtliche Betrachtungen*, Stuttgart, 1978

Buzzel, Robert D./Gale Bradley T., *The PIMS (Profit Impact of Market Strategy) Principles: Linking Strategy to Performance*, New York, 1987

Ceccarelli, Piercarlo/Roberts, Keith, *I nuovi principi PIMS: La gestione dell'impatto sul profito*, Mailand 2002

Clausewitz, Carl von, *Kriegstheorie und Kriegsgeschichte: Vom Kriege,* First print: Berlin 1832/34, Frankfurt, 1993, new edition, 2005

Deal, Terrence E./Kennedy, Allan A., *Corporate Cultures*, Reading, Mass., 1982

Drucker, Peter F., *Die ideale Führungskraft*, Düsseldorf/Vienna, 1967

Drucker, Peter F., *Landmarks of Tomorrow*, New York, 1947

Drucker, Peter F., *Management – Tasks, Responsibilities, Practices*, London, 1973

Drucker, Peter F., *Managing for the Future*, Oxford, 1992

Drucker, Peter F., *Managing for Results*, London, 1964

Drucker, Peter F., *The Practice of Management*, New York, 1954; new edition, 1982

Drucker, Peter F., *The Theory of the Business*, in: Drucker, Peter F., *Managing in a Time of Great Change*, New York, 1995, S. 21 ff.

Drucker, Peter F., *Managing in a Time of Great Change*, New York, 1995

Drucker, Peter F., *Innovation and Entrepreneurship*, Oxford, 1985

Drucker, Peter F., *Technology, Management and Society*, New York, 1958

Foerster, Heinz v., *Observing Systems*, Seaside California, 1981

Frankl, Viktor E., *Der Mensch vor der Frage nach dem Sinn*, Munich, 1979, 3rd edition, 1982

Gale, Bradely T., *Managing Customer Value: Creating Quality & Service that Customer can see*, New York, 1994

Gall, John, *Systemantics: How Systems Work and Especially How They Fail*, New York, 1975

Gälweiler, Aloys, *Strategische Unternehmensführung*, Frankfurt am Main/New York, 1990, 3rd edition, 2005

Gälweiler, Aloys, *Unternehmenssicherung und strategische Planung*. In: ZfbF Schmalenbachs Zeitschrift für betriebswirtschaftliche Forschung, No. 6, 1976

Gansterer, Helmut A., *Höfliche Vorschläge für Körper und Geist*, in: trend SPEZIAL, August 2005

Gomez, Peter/Malik, Fredmund/Oeller, Karl-Heinz, *Systemmethodik: Grundlagen einer Methodik zur Erforschung und Gestaltung komplexer soziotechnischer Systeme*, 2 Bände, Bern/Stuttgart, 1975

Gordon, Robert J., *Technology and Economic Performance in the American Economy*, Cambridge, Mass. 2002

Hayek, Friedrich A. von, *Der Weg zur Knechtschaft*, (Erstpublikation, 1944) Munich, 1971

Hayek, Friedrich A. von, *Freiburger Studien*, Tübringen, 1969

Hayek, Friedrich A. von, *Law, Legislation and Liberty*, Volume II, The Mirage of Social Justice, Chicago, 1976

Hayek, Friedrich A. von, *New Studies in Philosophy, Politics, Economics and the History of Ideas*, London, 1978

Heinsohn, Gunnar, *Privateigentum, Patriarchat und Geldwirtschaft*, Frankfurt, 1984

Heinsohn, Gunnar/Steiger, Otto, *Eigentum, Zins und Geld: ungelöste Rätsel der Wirtschaftswissenschaft*, Reinbek b. Hamburg, 1996, 2nd edition, Marburg, 2002

Henderson, Bruce D., *Die Erfahrungskurve in der Unternehmensstrategie*, Übersetzung der amerikanischen Ausgabe *Perspectives on Experience* (4th revised edition), Frankfurt/Main, 1972, and 2nd edition, Frankfurt, 1984

Hoffmann-Becking, Michael, *Münchener Handbuch des Gesellschaftsrechts*, Vol. 4: Aktiengesellschaft, Munich, 1988

Höhler, Gertrud, *Die Sinn-Macher. Wer siegen will, muss führen*, Munich, 2002

Kaplan, Robert S./Norton, David P., *The Balanced Scorecard*, Harvard, 1996

Keller, Stefan, *Aufgaben der Unternehmensaufsicht von Boards bei Verkäufen von wesentlichen Unternehmensteilen*, Diplomarbeit, University of St. Gallen, 2002

Krieg, Walter/Galler, Klaus/Stadelmann, Peter (Hrsg.), *Richtiges und gutes Management: vom System zur Praxis*, Festschrift für Fredmund Malik, Bern/Stuttgart/Wien 2004

Lattmann, Charles, *Die verhaltenswissenschaftlichen Grundlagen der Führung des Mitarbeiters*, Bern/Stuttgart, 1982

Lutz, Robert A., *Guts*, New York, 1998

Malik, Fredmund, *Effective Top Management*, Weinheim, 2006

Malik, Fredmund, *Führen Leisten Leben. Wirksames Management für eine neue Zeit*, new edition, Frankfurt am Main/New York, 2006

Malik, Fredmund, *Gefährliche Managementwörter. Und warum man sie vermeiden sollte*, Frankfurt, 2004

Malik, Fredmund, *m.o.m.® Malik on Management Letter*, published monthly since 1993

Malik, Fredmund, *Management-Perspektiven*, Bern/Stuttgart/Wien, 1993, 4th edition, 2005

Malik, Fredmund, *Management-Systeme*, in the series "Die Orientierung", No. 78, ed. Schweiz. Volksbank, Bern, 1981

Malik, Fredmund, *Strategie des Managements komplexer Systeme*, Bern/Stuttgart, 1984, 9th edition, 2006

Martin, Paul C., *Der Kapitalismus – ein System, das funktioniert*, Munich, 1986

McGregor, Douglas, *The Human Side of Enterprise*, New York, 1960

Mintzberg, Henry, *Managers not MBAs*, San Francisco, 2004

Müller-Stewens, Günter/Lechner, Christoph, *Strategisches Management: Wie strategische Initiativen zum Wandel führen*, Stuttgart, 2001

Nachtigall, Werner/Blüchel, Kurt, *Das große Buch der Bionik*, Stuttgart, 2000

Pelzmann, Linda, *Die Critical Incident Methode*, in: m.o.m.® Malik on Management Letter, Januar 2001 (9th year)

Pelzmann, Linda, *Führungsversagen aus Eitelkeit*, in: m.o.m.® Malik on Management Letter, September 2003 (11th year)

Pelzmann, Linda, *Triumph der Massenpsychologie – Rahmenbedingungen und Regeln*, in: m.o.m.® Malik on Management Letter, November 2002 (10th year)

Pelzmann, Linda, *Kollektive Panik*, in: m.o.m.® Malik on Management Letter, February 2003 (11th year)

Peters, Thomas J./Waterman Robert H. Jr., *In Search of Excellence*, New York, 1982

Popper, Karl R., *Die Offene Gesellschaft und ihre Feinde, Vol. 2: Falsche Propheten; Hegel, Marx und die Folgen*, 2nd edition, Bern, 1970

Porter, Michael, E., *Competitive Advantage – Creating and Sustaining Superior Performance*, New York, 1985

Porter, Michael, E., *Competitive Strategy – Techniques for Analyzing Industries and Competitors*, New York, 1980

Pruckner, Maria, *Die Komplexitätsfalle – Wie sich Komplexität auf den Menschen auswirkt: vom Informationsmangel zum Zusammenbruch*, Norderstedt: Books on Demand, 2005

Rappaport, Alfred, *Creating Shareholder Value*, New York, re-edition, 1998

Sloan, Alfred P., *My Years with General Motors*, New York, 1964

Sprenger, Reinhard, *Vertrauen führt: Worauf es im Unternehmen wirklich ankommt*, Frankfurt am Main/New York, 2002

Ulrich, Hans/Krieg, Walter, *Das St. Galler Management-Modell*, 1972; wiederveröffentlicht in: Ulrich, Hans, *Gesammelte Schriften*, Vol. 2, Bern/Stuttgart/Wien, 2001

Ulrich, Hans, *Die Unternehmung als produktives soziales System*, 1968; republished in Ulrich, Hans, *Gesammelte Schriften*, Band 1, Bern/Stuttgart/Wien, 2001

Ulrich, Peter, *Integrative Wirtschaftsethik – Grundlagen einer lebensdienlichen Ökonomie*, Bern/Stuttgart/Wien, 1997

Vester, Frederic, *The Art of Interconnected Thinking*, Munich, 2007

Vester, Frederic/Hesler, Alexander von, *Sensitivitätsmodell*, Frankfurt, 1980

Vickers, Geoffrey, *Freedom in a Rocking Boat*, Harmondsworth, 1970

Witt, Peter-Jürgen, "Corporate Governance", in Peter Jost (eds.), *Die Prinzipal-Agenten-Theorie in der Betriebswirtschaftslehre*, Stuttgart, 2001

Index